Morton Deutsch

A Life and Legacy of
Mediation and Conflict Resolution

Erica Frydenberg

Australian Academic Press
Brisbane

Publication of this work was assisted by a publication grant from the University of Melbourne.

ISBN 1 875378 55 3

Collating, editing, and writing assistance by Venetia Somerset and Stephen May.

Text design by Andrea Rinarelli.

Typeset by Australian Academic Press.

www.australianacademicpress.com.au

Contents

Abbreviations

ADR	Alternative Dispute Resolution
APA	American Psychological Association
AT&T	American Telephone & Telegraph
CCI	Commission for Community Interrelations
ICCCR	International Centre for Cooperation and Conflict Resolution
MIT	Massachusetts Institute of Technology
NTL	National Training Laboratory
NYU	New York University
SIPA	School of International and Public Affairs
SPSSI	Society for Psychological Studies of Social Issues

Acknowledgments

There are a large number of people who have contributed to this volume. Firstly, my appreciation goes to Morton Deutsch for being an inspirational subject who patiently provided the many hours of interviews. Mort answered an interminable number of questions, read copies of the manuscript and assisted in numerous ways. Lydia Deutsch gave interviews and insights while being a gracious host to my visits, in particular to the Hamptons. Tony and Nicholas Deutsch, Mort's sons, also gave their time for an interview.

Then there were Mort's many students and colleagues at the International Centre for Cooperation and Conflict Resolution at Columbia Teachers College and throughout the United States. Their contributions to this volume are greatly appreciated. In particular, Barbara Bunker, who was a most gracious host and who gave numerous hours of interviews during my visit. Pat Marshall, a colleague at the University of Melbourne made helpful comments on the text and colleagues in the legal field acted as reader-commentators on the manuscript. My appreciation also goes to Professor Dick Selleck, a distinguished historian who gave me encouragement and assistance during the time that I undertook the challenging task of writing a biographical piece.

The interviews, with Mort and his family, colleagues and students were conducted over several weeks during study leave from the University of Melbourne, an academic environment that has enabled this project to be completed.

I am indebted to Venetia Somerset who did much of the compilation and some of the writing of this book. Her enthusiasm for the task and appreciation of the subject made her a most valued contributor. As she commented recently, "I won't ever forget Morton Deutsch and his approach."

I would like to thank the editors at Australian Academic Press and the publisher, Stephen May, with whom it has been a pleasure to bring this project to fruition. Finally, I would like to thank my family, Harry, Josh and Lexi, who have come to know Mort and Lydia over the years and who have given me support throughout the undertaking.

Working for Peace and the Resolution of Conflict

I t was April 19, 2000, while flipping through the inflight magazine onboard American Airlines Flight 1473 to San Juan, that the importance of what I was actually doing finally hit me.

There in the dog-eared magazine, amidst the cheesy tourist stories, was a slick corporate consultancy advertisement for a business negotiation course. "We teach you to build solid long-term relationships that satisfy both parties by asking the right questions and delving into each person's *true* needs", ran the caption.

I had seen such ads before. "How to be a great negotiator" often features in expensive business and management seminar offers on negotiation and conflict. But now I was finally appreciating exactly where all the theory and techniques espoused by the people running these courses had come from.

They came from Morton Deutsch, the father of conflict resolution. The man with whom I'd just spent two weeks. The man I had casually asked of over lunch in New York a year before "Could I write your biography?". The man who should have won a Nobel Peace Prize.

Morton Deustch is one of the most distinguished psychologists of our time and has been honoured by his profession with numerous scientific awards. Yet today many human resource professionals working in the area of mediation, and most young psychologists, remain unaware of his great contributions to social and organisational psychology.

I saw this phenomenon myself when attending an address by Roger Fisher, author of the best selling book *Getting to Yes*. Many business students and devotees of Fisher remain ignorant of the name of Morton Deutsch despite much of Fisher's work being built on the foundations formed by the social science and ideas of Morton Deutsch.

So it was on that flight in 2000 that I realised I wasn't writing a biography. I was exploring a legacy that now stretched across the globe, generated by the continuing work of the man and his many former students.

This was quite a task for someone more comfortable writing psychological texts and research papers, but the willingness of Morton's former students, his family and himself to spend time talking with me led me to a wealth of stories and testimonials that helped piece together his life and legacy.

Once you start to delve into the world of Morton Deutsch, the superlatives flow easily. At Morton's retirement in 1990, Roger Myers, after twenty-eight years of working with him, said: "It is not ceremonial hyperbole to assert that Morton Deutsch is the most eminent psychologist that has been at Teachers College or Columbia University. In phrasing that sentence I am remembering the names of James McKeen Cattell, Edward Thorndike, and Robert Woodworth. These names were recognized as eminent when there were only maybe 400 or 500 psychologists in the world. Morton Deutsch has been recognized at that level and beyond when there are 100,000 psychologists in the world, an altogether different accomplishment."

Morton Deutsch's contributions to modern psychology have been no less important than those of Freud and Skinner. For over fifty years he has tested what he has called "grandiose theories" on cooperation and competition, and has been the pre-eminent authority on the dynamics of conflict, cooperation, and justice — central issues about human interactions and the improvement of social problems.

His life almost spans the existence of modern social psychology. Beginning his studies at the City College of New York in 1935, Morton Deutsch was introduced to social psychology at an exciting time. A time characterized by rapid development and great enthusiasm, when the potential impact that this young field could make on society was just beginning to be realized.

Social psychology flourished in America after periods of national adversity and social catastrophe. Events causing widespread social disruption such as World War I, the Great Depression and resulting grave class inequities, and the rise of Nazism, led to questions about the social influences on an individual's behavior and the possibilities of social change. Investigations into areas such as attitude change, prejudice, propaganda, and leadership all flourished.

Morton Deutsch's own research followed this development in social psychology and the realization of its potential to affect social behavior. He was inspired by the early pioneers of social psychology such as Kurt Lewin to engage in empirical research using a wide array of methodologies. Laboratory-based experiments were used to replicate real-life groups in controlled situations.

And yet Morton Deutsch has made an impact on the world in the quietest of ways. His name is not always recalled, but his ideas permeate the boundaries of disciplines such as law, international politics, education, business, and industrial relations; ideas so good that they have a place not only in the history of social psychology but also in the history of the twentieth century.

———

How an Australian Came to Write About the Life and Work of a New York Psychologist

I first met Mort, as he is affectionately known, in 1990 at a scientific meeting in Jena, Germany. The Berlin Wall had just come down and I had been invited some months earlier to join a group of psychologists to the third meeting of the Committee for the Psychological Study of Peace to talk about my own work on the psychology of coping. I was a young academic who had been schooled in Australia, a land of privilege and opportunity to which my parents had emigrated during World War II from my birthplace of Hungary.

As I crossed by train from the booming west to the grey eeriness of the east, I looked forward to meeting Morton Deutsch, whose name had immediately stood out from the list of 40 or so invited participants.

Jena was an experience that starkly contrasted with the comforts I had left behind. Tired from a 24-hour flight direct from Australia and the two-hour train ride, I headed down the corridor of the cramped country guesthouse where we were located, stripped off my crumpled clothing and got into the shower. It had only cold water, and as I dried myself on a small threadbare towel I wondered what exactly I had got myself into.

As the days passed, the cold showers didn't seem so important; the simple meals were a welcome part of the experience, as was the warmth of our hosts such as our colleague Wolfgang, whose opportunities for advancement were under threat of western domination in the reunified Germany.

The meeting featured distinguished scholars such as Ruben Ardila from Colombia who had written eleven books and had one child and expressed the regret that he had not written one book and had eleven children. There was Toshiba Irritoni from Japan, and Elena, from Russia, who talked about having no chalk in her classroom. There was a man and his wife, an English literature PhD, who were desperately trying to leave Russia for a better life with their 6-year-old son.

And there was Mort and his wife Lydia. Lydia was an elegant, sociable lady with ready conversation, while Mort was considered in his speech. He exuded a cool deliberation behind a generous and easygoing nature. There was a spark in his eyes whenever the group talked about his favorite subject — improving the lives of ordinary people through living cooperatively and working toward world peace. He was asked to contribute to the discussions at every point as the elder statesman, the distinguished scholar. He did not complain about the cold water, or having to walk to the bathroom, or the modest feasts that our hosts negotiated. He just accepted things as they were.

As the four-day meeting drew to an end I summoned the courage to ask Mort if he would like to come to Australia. To many US-based academics it is still a far-flung place requiring much time and effort to visit. Mort himself had already turned down an invitation to attend the 1988 International Congress of Psychology held in Sydney, the biggest event in the history of Australian psychology. However, he seemed pleased at my invitation and said he might just make it this time.

The time came three years later when Mort travelled to Australia as a guest of the Australian Psychological Society (APS). He gave a keynote address at the 28th APS Annual Conference held in plush surroundings in the heart of Australia's glamour Gold Coast beachside resort town, Surfers Paradise, as well as speaking to several gatherings in Melbourne hosted by the Psychologists for the Prevention of War. Lydia travelled with him and they took time to visit wildlife sanctuaries, vineyards, and other scenic spots.

Another visit to Australia followed in July 1997 when Melbourne hosted the biannual meeting of the Fifth International Symposium on the Contribution of Psychology to World Peace. By now Mort was seventy-seven and he had journeyed from New York to be part of a modest group of fifty or so students and scholars. When his hosts placed him in student accommodation, he accepted it with grace, despite being more accustomed to his New York lifestyle of an upper Westside Manhattan apartment and holidays in the Hamptons.

By this time, I had got to know Morton as a colleague and friend. In April 1999 I visited New York, meeting over lunch with Mort and Susan Opotow, a former graduate student of Mort's, to talk about a chapter they had contributed to a book on the psychology of coping that I was editing. He and Susan seemed pleased with the product but I was at a loose end now my editing task had finished.

I had written thousands of words on the subject of coping and had put into circulation a number of psychological tools, instruments that could be used by clinicians and researchers to investigate coping. Now was the time for a new challenge. Something that was worth doing and could engage my interest for some time.

That's when I somewhat impulsively decided Mort might be an interesting project himself.

Six months after searching the library for articles, scouring the internet for students' addresses, and writing to students to arrange interviews, I walked into Mort's office at the International Center for Cooperation and Conflict Resolution in New York on April 1, 2000 for the first interview.

The Center that he had founded in 1986 at Teachers College, Columbia University consisted of a series of crowded, rambling offices — too many people, too few desks, computers old and new jumbled together, groaning bookshelves, and numerous telephones scattered around. But the faces that greeted me were bright and friendly as I was introduced as that lady from Australia who was writing Mort's biography. People were curious. What had prompted me and what was I going to do with it? Where was it to be published? Why was my university in distant Australia interested?

There was a particularly jubilant atmosphere in the Center that day. The latest "offspring" had arrived — a large box holding ten copies of the *Handbook of Conflict Resolution: Theory and Practice*. Everyone had contributed something to the book, writing, editing, or organizing the twenty-seven chapters of this impressive tome. The striking green and buff colors of the dust jacket balanced the title which had been picked out in red and green lettering.

I glanced at my inscribed edition of the book and saw the diverse chapters on cooperation and competition, justice and conflict, constructive controversy, power and conflict, anger and conflict, change process, and mediation. There was hardly a topic not covered. Many of Mort's former graduate students, whom I was to interview in the weeks to come, were contributors. As I read the chapters it became clear that this volume alone provided a rich source of information and evidence about the many areas of Mort's influence.

After returning from lunch at the same Indian restaurant where I had first proposed to write Mort's biography we went into his office. This was where so many books and articles had been written, and where each of the doctoral students had sat. A smallish office by any standards, let alone that of a distinguished scholar — a mere twelve feet by eight. Behind the man there were shelves stuffed with books, some resting in precarious positions.

He sat at his desk with little ceremony. I sat beside him and behind me on the floor was a clipboard with photographs of students and events. The rest of the room was taken up with a couch and some open shelving on which sat the dozens of articles he had written, some collecting dust and others representing more recent editions. I started the tape.

Over the next two weeks the tape recorder racked up twenty-four hours of interviews, mornings and afternoons. Outside pneumatic drills sometimes threatened to drown out our speech. New York City had decided to replace much of the road on 120th Street just outside the Horace Mann building where we were sitting. At regular intervals the buses would grind to a halt right outside his window, only to rev their engines up a few minutes later. At other times the rain pelted down. It is never quiet in Mort's office, the outside always strains to enter. In this atmosphere Mort has done much of his writing since arriving at Columbia in 1963. His voice was soft and deliberate, sometimes faltering in speech but never in ideas.

After that first day Mort did not share lunch with me. Lunchtime was the respite from talk and Mort's time to take his daily swim. And when he returned from his swim he would open a small can of fish as he had done for almost twenty years, as I later found out to keep his cholesterol in check. The tuna, herring, salmon, or sardines would come out each lunchtime, sometimes during a meeting.

But it was not all work. Mort and Lydia graciously invited me join them on one of their regular visits to their seaside retreat at East Hampton. Mort drove, as I sat in the back with Lydia watching the scene outside as the city faded away and morphed into green countryside. Here, where the rich and famous holiday, you can stroll by water and on green lawns unfettered by a fence of concrete roads choked with traffic. My own visit was a touch less idyllic, marred by constant rain which afforded only smudgy glimpses of the numerous coves and grand "beach-shacks" of the likes of Barbara Streissand, Steven Spielberg, and Jackson Pollock. We went out to see a Japanese arthouse movie and celebrated

Lydia's birthday overlooking the water at East Hampton Point restaurant, before returning to the city.

Nearly a year later I was back in the US. In twelve months there were some differences. George W. Bush was in the White House, Hilary Rodham Clinton had become a senator. But in the Middle East there was still turmoil with an intifada that had left 445 dead, with homes and the hopes of countless people destroyed.

Back in Mort's office, the sun was shining through a new set of windows, replaced since my earlier visit, but the bathing suit and towel were still hanging there. The wall proudly displayed a framed award from lawyers for the *Handbook of Conflict Resolution*. The New York Academy of Science was on the phone inviting Mort to do a presentation on any topic of his choosing.

My final visit to New York for the book followed my attendance at the 2002 Annual meeting of the American Educational Association in New Orleans. The world had now changed. Airport security was palpable as armed military were visible at every turn. Queues seemed longer and slower than before. Yet the country retained a sense of optimism. The colorful city of New Orleans was still replete with tourists promenading down Bourbon Street, drinking beer or taking in the street theatre. The young and not so young were still dancing the night away on the bulging narrow balconies of the French Quarter.

I flew in to New York on April 5, 2002. The city seemed to have recovered from the shock and trauma of 9/11. The tourists were out in full force, a hotel bed was not easy to find, and the streets around Times Square and 5th Avenue were jam-packed with people. The Museum of Modern Art, around the corner from my hotel, had a typical New York snake queue waiting to enter an exhibition of the German artist, Gerhard Richter.

Mort met me for a prearranged lunch. We discussed September 11 and the escalation of the Middle East conflict. Mort being an old hand in New York had booked a table for lunch at the Museum of Modern Art, thus affording a queue-free entry into the Richter exhibition after lunch.

I returned to Australia a few days later and began the mammoth task of piecing together the wealth of information and experiences I had gathered over the past two years.

Personal Reflections on a Life's Work

Mort is now in his eighty-forth year and still very active. He explained his driving force way back on April 11, 1969, in his presidential address "Socially Relevant Science: Reflections on some studies of interpersonal conflict" before the Eastern Psychological Association in Philadelphia, Pennsylvania:

> I have deliberately borrowed the phrase 'the welfare of man' from the ethical code of the American Psychological Association. In my view it is the ethical responsibility of all psychologists — as individuals and as members of their scientific and professional association — to see to it that psychology is used for peace rather than war, for reducing the arms race rather than intensifying it, for eliminating ethnocentricism and prejudice rather than fostering them, for removing social and economic injustices and inequalities rather than perpetuating them. Since Hiroshima we can no longer pretend that science or scientists can plead innocence with respect to the social consequences of their scientific activities.

Mort sees two constant themes in his work: his intellectual fascination with cooperation and competition, around which he has done his theorizing and research and which classes him as a *social* social psychologist rather than an *individual* social psychologist; and the relevance his work has to important social problems.

Apart from occasional sallies against some of the fashionable theorizing and research, he says he has not been energetic enough to take on additional themes. What he has attempted is to "get at fundamental processes that are involved in all aspects of social life, and study them in different forms." The way to proceed, he says, is to think in general terms about what ideas you want to investigate and then try to capture, in your research design, some central feature of the idea you want to work on. He has been very much influenced, as a lot of the early Gestaltists were, by the notion of wanting to understand and explain everyday life.

What I do is try to capture some feature of everyday life which I think is important and to translate that, to tame it, so to speak, by putting it into the enclosed box of a research design. That is a transformation but it starts off with some experience, some feeling that this process — whether it has to do with trust or suspicion, cooperation or competition, something going on in the family, something going on in the larger world that captures my interest — is also something that is universal, and then I try to think of a way of transforming it into research.

Mort is aware that his work has been influential and sees its application as what, in the end, gives it meaning. Not all areas, however, have a clear application. He is unsure exactly how much influence his work in justice has had, and is pleased that his students, at least, have done a lot of writing and research in this area.

While his work did help to broaden the justice field from its sole focus on equity, Mort does not think that it has been as productive as he would have liked. He had hoped that he could come up with some basic notions of how to overcome injustice, to look at injustice in different contexts, such as family, work, school, and the broader society, and see if there were some basic principles that could be drawn out.

Some of his colleagues who were in pure experimental social psychology tended to look askance at his involvement with social causes, seeing this as putting him outside the academic circle. It is a criticism he waves aside.

I did hard-nosed research that I thought related to central problems which then had implications for social issues. These social issues are soft from the point of view of science. To deal with them adequately, you have to make a lot of extrapolations, you have to think politically and economically as well as psychologically. But cooperation, competition, conflict, and justice are central areas in the social sciences. They have implications for a wide range of world problems, and I don't see these problems as soft — not in any sense.

Inevitably, he says there is a tension between these different arms of psychology. This produces a dilemma for academics in terms of how strong they are as advocates with regard to particular social issues and surfaces within professional organisations such as APA.

> There are people who say that you should never take any stance on social issues and there are others who say it's the professional's responsibility to take a stand when you have particular knowledge or information as a result of your work. This is a constant dilemma. How far can you go? In my work it's not been an issue because I've been quite free to speak out on war and peace, on discrimination, to help overturn segregation policies, and I've felt that psychological knowledge really supported the kinds of positions I was advocating. It can be dangerous if you feel that you can speak out as a professional on any kind of issue that you have no particular professional knowledge of. You can speak out as a citizen, but not necessarily as a psychologist. But I think psychologists do have a wide-ranging knowledge about the effects of social injustice, the effects of war, and the kinds of attitudes that can promote war, and in my view it's irresponsible not to speak out.

In addition to his scientific research, Mort ran a psychoanalytic practice for about thirty years until he officially retired from Teachers College. When he started private practice he was seeing patients for up to twelve hours a week. They varied from borderline schizophrenics to obsessive and hysteric personalities. He found it a very valuable experience for a number of reasons. One was that he saw people from a different angle.

Social psychologists, he says, tend to see people from a relatively narrow cross-section of their lives, though perhaps in a wider arena beyond the intrapersonal. From a psychoanalytic perspective you see people from a developmental point of view, as well as a longitudinal, historical point of view. In addition, psychoanalysis deals with matters that are profoundly important and emotional for the people involved and which are not able to be experimented upon because of ethical restrictions.

An important aspect of psychoanalytic work is that it requires you to be constantly aware of your own feelings and your own reactions to patients, so that you don't experience counter-transference in a way that interferes with your work. It's very valuable to be constantly in touch with your own inner life. You're exposed to life stories that are quite different from your ordinary life stories. One patient I worked with very deeply was a woman who had been through the Holocaust as an adolescent, and I could almost get the experience of having been in that situation — much more directly than you would from just reading about it. And that's true for many different life stories. It has been an interesting way of peeking into other people's lives.

In 1962, Mort also co-edited a book with William M. Evan and Quincy Wright called *Preventing World War III*. The book consisted of invited essays by well-known experts. It had three parts: Stopping the Arms Race, Reducing International Tensions, and Building a World Society; there was also an editor's epilogue consisting of essays by each of the three editors. The book was published during a very "hot" period during the Cold War and it received a good deal of attention. In 1963, during the height of the Berlin crisis, the American Friends Society hosted a conference outside Washington DC during which the book was to be discussed. Mort was invited to attend along with high-level diplomats from the State Department, including an Under-Secretary of State, a Deputy Ambassador from the Soviet Union, Ambassadors from Poland and France and other countries, and several senators and congressmen.

> Senator Pell from the Foreign Relations Committee came directly from a meeting with President Kennedy. I had been talking about role reversal as one of the techniques used in conflict situations — something that Anatol Rappaport's contribution to the book discussed at some length. Pell said, 'Why don't we have a role reversal here between the Russian Deputy Ambassador and the Deputy Under-secretary of State?' I described the procedures and orchestrated the role reversal. It was very interesting because the two could well represent each other's perspective, but they didn't seem at all to be able to characterize

the perspectives of the ambassadors from Poland and France and other surrounding nations who were being affected by this, so a very lively discussion was generated.

On another occasion a meeting was organized by the Rand Corporation near Washington, where Mort and others met with the Chief of Staff of the armed forces. When the talk moved to the need for deterrence, Mort and his fellow psychological colleagues put forward an alternative perspective, claiming that deterrence was a very weak reed to put much weight on. They talked about the need to develop cooperative relations, and tried to present a role reversal. Mort would say, "Well, how do you think China feels about this? Or how would Russia view this?" That kind of orientation, trying to bring in the perspective of the other, was what such psychologists such as Charles Osgood, Ralph White, Jerome Frank, Herbert Kelman, Irving Janis, or Mort would do at the many conferences that one or another of them attended. The conferences were generally sponsored by Defense Department think-tanks. "It was not uncommon for one or more of us to be invited as the critical voices at conferences whose participants were mainly intellectuals working for or supported by the Defense Department.

Asked what he thinks is the future of psychology, Mort speaks of the development of instrumentation that would give a clearer picture of the internal environment, of the biological environment, and also of psychosocial development. He has read a paper in an MIT magazine on microprocessors and other techniques that would allow understanding, in considerable detail, of the nature of physical, physiological, and neurological processes. There would, he says, have to be a similar development in characterization of the nature of the social world, the external environment, from a psychological point of view.

He believes that this combination of technological development in the inner and outer environments is where psychology will go. It will be easier to develop the internal aspect because it is easier to assemble good data in that area. It will be much harder conceptually to develop a good characterization of the social world that people face, something that has been neglected in psychological theory. If psychology is to develop well, this is an area that has to be worked on.

According to Mort considerable progress has been made in the social psychological study of conflict over the past seventy years, however there is a long way to go.

> The progress does not yet begin to match the social need for understanding conflict. We live in a period of history when the pervasiveness and intensity of competitive conflict over natural resources are likely to increase markedly. And currently ethnic and national conflicts pose great danger to peace in many areas of the world. We also live in a period when hydrogen bombs and other weapons of mass destruction can destroy civilized life. The social need for better ways of managing conflict is urgent. In relation to this need, it is my view that too few of us are working on the scientific issues which are likely to provide the knowledge that will lead to more constructive conflict resolution of the many intensive conflicts which await us all.

If he were starting his career today Mort says that while he would still focus on the issues he has focused on, he would probably be more involved in multidisciplinary work. Then, he says, he would be a better political scientist and sociologist as well as a social psychologist. He would try to integrate more of the social sciences than he has done because he thinks that what is needed in the world is more integration of the ideas that do exist — there are a lot of good ideas around but they tend to be compartmentalized.

> If I started now I'd probably — and I admit it sounds over-ambitious — try to have more of a background in mathematics and physiology and some of the other social sciences than I do now. I'd want to be more of a Renaissance person, a polymath. I don't know if that's possible any more, but I feel the gaps in not having a broad-based knowledge, all of which has to be relevant to the kinds of issues I want to think about and work on. Donald Campbell had this fish-scale model of the Renaissance person who had overlapping knowledge of many subjects. He feels it's no longer possible the way it was two or three centuries ago for any single person to have a real embracing knowledge of the fundamentals of the various sciences.

Many have remarked on Mort's openness to ideas no matter where they come from.

> The real genius of science is being open and flexible, able to go in the directions that seem promising. Orthodoxy tends to stifle you, and I think it's a betrayal of the original ideas and impulse. Take orthodox Freudians. Freud was an inventive, creative character who would not have been an orthodox Freudian all his life. And the same goes for Karl Marx or any of the leading social scientists. I have a prejudice against orthodoxy in religion in the same sense, because it takes as written in stone ideas and practices that were maybe appropriate for given periods in history, a given culture and so on, but don't allow the kinds of innovations and developments that make it a more living, adapting, creative force. So I tend to be against orthodoxy in whatever form it takes, but I think it's particularly inappropriate in science; it just negates the whole idea of science.

The same openness and flexibility are his gifts to his students.

> It would be terrible if my students were all simple replicas of Morton Deutsch. They have each done original, creative work in their own domains. That's been my approach. It would be terribly presumptuous to say that I have any final answers to anything. I don't. So it's really important for people to be able to develop in their own way. It frees their creative energies.

Morton Deutsch's modesty is the common sense of a man who knows who he is and how wide the world is. He has neither arrogance nor false modesty but accepts the value of his work with equanimity.

The examination of his life and legacy that follows shows he has been as capable of standing up for himself as he is of making way for others. He is, above all, a balanced man who exemplifies his theories about cooperation and the resolution of conflict.

Part One

A Life

Chapter 1

The Man and His Family

Ahead of His Time

Mort describes his premature birth on February 4, 1920 as an emblem of his desire to be ahead of his time. The young Mort raced through his schooling, skipping three grades, 2, 4, and 6, going to a special three-year high school, and ending up in college at the age of 15.

He was born into comfortable, middle-class circumstances in the Bronx, which was then a mainly Jewish area of New York City. Both his parents, Charles and Ida, were Jewish immigrants from what is now Poland and what was then part of the Austro-Hungarian Empire, near Lemburg. They came from the same *shtetl* (village) and arrived in the United States in 1908. Mort never knew his grandparents because they remained in Poland. His maternal grandfather was a reasonably affluent grain merchant, while his paternal grandfather was a scribe in a synagogue.

John, Charles and Ida's oldest son, was about twelve and a half years older than Mort, Jack was about ten years older and Henry two and a half years older. Because of the age difference between him and his brothers, the adventurous Mort spent much time in the neighborhood alone, without close supervision. Just north of where they lived there was a large flight of steps which led to a wooded, undeveloped area where Mort and his friends played. Although he was younger than the other children on his block, he wasn't completely excluded. He recalls playing kickball and other games on the streets. In the 1920s, with fewer passing cars, they could play on the streets without danger.

Mort has an ongoing love affair with New York. To him the New York of the 1920s was as exciting as it is today. Colorful street scenes reflected the ethnic diversity provided by the Irish, Italian, and other European immigrants. The family moved from the Bronx when Mort was five to an apartment on 181st Street in Washington Heights near the George Washington Bridge. In winter there were sleigh rides down a big hill on 181st Street that went for ten blocks. There was more snow then than there is now.

Mort's early life encompassed the Great Depression, World War II, the ghastly revelation of what lay behind the walls of Buchenwald and Auschwitz, and a host of other twentieth-century traumas. He remembers the Depression, when people lived in the parks in shacks known as "hoovervilles" and stood in the street selling apples. Life was less sanitized then and people were more visible on the streets. There was a greater sense of community, but suffering and destitution were also close to home. By the age of 10, Mort had read a lot of Karl Marx and Freud and socially conscious poets such as W.H. Auden. He was repelled by the systematic discrimination against African-Americans.

Mort was a great walker when he was young. As a child of twelve he discovered the joys of walking around New York. Townsend Harris, his high school on 23rd Street, was a long way from his home on 181st Street, on the Upper West Side. Sometimes he would take the subway, but often he would make the two-hour walk home from school, up Lexington Avenue, across Fifth Avenue, then through Central Park to the West side and up Broadway. In those more innocent days before World War II, you could walk safely through Central Park even at night. New York was such a diverse city in its people, its architecture, its sounds and smells. You could go to art theatres to see the latest Russian or French films. There were a lot of places offering free music, free dance and free theatre. Mort later missed his beloved New York acutely when he was in the army and away from the city.

In later years he took part in the lively social movements of the day. For Leftists, there were many radical events, with groups doing things that were free or mostly inexpensive. With the little money that he earned as a waiter during the summer, he was able to enjoy

New York's abundant resources — walking down the street and hearing different languages, walking past food shops with their varied aromas, and going into the greatest museums in the world. He drew from the city's fast pace and human richness a life-affirming energy that drove his long career.

Few early childhood memories stand out, but the ones that do seem to signal his interests in later life. A pivotal experience occurred during a summer holiday in the Catskills with his brother Henry. John and Jack, being so much older, were not there. His father and the two older boys came to visit on the weekends. A counsellor organized a little baseball game with the six- and seven-year-olds. Mort, then just three and a half, was left out while Henry was allowed to play. Mort felt mad, and when someone hit a foul ball to the sidelines near him he threw it away, out of the game. This was his first conscious memory of experiencing anger and injustice, and he sees this as fuelling his later interest in justice and in overcoming discrimination.

Mort's father worked as a partner in a successful wholesale butter and egg business. He was not overly wealthy, but when he later refused an offer to partner in the eventually highly successful retail dairy store called "Daitch", Charles gradually lost his relative affluence.

Ida Deutsch (née Prager) had only the equivalent of an elementary school education, but along with Charles was interested in books and ideas, part of the Jewish cultural heritage that emphasized the close study of the Torah. Their household owned books and the public library was easily acessible. For Mort there were visits with Ida to the art theatres and, now and then, to the movies. Ida wasn't involved in the family business because the downtown workplace was quite a distance from the family home.

The book-learning that was so much a part of the Deutsch household was also part of the background of many of the young people with whom the Deutsch boys went to school. New York City, particularly at that time, was much more Jewish than it is now. Mort's heroes were Einstein, Freud, and Marx — three eminent intellectual Jews — rather than baseball players. He did, however, have an interest in baseball and talks knowledgeably about Babe Ruth and Lou Gehrig, the stars of the New York Yankees.

By the age of 12, skipping grades had made Mort stand out from his peers. His high school, Townsend Harris, offered a three-year program designed to accelerate bright students, and it precipitated Mort into an older, adult world. His high school was located in the Business School of the City College of New York. To get into the crowded elevators, to go to the 9th and 12th floors, where Townsend Harris was located, he often had to squeeze himself between 18- or 20-year-old college students two or three feet taller than he was!

The years he spent at Townsend Harris, 1932–1935, were the years of the Great Depression. It was a time of political ferment, marked by the rise of the union movement in the United States. The struggle for survival, for justice, affected many families. Marxism and socialism were in the air. Townsend Harris was no exception. The students, unhappy with the food in the cafeteria, organized a strike. For the young Mort it was exhilarating to help organize the strike and to participate in it. For a youngster destined to make his mark in the areas of conflict and justice, there was much to absorb in 1930s New York.

The Brothers

Mort was influenced a great deal by his three brothers, particularly Jack. Jack was more intellectual than John and was to become a teacher. He was interested in mathematics and probably would have done very well as a mathematician except that the Depression hit and he decided to seek the security of employment as a high school teacher rather than finishing his doctoral degree. Jack was always interested in ideas. Mort remembers his brother as somewhat radical — not a communist but oriented toward Leftist ideas. John completed a law degree and then went into business as a successful insurance broker. Henry, having done well in school, Phi Beta Kappa, became an accountant. Jack and Mort were the intellectuals of the family. John, Henry and his father, Charles, were more business-oriented and consequently were perceived as aligned, while Jack, Mort and his mother, Ida, were the intellectuals.

Mort regrets that he never learned Yiddish. The older brothers insisted that English be spoken at home. Their aim was to protect

Mort and Henry from speaking the Yiddish of their parents so that they could blend better into American society — a common phenomenon among European immigrants. His parents had learnt English quite well, so Mort grew up in a family where speaking the new language had become natural.

Mort did not grow up as an observant Jew. Charles had rebelled against the religion of his scribe father, so imposed no religious observance on Ida and the children. Mort was sent to a Reform Hebrew school on Sundays for several years but neither he nor his older brothers had a bar mitzvah. This was not seen as atypical in a non-orthodox family in New York in the first half of the twentieth century; while religiousness was denied, Jewishness was not.

Mort saw his older brothers as supportive but was not close to them. His relationship with Henry was deeply ambivalent, and in fact became a seedbed for Mort's later passionate concern with justice and conflict resolution. Mort expresses it as a kind of unspoken rivalry between them. There had been the baseball incident, where Henry was preferred, and he seemed to get certain other privileges that were denied to Mort.

Mort did not fit easily into any age group. Many of the children in the neighborhood were Henry's age. While Mort was younger, his rapid progress through school grades meant that in schoolwork he was not far behind Henry, so he was constantly associating with older children. To make matters worse, Mort was smarter than his brother. Henry would come home from algebra class and give Mort an algebra problem before he had learnt any algebra, and Mort could figure it out — a triumph for Mort and a source of annoyance for Henry. Henry and his neighborhood friends formed a gang that went in for cruel initiations with physical beatings. After a while Mort refused to be involved and chose not to be part of the group. It was an early and painful lesson in conflict: wanting to be part of the group but being unable to put up with the constant humiliation. Henry was maintaining his status as the older brother while being challenged by Mort in different ways. This need to outshine those who were trying to put him down gave Mort a strong push to achieve.

The Family

There were other tensions within the Deutsch family. Family quarrels happened with no attempt at resolution. Early in his life Mort remembers his father as being quite liberal and socialist in orientation, but when he grew disillusioned with union activity he became somewhat reactionary. There were some bitter arguments during Mort's college years, which ended with feelings of estrangement on both sides. It was not an unusual picture: the radical son and the conservative father. Sometimes the quarrels led to heated exchanges, reinforcing already existing attitudes; at other times they were just shrugged off. It was part of the atmosphere. Nothing got dealt with in a way that everyone could feel happy about.

Neither was the relationship between Charles and Ida a close one. Again, there were unexpressed tensions. Ida was a very attractive woman, and Mort describes how, at the age of 12, walking behind her without realizing it was his mother, he noticed with approval her excellent figure. He was shocked to find it was his mother! Mort saw a good deal of rage in her, which might have accounted for her high blood pressure. Unspoken, he believed it used to come out in her facial expressions.

To Mort, his mother seemed to have a sense of loneliness about her, an absence of the affection and attention she needed. He was aware of his mother's awkward and somewhat over-affectionate response to tradesmen who occasionally did work in the apartment, as though she had a need that she could only express clumsily. He felt an unspoken pull from her to fill that void and at the same time was afraid of getting sucked into a vortex. Much later in his psychoanalysis training, which he started when he was 34 years old, he became aware of how this theme affected his most intimate relationships.

In 1937, she died suddenly of a stroke at the age of 57. It was a shock to the 17-year-old, who left for college in the morning to be greeted on his return by a strange hush in the family home.

It soon became apparent that his father had been having an affair with his secretary, Esther. Mort remembers Esther as a pleasant, friendly woman. She was much younger than Charles and in fact younger than his older brother John.

After Ida's death Charles married Esther. Not surprisingly in such a context, Mort and his father at times had a strained relationship. His father was in his forties when Mort was six or seven. He remembers him as solid of figure, with the small belly associated with a hernia. He wasn't the relaxed, informal kind of father one might have seen in the latter half of the twentieth century. He did take his son to visit friends and to places like the Bronx Zoo, but the hard pinch he gave Mort's chest when he was a chubby 10-year-old engendered in Mort an anger towards his father that stayed with him. Their later political differences drove them even further apart.

Charles died in 1950 at the age of 72 from a coronary occlusion. Most of his money, of which there wasn't a great deal, went to Esther. He left Henry $1000 in his will and Mort $500. This was a clear statement of dismissive displeasure toward the youngest son, which reflected the estrangement.

The tensions in Mort's family were tempered somewhat by the presence of sundry uncles, aunts, and cousins. On his mother's side there was Aunt Clara who lived with them in Washington Heights for some eight years. She had emigrated from Poland in the 1920s. Uncle Alex didn't live with the family but was around a lot. Then there were Pauline and Isadora, who lived in New Jersey. On his father's side, Cousin Irma was a very beautiful young woman who looked like Hedy Lamarr. Charles had one brother, Louis, who owned a candy store in Brooklyn and the family used to visit there often. When the Deutsch family had a cottage at Rockaway beach Louis and his family used to stay with them. There were visits to another aunt, Tanta Bella, who sold pickles and sauerkraut in a wonderfully appetizing store in Brooklyn; the young Mort would go there to savor the aromas. There are no recollections of family rituals or feasts on holidays — religious culture was not part of family life.

The Deutsch brothers didn't have family weddings. The family were not the kind that had expectations of grandeur or went in for ritual or formality. Mort got to know John's wife, whom he describes as a "very beautiful and friendly woman," simply because she introduced herself on the street. Jack, a high school teacher, married a woman who was working in his school as an administrator. When Mort met her he found her to be warm and motherly.

Marriage and a Family of His Own

Mort met his future wife in 1945, shortly after arriving at MIT. He noticed a very attractive young woman, named Lydia Shapiro, who would occasionally pop in to the Center. She was working as an interviewer for a study on self-hatred among Jews under MIT's research center's director, Kurt Lewin.

As Mort says, "We started to get to know one another over cherry cokes and jelly donuts. Being supported on the GI bill, I was a cheapskate and she did like jelly donuts." Mort was assigned to supervise her work, and fired her after learning that she spent much of her time sunbathing on the banks of the Charles River. They were married a year and a half later. "In moments of marital tension," he later wrote, "I have accused Lydia of marrying me to get even, while she asserts it was pure masochism on her part. In our 50 years of marriage, I have had splendid opportunities to study conflict as a participant observer."[1]

Madeleine Heilman, one of Mort's later students, recounts her expectations of Mort's wife. "Our conception of this great scholar's spouse was that she'd be a very serious, rather stodgy kind of person. The first party of theirs that I went to wiped the floor with this notion. It was in my first year, at Christmas time, and there was this absolutely stunning, dramatic creature — flawless, but very animated. It turned out that she was Mort's wife. I loved her instantly. It was just so great that she defied everybody's expectations so much, and yet she's so intelligent and so able to be everything that she needs to be, and yet still have all these extras. She brought beauty into his life. She's a painter, a woman who enjoys art and things that are beautiful. She has really rounded out his life. I liked her immensely and we really got along right away. She's marvellous to go shopping with. This is the woman who has been a fashion designer. Going through a rack of clothes with Lydia, she sees things that I don't. She sees fabric, she sees lines, she sees subtle details that most people would miss. She's just terrific. We've had a lot of fun with Mort and Lydia over the years."

Lydia was born in Boston at a place called Mattapan. Her father owned a clothing store, in Lawrence, Massachusetts, to which he commuted daily for a couple of hours each day by train. Lydia had a brother, four years younger. The family home was in Methuen, a middle-class suburb of Lawrence, which was a mill town in Massachusetts. The family lived in a small house on a small block of land, where her parents were keen gardeners. Lydia's mother clearly liked men better than she liked women. Once Lydia introduced Mort to her mother she gave Mort more attention than she did her daughter! She was an anxious woman, a gracious hostess and a wonderful cook, but her eagerness to please bordered on dysfunction. During Lydia's childhood she would get exhausted and depressed and would take to her bed, although not during the time Mort knew her.

When Lydia met Morton Deutsch she was living in a rooming house run by a French woman, not far, as it turned out, from an apartment that Mort shared with two graduate students from Harvard, Bernie Kramer and Dalbir Bindra. Lydia took some courses at Harvard in anthropology after meeting a professor from the anthropology department who sometimes ate at her rooming house. She met all kinds of people at Harvard and had an active social life.

Before getting married she worked for about a year as an admitting officer at a small hospital near Boston. Not having much to do, she would walk around and talk to the patients and tell them how wonderful they looked, soon becoming the head of public relations. After her marriage she got a job, through a friend of the family, as an assistant to a radiologist at a different hospital. She worked for the radiologist only for the first half of each day. On her way home she would stop at Filene's Basement, Boston's famous store, where she would shop. This carefree life was further filled with many social events with family and friends.

Mort's family tradition of minimal weddings was not the preferred style of Lydia's parents. They were much more formal and wanted a proper wedding, with black tails and white tie. The date was set for June 1, 1947. Lydia's uncle owned a nightclub, in Boston, the Fox and Hounds Club, and they arranged to have the wedding there.

Al Pepitone and Stanley Schachter were fellow MIT students who were Mort's roommates during1946–1947 after he moved from Cambridge to Boston. Being unable to choose between them who would be best man, he decided both would be, but when he went with them to hire clothing for the wedding, Mr Goldstein, the shopkeeper, just couldn't adjust to the idea. Ultimately, Schachter, because he was Jewish, became the official best man.

For their honeymoon Mort and Lydia toured Quebec in a borrowed car (Lydia's father's). They stayed the wedding night at the Sleepy Town Motel in Maine, on the way to Quebec. Driving around the Canadian state, they found it quaint and charming.

Straight from the honeymoon Mort and Lydia went to Bethel in Maine to attend the first National Training Laboratory. Lydia and a woman who was the wife of another conference participant were the "rum runners". Bethel itself was a dry town so the rum runners had to drive about 20 miles to provide the continuous supply of alcohol to lubricate the conference. Lydia didn't enjoy the conference; she felt on the margins while the participants were so intensely involved.

The newlyweds moved into an apartment in Cambridge, Massachusetts, obtained through Lydia's uncle, who owned the building. When they decided to move to New York they were able to find a one-bedroom apartment in Manhattan on 20th Street and 7th Avenue. It was ten or fifteen blocks north of Greenwich Village and New York University. Mort worked at the Commission for Community Interrelations of the American Jewish Congress (CCI), and also at the New School.

In New York, Lydia's aspiration was to find a job that would be enough to make a substantial contribution to the rent. She did a six-month course at a design school, and on graduating worked as a designer for a lingerie and lounge wear company. The business, Blue Swan, was owned by the McKay brothers: two brothers whose name had originally been Konigsberg. They had anglicized the name to Kay and then to the Irish, McKay, and converted to Catholicism, which meant that there were often Catholic priests wandering in and out of the office. It was 1950, and the McKay boys made a fortune selling "suspants," snug-fitting woven panties that acted as a girdle complete with stocking garters. They would fly Lydia and her assistant in their private plane to the factory in Pennsylvania so they could direct the pattern-makers.

Lydia's life took on a Hollywood quality: lavish offices, manicurists to do her nails while they watched fashion shows, parties and champagne — it was straight out of the movies.

This lifestyle was not to last. Despite her talent and interests, Lydia did not feel a drive for success that said, "This is what I want to do. This is my highest priority." And then the children began arriving, and life changed.

When Lydia fell pregnant the couple was able to move into a comfortable two-bedroom apartment because a friend that Lydia worked with knew a Polish gentleman who owned the building. Apartments were very scarce after the war, and she arranged for Lydia to meet him. Lydia was four months pregnant. "He was to take me to lunch," Lydia says, "but he wasn't to know that I was pregnant, and so I moved the buttons about six inches on my jacket, squeezed into a suit and went to lunch with him, and he gave me the stamp of approval."

The young couple's first child, Tony, was born on September 20, 1950. Mort's father had died a few months earlier. Lydia was still working for two and a half days a week but found that there was constant pressure to come up with a design that was going to make a fortune for the company at least for that year.

It was a difficult time. Tony had celiac disease from nine months of age until two years as it took some time to diagnose the condition. He had constant irritability of the stomach and diarrhea until finally a pediatrician diagnosed it and put him on a very strict diet. After eighteen months on this diet he was cured.

The couple found that parenthood brought inevitable changes to their lives. Having a young child meant that they didn't have their evenings or weekends free to do whatever they wanted. The young family spent several summers in Ogunquit, Maine, near where Lydia's parents lived in northern Massachusetts. Here they rented a house for a month. The combination of being a mother and working in the fashion industry led to Lydia having a number of quarrels with her bosses, who were putting pressure on her to work more hours. At that time Mort was involved in parenting Tony, taking him out to the playgrounds and climbing the rocks in

Central Park, but the responsibility for managing the nannies and the baby rested with Lydia.

From the beginning of Mort's career he was very absorbed in his work, which he loved. It was just as well for Lydia that she had her own career, otherwise she might have found Mort's periodic absences very difficult. Mort's heavy involvement at Bethel, while he was still a graduate student, just a week after they had been married, was an omen of what was to come.

"I was well trained by my mother to think that men are supposed to do what they're supposed to do," says Lydia. "That's their privilege. Women were just supposed to sacrifice or something like that. Marriage came first, nothing else was really important, and whatever feelings I had about a career, they were always secondary, and the money I regarded as just extra money to buy clothes or other things, so I didn't really take my career seriously. When I look back on it I envy women today who are really serious about their careers, because my generation wasn't."

After another two jobs, one with Christian Dior, Lydia went back to painting, studying at the Art Students' League at the same time as she was doing her master's at Columbia and working part-time. She stayed at the League for about ten years and has been painting ever since.

When he was four years old, Tony went to a nursery school, Emerson on 96th Street, not too far from where the family lived on 72nd Street. After a year or two he went to the local public school. Once he started regular school he went on to playgroups between 2.30 p.m. till school ended and 5.00 p.m. when Lydia or Mort would be home.

Tony had a certain original flair that matched a determination to do things in his own way. When Tony needed some psychological tests done to gain entry to a school, Florence Halpern, a distinguished psychologist at Bellevue Hospital in Manhattan with whom Mort was doing an internship, conducted the tests. Mort remembers Florence asking Tony if he'd like to draw a house, boat, tree and so on. Tony, however, would do something different. When later challenged about not doing what he was asked, he said, "I wanted to do something else. She asked me what I wanted to do!"

There was also a premature independence that caused his parents some concern. And when Nick arrived nine years later, it seemed that like so many elder children, Tony was put out by the birth of a sibling. As the only child who had traveled with his parents and been very close to them, Tony understandably carried some resentment towards Nick. The age gap, however, meant that Tony was at elementary school while the household focused on the new baby, and he also spent many of his summers away at school camps.

Tony is like his father in a number of ways, especially in this independent nature. When he was four years old he used to call himself "Mort"! His insistence that he be called by the same name as his father is perhaps something more than merely amusing. For a boy to identify with his father is not unusual but to insist on having the same name is taking the identification a little further than most.

He had an innately sharp wit. Before Nick was born, his parents talked about having a contest to name the baby, and what kind of a prize they would give to the person who thought of the best name. Without hesitation, eight-year-old Tony said, "the baby!" One time when Mort and Lydia were talking about Nick's chubbiness Tony said "You may call him Buddha but I call him Budapest!" He had a keen sense of humor and as an adult he has an engaging originality about him. In high school he was already a senior chess master and when he was seventeen played in the National Open Chess Tournament and tied a grand master in the game. His parents were impressed by this achievement but were happy when he decided not to continue with chess as his main occupation as they saw it as an isolating activity.

Lydia tells a wonderful story about Tony's prowess at chess. One summer she took him to a beach in East Hampton, near their summer cottage, where a lot of artists were congregated. Tony noticed that all the artists were playing chess with each other, so he challenged the winner, and of course he won because he was a much better player. The wife of the man who was beaten, who was a well-known artist, came over to where Lydia was sitting with some other artists, and said "Does anyone know who that little son of a bitch is who's beaten my husband?"

In 1959 Mort and Lydia's second son, Nicholas, was born. Nick was quite a different child from Tony, and his parents' experience of him also differed. Perhaps most significantly, Lydia stopped working for several years after Nick was born. Being around and knowing what was happening all the time made her feel much more relaxed and confident. She enjoyed motherhood more this time, and the baby thrived. However, she was happy to eventually get back to work. She was never someone solely oriented toward house and children.

Nick's childhood progressed smoothly. He went to Columbia Greenhouse school when he was three and a half and then to elementary school (until 6th grade) in the Horace Mann building at Teachers College. Mort's office was in the same building and if Nick had any problems he'd just come up and talk. He was much easier to get on with than Tony, more huggable, and he did fairly well in high school. He had no difficulty getting into Columbia where he graduated Summa cum Laude. He attended Columbia College, and then Columbia Medical School. His tuition was completely paid for by Columbia University's Teachers College, because Mort was on its faculty; the family, however, paid for his room, board and books.

Tony graduated Magna cum Laude from SUNY at Stony Brook. Like his father, Tony skipped classes. He could study on his own and do well generally but he only went for the things in which he was really interested. Tony is now a partner in a large human benefits firm in charge of the East Coast Actuarial Division.

Nick was less rebellious and had a superb academic record. His academic undergraduate record was almost all As or A+s and his professor in biochemistry hoped he would go into research, but he decided to become a medical doctor. Today he is a cardiac anesthesiologist and does two or three operations each day.

Lydia says that they are both sons that she and Mort can be proud of in terms of what they've accomplished. Mort adds, that they have been excellent fathers and partners and very successful in their occupations. Nick is the practical and managerial character in the family. He was always good at thinking things through in a practical way and fixing small appliances. While he was in college the family often went to their holiday house at East

Hampton, while he stayed behind. Mort and Lydia later learned, at his graduation, that a lot of parties were being held in their apartment while they were gone, and they never knew because Nick had cleaned up so well!

Did Mort's political and social justice ideas rub off on his children? Tony remembers a lot of political discussion in the house but no acrimonious disagreements. He was very much aware of the civil rights movement — in 1964 one of the civil rights workers who lived in their building was killed. He remembers that his father was active and aware, and that the civil rights movement was very much part of the environment at school. Later Tony was involved in some of the early anti-Vietnam demonstrations and was conscious of Mort's opposition to American foreign policy at that time.

It doesn't appear that Mort's work had any large impact on his role as a parent. Much of his work on conflict theory came after the children were grown. *The Resolution of Conflict* was published in 1973, fourteen years after Nick's birth, and it was a general, theoretical research book. Lydia and the boys attest that Mort never talked about his work at home. When he won awards he often went off and collected them without involving the family. As a result, Tony and Nick knew very little about the details of his work.

Just as he did with his students, Mort tried not to tell his sons what to do except where he felt it was necessary. He feels he didn't do too well on that score with Tony. He thought Tony would be better off as an academic than if he went into business.

"I tried to persuade him that there were opportunities for him in the academic world, but he was not really open to this. I think at a certain point he wanted to be in a field where he would make a significant amount of money, and he didn't think he could do that as an academic."

In general interpersonal communications Mort's style is what psychologists call "conflict-avoidant," while with Lydia his style is conflict-avoidant up to a certain point and then, because Lydia's style is "conflict-escalating," he steps in strongly at an escalated point and that tends to bring the heat down. Sometimes they talk rationally about what the issues are and sometimes the issues are forgotten. Because he is focused on the sensitivities of other people in identifying what will make them angry or anxious, he is able to avoid doing that himself. He often avoids doing things that would necessitate him having to deal with a conflict.

Travel was a significant part of Mort and Lydia's early years together. Frequent work meetings in Europe offered opportunities to go to different places. In relation to the European currencies after the war, the American dollar was so strong that everything was cheap. They were able to travel in a style that they couldn't have afforded later. In Venice they stayed at the Hotel Monaco in a beautiful suite, fronting a canal. They were able to stay at expensive hotels in Switzerland, France and Italy and enjoy excellent food and wine. Tony was with them on many of these visits and has vivid memories of Europe and, once, Mexico.

Mort has always been a Francophile. This goes back to his early boyhood when he had a French friend whose mother would bring back presents from Paris when they went over for the summer. He loves the food, wine and beautiful countryside, and finds Paris a wonderful city to walk around. He and Lydia were an attractive young couple who found that places and people just opened to them. The one problem was that Mort didn't have any talent for languages. He had problems pronouncing English words, let alone foreign ones!

Home and Friends

In 1964 the family stopped traveling overseas so much and instead began taking summer holidays at East Hampton on Long Island. A large contingent of New York artists, academics, and business people used to go out there for the summers, among them Max Deutscher, a psychoanalyst, who had a house in East Hampton. Mort and Lydia went to visit him and he suggested they rent a house for the summer. Tony was then fourteen and Nick about five. They rented for two years then bought a house. Six years later, in 1972, they bought another house which they still own. East Hampton had probably the nicest beaches in the country, and a variety of wonderful scenery — the bay, the ocean, and beautiful farmland in the back roads.

At East Hampton there was a rather hectic weekend social life. Sometimes Mort would come out by train on a Friday night; Lydia would pick him up and they would go to three or four parties. In New York part of their social life centered on the people Lydia worked with, part of it on the people Mort worked with. This created an interesting clash of cultures between the garment industry and the academic world, where the pressures that existed in the commercial world contrasted with the slower, longer view of things in academia. Tension between Lydia and Mort came out of this difference in their ordinary surroundings during the day.

Lydia was also, at that time, studying at the Arts Students' League, and some of her fellow students and their husbands became lifelong friends. Mort, via his research on interracial housing, met Ed Rutledge, an official engaged in anti-discrimination work. Lydia and Mort introduced him to Renata, one of Lydia's fellow art students. They married and have been close friends of Mort and Lydia's ever since.

Compared to the orthodox Jewish community, which has a certain kind of cohesiveness and a sense of belonging to a clearly identified group, Mort characterizes his own social life as being more fragmented. The book club he and Lydia belong to is one of several separate friendship groups to which they belong. The club consists of four couples, of which he and Lydia are one. Another is Amnon, a psychiatrist and Dora, a professor specializing in Latin literature. A third, Bob and Ruth, are both psychologists who run psychoanalytic practices. Phima is also a psychoanalytic psychologist, while her husband Stanley is a very successful businessman, an intellectual who has always rather regretted not being an academic.

"They are an interesting group and we meet socially and talk about a book that one of us has selected. We take turns selecting books, and sometimes if the book is interesting we have a really good discussion; other times it's mainly a social occasion. We've been meeting once every month or two for the past fifteen years. In winter we meet in New York City and in the summer we meet out in East Hampton, where we all have houses."

Another social group is a New Year's Eve party group that Mort and Lydia have been going to for many years. And then there is the group Mort calls his "rich friends." Then there's the academic social circle, a group which has very little overlap with any of the others, and another set of friends who know each other from East Hampton and New York.

Mort has a profound sense of privacy that kept his rich social life apart from his professional life, according to Barbara Bunker, one of his past students. She feels she could have been a better friend of Mort's, though not necessarily a close one, if she had not been his student. She feels Mort had a very conscious sense of standards, probably out of his therapy training, about what is appropriate for people in authority to do with people over whom they have a kind of control. Some people, she says, are more skilful than he is at both maintaining the boundary and also being warm and "toasty."

Mort keeps this separation for a reason, which has to do with equity across students. "If you have favourites," Barbara says, "you set up dynamics. I always felt very comfortable about my relationship with him, but I always felt that it would be an imposition and inappropriate to push it in any way, because Mort had this sort of even-handed sense of equity that I liked. I used to think, this guy is the kind of person you'd like to have as your boss, because he isn't going to single out anyone for special treatment. Occasionally, however, I'd be with him and he'd make a really pejorative comment about some student, and I'd be astonished because he wasn't like that in his demeanor toward people in general. So there was the Mort who made evaluations, and then there was the Mort who played his role as the sort of even-handed mentor whose job was to help people get through. I think he did both things reasonably well."

Madeleine Heilman and Harvey Hornstein, both students of Mort's who married, have a particularly close relationship with Mort. "Our children treat Mort and Lydia like their grandparents. We were both very prized students, and he was just thrilled when the two of us got together," Madeleine says. Although Mort was committed to not having religious rituals in his house, he and Lydia would go to the Hornsteins' Seder every year at Passover, as members of the family. "Harvey and I have been very close with Mort and Lydia over the years. We've taken Mort out for his birthday to a surprise restaurant every February for twenty years. Mort's eightieth birthday party, to which I was privileged to be invited, was just a small group, his wife and children and a couple of friends. He toasted Lydia very beautifully, and talked about how she brought all these things into his life."

Barbara thinks that this close relationship with Madeleine and Harvey was because Harvey was his first student and colleague, and because Harvey and Mort are both Jewish New Yorkers. "Mort did something for Harvey. Harvey would never have made it, not because Harvey isn't smart, Harvey is very smart, but Mort saw in him something that he didn't see in himself. And more than anybody else, I think that it's like a father and son relationship in a very nice way. Harvey's like Mort's first-born, so it's a special relationship, and I think Mort allowed himself that relationship."

Mort and Harvey were good friends even before Harvey's marriage to Madeleine. Barbara says Madeleine is a warm, interpersonally competent, delightful woman who is easy to relate to, and thinks that her warm friendship with Lydia is the complement of Mort's friendship with Harvey. "Mort and Lydia took them on as a young couple and did things with them, and over the years they've developed a very nice couple-and-couple relationship."

Mort was known for loving parties although he can sometimes seem a shy man. He enjoyed watching other people have a good time, and hearing people talk about parties where he danced. In his youth he wasn't a particularly good dancer, but he says a number of students used to want to dance with him so he would get in the mood and enjoy it. He had the discipline to be pleasant and gracious on any such occasion. His shyness endeared him to people all the more because of this willingness to be outgoing when it was asked. And he surrounded himself with people who were outgoing. Lydia represents that other side of Mort that was rarely expressed.

Barbara says that although Mort is not an expressive, affectionate person, you know when he holds you in a kind of warm esteem. In contrast, he draws a great deal of warmth toward himself. Other people find him sensible and down to earth but in a soft, almost rabbinic way. More than one person has remarked that Mort has a kind of "Solomonic" wisdom into which people can just relax and know that they are safe.

Chapter 2

The Shaping
of a Psychologist

Light Bulbs Going on in the Mind

By the early age of 15, Mort was at college in his beloved
New York. As he walked the familiar streets, delighting in
the colorful tide of humanity and the energy of a great city at
work, he began a journey to seek resolutions to human conflict.

The main campus of the City College of New York was at 137th
Street. It looked like an imitation English university and was an
exciting place to be in the 1930s. City College attracted bright
students, among them the relatively poor Jewish students who
couldn't afford to go to Yale or Harvard or the other Ivy League
schools. Applicants usually had to have an A minus average to get
in, Mort did not have that sort of average but was able to qualify
automatically from his high school, Townsend Harris.

The college at that time was a breeding ground for a number of
well-known intellectuals. The most exciting places on campus
were the alcoves where students had lunch and where there was
always keen political discussion to be had. Between 1935 and
1939 political turmoil swept the world — communism in the
Soviet Union, the rise of fascism and nazism in Europe, and the
fascist invasion of Spain triggering the idealism of a whole generation of youth. It was a campus humming with political activity
that was supported and enhanced by the political orientation of
particular faculties.

So Mort began his university life in a place where neither opinions nor political action were stifled. That freedom he was to give back a thousandfold. At one point Frederick Robinson, the President of the College, invited the Italian ambassador, a fascist, to visit City College. The students went on a sit-down strike in front of the President's office and the visit was cancelled.

The students saved their lunch money and contributed funds to the Spanish cause. Some faculty members joined the Lincoln Brigade, a group of Americans who went over to fight for the Spanish Loyalists against the fascists. Some of the students were anti-Nazi and anti-fascist but not anti-Soviet. In those days Leftist opinion had considerable sympathy for the Soviet Union, and City College students were no exception. Mort was in his element, closely involved in the causes and groups.

In the midst of all this, he encountered people and ideas that set him on his life path. The first was Morris Raphael Cohen, a distinguished philosopher of science and the leading intellectual figure at City College, whose influence, Mort says, "permeated the atmosphere."[1] Cohen was well known in other fields as diverse as history, physics, and chemistry.

Certain faculty members seemed to resent Cohen's intellect, annoyed that whenever any subject came up Cohen was always able to talk about it with more knowledge than anybody else. Legend has it his colleagues once decided to get even by all studying an esoteric subject — sixth-century Chinese armor. When the time came to talk about it at a faculty meeting, Cohen was at first unusually quiet, but then declared that he had actually written an article about the very same subject for an encyclopedia.

More in line with his main work, Cohen wrote a wonderful book with Ernest Nagel, a distinguished professor in philosophy of science, on scientific methods, *An Introduction to Logic and Scientific Methods*.[2] The book had become a kind of bible to students at the college, and Mort was thoroughly indoctrinated in the book's approach, particularly because it presented a very clear and profound way of thinking about science and how it could be applied to research on important social issues.

Cohen and Nagel's scientific method was an examination of theory and research and how the two could be integrated. Research needed a theoretical context, they said, otherwise it would have no real implication. It was the theoretical structure used that gave generality and significance to any particular research study, so it was of the utmost importance. They had many ideas about the nature of theory and the role of empirical work. It was a brilliant book and steered Mort toward the need to combine research with theory and toward his lifelong insistence that theory was crucial. Cohen and Nagel also gave him the notion that you could never approach research in a merely hunch-wise fashion without trying to explicate the ideas behind the hunches.

At that time also, because psychology was taught within the City College Philosophy Department, Mort encountered the ideas of Kurt Lewin, a man who, even more than Cohen and Nagel, radically shaped his life's work. Kurt Lewin, an innovative experimental psychologist close to the Gestalt movement, had fled Nazi Germany for the US in the early 1930s. Mort was immediately attracted to Lewin's ideas after reading J.F. Brown's *Psychology and the Social Order*, as Mort describes it:

> an ambitious, challenging, and curious text that tried to apply Lewinian and Marxian ideas, with a sprinkling of the Riemanian geometry employed by Einstein in his theory of relativity to the major social issues of the 1930s. To a naïve 17-year-old undergraduate student like me, it was a very impressive and inspiring book showing how social science could shed light on the urgent problems of our time.[3]

In another course Mort read Lewin's *A Dynamic Theory of Personality* and *Principles of Topological Psychology*. He describes these books as "mind openers," "permeated by a different view of the nature of psychological science than the then traditional one."[4] Lewin also appealed to him as a profound scientist who was concerned with basic issues, such as authoritarianism and democracy, issues already sharpened by the social surroundings of Mort's youth. J.F. Brown's high-flown theoretical language was exactly to his taste, and to a bright and ardent student of 16 or 17, Einstein was, along with Darwin, Freud, and Marx, an overarching intellectual demigod. Mort was in heaven.

Mort had started college with the idea of becoming a psychiatrist because, "it appeared to be so relevant to the personal issues with which I was struggling, and also because it was so radical and rebellious."[5]Already in high school, on his own initiative, he had read a good deal of psychoanalysis. His interest in psychology and psychological issues was propelled by an interest in internal dynamics — an understanding of how people think and feel and what drives these functions. Early on, he had thought of studying psychiatry through a medical school, but the experience of dissecting a pig had revolted him and he had abandoned his idea of joining the medical profession. The more important influence in psychology at City College was not so much the courses, because he did a lot of his own reading, but the intellectual ferment and the continuous vigorous discussion with other students in the alcoves and outside classes. It was here that he found his attention focused, and with the arrogance of youth he found the students more interesting than many of the teachers.

Mort finished college at 19, in 1939. His mother had died in 1937 and the family moved out of their apartment in Washington Heights to a hotel apartment on the Upper West Side of Manhattan. During the summers he worked as a waiter at Camp Copake, a resort in the Catskills made famous by the 1938 movie *Having a Wonderful Time,* play and screenplay written by Arthur Kober. The resort was run by two men who claimed that they were communists but were rather authoritarian and exploitative. The work was not easy. Waiters had to pay about $60 for room and board (which was terrible) and the only money they earned was from tips. At some point Mort and his friends organized a strike and eventually the management changed the way they went about things and hired professional waitresses.

"In many ways it was a good experience," Mort says, "because you were part of a close-knit group. There was the expectation that you entertain the guests, dance with them at night, and that was fun. The norm was that you never dated a guest who sat at your table, because then you couldn't accept a tip, but you dated guests from other people's tables so you could talk up a tip. There were a lot of talented people there, including the comedian-actor, Jack Guilford, who acted in several movies and Broadway shows, and groups doing modern dance. We were young, we could work all day and stay up all night."

In 1939, Mort went to the University of Pennsylvania to take a one-year master's in clinical psychology, one of the few clinical training programs that then existed. Because of his keen interest in psychoanalysis, he also attended lectures at the School of Social Work and, when he was in New York, at the New York Psychoanalytic Institute, and kept abreast of the psychoanalytic literature. It was a mistake to go to Pennsylvania, however, because their clinical program was very narrow and dry. There were a couple of younger faculty members, Frank Irwin and Malcolm Preston, who had heard of Lewin and were sympathetic to his work. They were more experimental and Mort found some interest in their work. But as a whole, he saw the program as being old-fashioned and not based on psychodynamics, something Mort had hoped for. He also did a little work with children in a speech therapy clinic.

At Pennsylvania he also took a course on tests and measurement with one of the professors, Morris Viteles, a well-known industrial psychologist. When Viteles said one day that there was no evidence that Blacks were not lower in intelligence than Whites, Mort, armed with his City College radicalism and youthful brashness, simply replied, "that may be true but it's a misleading statement unless you add that there is no evidence to indicate that they *are* of lower intelligence." From then on he was labeled the "City College Radical" by the other members of the program.

After completing his MA, Mort joined the New York State Internship Program, which offered a rotating internship at three institutions. One was New York State School for delinquent boys (called Warwick), another was Letchworth Village for the feeble-minded, and the third was at Rockland State Hospital for the insane. He found these experiences fascinating.

"I had a lot of different kinds of interactions with the kids at Warwick, who were not much younger than me. I not only did testing but also I did some remedial teaching and led some groups, and they would sometimes tease me. I remember a boy tapping me on the shoulders, with a baseball bat in his hand, and saying, 'Look, Mr Deutsch!' It was a very rich psychological experience, at that stage of my life, to have contact with people who were mentally retarded, people who were psychotic, and boys who were delinquent."

He found his time at Warwick very interesting because he was young enough to be able to relate to the boys. Most of them were African-Americans from economically disadvantaged backgrounds, and he became well acquainted with their stories. Their descriptions of their lives fitted in with his view of what factors led to delinquency. During his undergraduate course he had written on delinquency and the cultural and socioeconomic factors contributing to it.

At Letchworth he mainly did testing and remembers, in particular, one youth who was then about twenty years of age and had been in the institution since he was six or seven. He was clearly not at all mentally defective and was functioning as a kind of handyman around the place. Mort saw that he didn't belong in the institution and brought his case to the attention of the authorities.

"Nothing was done," Mort recalls, "and at some point — this was when the United States was enlisting soldiers before our entry into World War II — I suggested that he run away. I don't know what happened to him. I thought it was terrible that here was a kid who, probably because he had no relatives who were interested in him — he may have been a problem child and may have tested badly — was put into this institution and simply forgotten." It was an early confrontation with inhumanity, and Mort never forgot it.

The third internship was at Rockland State Hospital for psychotic children and adults. Here he worked in the Children's Unit, where there were a lot of practicing psychologists. The informal seminars were stimulating and he met a number of psychiatrists and social workers who were doing psychoanalytic work and were connected with the New York Psychoanalytic Institute.

At Letchworth, Mort had the good fortune to meet Clark Hull, the famous learning theorist. Mort says that he was a "remarkably generous and tolerant person."[6] They had several long discussions. "Hull seemed genuinely interested in what I had to say about his recent books despite the fact that I was an overly brash twenty-year-old pipsqueak. We had another interesting discussion in which he gave me advice on how to seduce a woman. He told me that, on a date, I should carry a handkerchief permeated with perspiration. He explained that sweat and sexual feelings were associated together because of their joint occurrence during sexual intercourse and that sweat would arouse sexual feelings. In retrospect, I realize that he must have been joking since his suggestion never worked for me."[7]

Wartime

The United States entered World War II on December 7, 1941. Mort enlisted in the airforce the following January, although he would have been drafted anyway even if he had not enlisted. His brother Henry also enlisted. Mort preferred to fly than fight in the trenches so he joined the Air Force and was trained as a navigator. He spent a summer in Idaho with a training group and flew a great deal over the western part of the United States. To get to his combat base in England, he flew from Idaho to Florida, to the Caribbean, and on to Brazil. There were a couple of stops in Brazil, and Dakar and Marrakech in Africa, Scotland, and finally England.

Until that time Mort had not been out of New York much. The trip was an eye-opener in several ways. "I had been mostly with Jewish kids in the various academic places — not exactly true in my internship, where there were mostly non-Jewish kids. In the airforce I never knew actually who the Jewish kids were. I found myself in a non-Jewish environment really for the first time. I was the only Jewish kid in my bomber group and the only Jewish kid in my hut. There were other Jews in the heavy bombardment group, but in my particular plane I was the only Jewish guy." In the airforce at that time all the enlisted men he came into contact with were Whites from Euro-American backgrounds. During the war there may have been one or two units that were racially mixed, but soldiers were mainly segregated. The army helped to start the process of racial integration after the war.

As lead crew navigator with the 467th Bombardment Group he flew thirty bombing missions over Europe. He was eventually awarded the Distinguished Flying Cross, with cluster, for superior navigation on leading his Squadron, Group and Combat Wing. He reflects on the war as being a confidence-boosting and maturing experience, "I certainly felt the war was serious business but I wasn't humbled by it. I felt I gained a lot of personal strength, having gone through the war, having survived it, with all the tensions and problems. I felt stronger psychologically as a consequence of having gone through it successfully and faced the fears."

He recounts an incident when a drunken pilot was riding his bicycle through the base and, wavering, fell over a tree stump and broke his arm. He had been going to fly Mort's plane but Mort refused to fly with him and had him grounded — it wasn't right for the crew to be put in danger. So what was an act of disloyalty to the pilot was to him an act of concern for the crew. Despite the privations and danger, he describes the airforce years as a good period of his life. He felt that the cause was a good one, something worth doing.

"I'm not a pacifist," he says, "otherwise I wouldn't have fought in the war. I believe that under certain circumstances you have to resort to violence, but I think people resort to it much more often than they need to, and often it defeats its objectives."

"The war was such a destructive business. I saw planes that we were flying with shot down. I saw the bombs we were dropping destroy whole areas, and a sizeable number of my crew were killed, though not when I was actually flying in the plane with them. Other people that I knew were killed during the war. When we dropped bombs from our B24s you could see a large part of the city under us just disappear. It was sheer destruction."

"When we saw what the atomic bombs had done in Japan, war seemed such a serious problem that it had to be thought about. Something had to be done to prevent it. I was preoccupied with this, not in any obsessive way but because of my social interests. For me this became, particularly at this time when the UN was being formed, an area that I thought really deserved a lot of hard thinking. When I was in London I saw the results of the bombing — devastation in area after area, having to hide in an air-raid shelter when the bombers came over again. And then being in combat where planes and anti-aircraft guns were shooting at us."

Despite his service time, Mort doesn't see the war as con-tributing greatly to his interest in social psychology. But he did see war as a crazy response, like something out of Joseph Heller's *Catch 22*. "There was a lot of that insanity during combat," he says. "A lot of the things that were happening seemed so stupid and so dangerous. I'd always been interested in social issues from early on, and this had been reinforced by experiences in high school and the strikes at Townsend Harris, City College, and Camp Copake, then being in a highly politicized atmosphere at college. So I wouldn't say that apart from a generally maturing, interesting experience the war changed me in any substantial way. With the advent of the atomic bomb, it just seemed so obvious to me that war was becoming increasingly impossible if we were going to survive as a species."

Mort returned from war in late June of 1945. He was discharged early because, after finishing his tour of duty, he was reassigned as a psychologist in an Airforce Convalescent Hospital program. He was one of the few people on the staff who were eligible to be discharged after earning the required points.

Mort returned to civilian life with his many combat ribbons and medals, his proud father eager to show him around to everyone at the market. Charles had married Esther before the war and Henry was also married. Henry had trained to be in the A bomb group, though he wasn't in one of the planes that dropped the bombs on Hiroshima and Nagasaki. When Mort was discharged he lived with his father and Esther until he left for the Massachusetts Institute of Technology (MIT).

MIT

Mort went to MIT in late August 1945 after teaching a course in abnormal psychology at City College in the summer session. As one of the early returning veterans, he was able to gain entry to graduate school easily. He had narrowed his selection down to three. One was Yale, where Clark Hull had been (he had been impressed with Hull even though he disagreed with a lot of his ideas). Then there was Chicago, where he thought of continuing his clinical work. The third place was Kurt Lewin's new Research Center for Group Dynamics at MIT in Boston.

The appeal of Chicago was Carl Rogers, one of the few psychologists who offered clinical training in therapy. Mort went to Chicago and sat in on some therapy sessions Rogers was conducting with patients. He was not impressed. Rogers' approach did not have the kind of psychodynamic flavor that appealed to Mort. To Mort, Rogers appeared to be working on the surface rather than in depth, which failed to fire Mort's enthusiasm. Chicago was crossed off the list. Mort then visited Don Marquis, Chairman of Yale, but Yale failed to catch him also, mainly because he had by then met Kurt Lewin and sensed that this was the man to follow.

Mort dates the start of his career as a social psychologist to his first meeting with Lewin, in which he committed himself to studying at Lewin's MIT Research Center.

> He had arranged for me to meet him for breakfast at a midtown hotel in New York in August 1945. Even though it was very hot, I dressed formally — with jacket and tie — to meet with this very distinguished professor. Our meeting time was 8.30 a.m., but he did not appear until about 9 a.m. He came bustling in, cheerfully looking around for me, his face bright pink from a recent sunburn. He was not wearing a jacket or a tie, and his manner was quite informal ... I do not remember much about the conversation other than that I described my education, experience, and interests, and he described his plans for the new center. I was being treated as an equal; I felt somewhat courted; I was experiencing a trance-like sensation of intellectual illumination with new insights constantly bubbling forth from this brilliant, enthusiastic, cheerful, effervescent, youthful, middle-aged man. He spoke a colloquial American, often with malapropisms, and he was both endearing and charming. I left the interview with no doubt that I wanted to study with Lewin."[8]

A second meeting, after arriving at MIT, confirmed Mort's impressions. Lewin asked him to prepare a review of the essence of the literature on prejudice, and to do it in three days. "I felt good," Mort wrote.

I was being treated as a serious professional, and was given a responsible and challenging task. Lewin's treatment of me was, I believe, typical of his relations with his colleagues and students. He would discuss a topic with great enthusiasm and insight, he would ignite one's interest and he would encourage one to get involved in a task that was intellectually challenging, giving complete freedom for one to work on it as one saw fit.[9]

It was a manner that Mort was to replicate with his own students.

"Lewin had a good deal of charisma," Mort says. "He was excited about the new thing that he was involved in, and he talked with you in a way that made you feel light bulbs were going on all the time in your mind." Gestaltist and Lewin's biographer, Alfred Marrow quotes Mort as saying that Lewin "communicated an intense enthusiasm and the feeling of being engaged in work that was scientifically pioneering as well as socially significant. He was irrestistible."[10] Mort was particularly impressed with Lewin's conviction that social psychological ideas ought to be applied to bring about positive social change. This also had immense implications for his career.

Mort came to MIT with David Emery, a PhD from Swarthmore whose father-in-law was a very well known mathematician, and Gordon Hearn, an influential social worker. Lewin was seeking a diverse group for the new center. Gordon was not a trained psychologist like most of the others in the student group. He didn't have a master's in psychology; he was not primarily a researcher but was involved in community work.

There was also Stan Schachter who had been at Yale and had first been interested in medicine, and Harold Kelley from the University of California. This small group of students became very close, engaging in intense discussion — a central part of the academic experience. They interacted with one another continually, talking about theory and research, and helping one another with their experimental work.

The psychology researchers were considered oddballs at MIT because it was an engineering school. The students were housed in what had been the radiation laboratory's temporary buildings. Before Lewin came to MIT there were three psychologists on the faculty and all were industrial psychologists. They had been instrumental in recruiting Lewin.[11]

With its small group of specially recruited faculty and students, Lewin's Research Center played an important role in the origin of experimental social psychology. Thus, as a young man Mort was given the exciting opportunity to work alongside such notable figures as Leon Festinger, Stanley Schachter, John Thibaut, Ronald Lippitt, Kurt Back, Dorwin Cartwright, Albert Pepitone, Alvin Zander, Alex Bavelas, John R. P. French and Harold Kelley. Such an environment — its prolific publications dominated experimental and applied psychology in the US — clearly stimulated Mort's thinking and research.

Mort has reflected on the fact that the group was all male. "This was quite a change for Lewin; in Berlin, most of his students were female. It is interesting to speculate how modern social psychology's development might have differed if the student group [had] included a substantial number of women."[12]

Lewin died in his sleep of a heart attack on February 11, 1947, at the age of fifty-seven. Mort recalls that he was due to have an oral exam by the faculty on the morning after Lewin died. "I didn't know that he had died late that evening, and they didn't inform me. They went on with the exam, and it was a very strange atmosphere. I knew something was wrong, but I couldn't tell what it was until afterwards when they told me, and it was quite a shock. He was not that old."

At MIT most of the research did not take individual differences into account but treated subjects as though they were a homogeneous group and tried to induce an independent variable in all of the subjects regardless of their personality. This was true for Mort's research also, although one of his papers published while at MIT[13] analyzed how the leader's personality affected leadership behavior.

Mort believes that you cannot talk clearly about personality without also talking about situations; personality measures tend to be devoid of situations, and therefore they do not capture what is going on. Kurt Lewin's formula was "behavior is a function of personality as interaction with environment." But for practical reasons, most of the MIT researchers found that it was easier to do the kind of research where they tried to have strong experimental variables that would minimize personality differences.

Mort sees two streams emanating from his work at Kurt Lewin's prestigious Center. One was the very influential research, the other was a wide field of social applications. Appropriately, Mort became an early member of the Society for Psychological Studies of Social Issues (SPSSI). Later, at New York University (NYU) he became involved in war and peace issues and was chairman of both the SPSSI and the American Psychological Association's (APA) committees on international relations. Discussions in these committees contributed to the formation of the US Arms Control and Disarmament Agency. Through its staff, the APA committees were able to have discussions with aides of the very influential Senator Herbert Humphrey, who played a leading role in creating this agency.

The NTL Movement

The NTL or T-group (training group) movement started almost accidentally at a Workshop on Intergroup Relations conducted in Connecticut in the summer of 1946 by the MIT Research Center. This workshop was organized to deal with racial problems that had arisen in Connecticut and turned out to be the precursor to the NTL workshops. The participants were people involved in interracial, intergroup relations as part of their regular activities — government officials and heads of civil organizations that dealt with intergroup relations and various people of different racial backgrounds.

The original aim of the laboratory (as the workshops were known) was to help people deal more effectively with complex human relationships and problems. The method was called "sensitivity training" or sometimes "laboratory training" or "group dynamics training." It was generally believed that it had promise for alleviating social problems. Participants hoped to develop their skills in dealing with other people, changing people's attitudes, gaining insight into people's resistance to change and greater insight into their own attitudes and values. The workshop began with a program that encouraged discussion and decision by the entire group; the staff treated the members as peers. There were participants and there were researcher/observers who talked among themselves about what they had noticed, but the practice developed of giving the group participants feedback about their own behavior.

Mort has described the genesis of the T-group at the Connecticut workshop:

> One evening following a lengthy workshop day, we (Lewin, the workshop participants, the trainers [Ron Lippitt, Ken Benne, and Lee Bradford] and the researchers [Murray Horowitz, Mef Seeman and Mort]) were all sitting around a conference table when one of the participants turned to the researchers and asked what we were doing. We said that we were keeping track of the patterns of interaction among the group. He then asked us to describe what we had noted and Lewin suggested that would be an interesting thing to do. We then summarized our impressions and this led to a very lively, productive discussion among the participants which all of us felt was a very valuable, insightful learning experience. This was the embryo of the T-group and sensitivity training which was given birth at the first NTL in 1947.[14]

There was always an air of openness at the NTL groups. Mort had a psychodynamic viewpoint and was identified as the social psychologist and the clinical person in the MIT group.[15]

Colleague Barbara Bunker describes it another way. "There were lectures in the morning, then there was group discussion. At the group discussion there was a researcher or two from Lewin's staff, so Lewin had a core of his graduate students there, and Mort was one of them. The discussion groups met once or twice a day, and the researchers were sitting in the background taking notes and watching what was going on. Then in the evening they would meet with Lewin and talk about what happened in the groups.

"Well, then what happened was that about day two or three, at lunch, a researcher and some teachers who were in a group that he was observing were having this discussion and the teachers asked the researcher what he thought was going on in their group, and he said a few things, and they disagreed with him, and a very lively conversation ensued."

"That evening these teachers went to the research meeting, knocked on the door and said, 'We understand you're talking about our group and we'd like to hear what you're saying,' and Lewin, being a very generous, delightful person, said 'Come on in' rather than 'No, this is a research meeting.' An immensely stimulating discussion followed, so the next night another bunch of people showed up, and by the third or fourth night an enormous part of the conference was coming to these evening discussions about what happened in their discussion group. It was unbelievably lively, and for many it became the best part of the conference."

It was out of this experience that the next summer Lewin, Bradford, and Benne created an institute at Bethel in Maine to study group dynamics. They knew from their time at the conference that if you allow a group to have an experience and then go back and reflect on it, you can help people to understand the group they are in, and they learn experientially what group dynamics are about. Essentially, a T-group is a creation of data or information based on experience and ideas; you think about it and then you create some more data, and you think about that and talk about it in a simple form.

The NTLs were a forum where people with applied interests, mostly university professors, provided training, tested concepts, gave theory sessions, and then helped people understand how to use the theoretical ideas that arose. A lot of ideas were explored. For example, there was research about whether groups function better than individuals, and people began to develop all kinds of activities that demonstrated that you could examine, experientially, whether a group functions better than a collection of individuals to solve a problem. There were ways of translating what people thought they knew about groups and interpersonal relations into experiential exercises that allowed students to feel it and to learn it at a deeper level than just reading a book about it, and then to taking it into practice.

The classic T-group focused on group dynamics. People discovered that in the middle phase of the T-group it was possible to give a lot of interpersonal feedback. There was potential for a great deal of learning about individual style. Some people jumped on this idea, but they were primarily interested in the interpersonal growth, individual development, and growth processes that happened for the individual participants. But those processes don't happen unless you have group development, because people don't want to disclose and talk to each other unless they have been in a group where trust has been established and people feel others will support them. The applied T-group movement went one way, and the research on small groups went another, so that people who were not university researchers became interested in the practical aspects of personal development and interpersonal relationships, and the researchers began work on the social psychological processes occurring within groups and between individuals.

The NTLs had their heyday in the 1960s. Everyone went to sensitivity training or to T-groups. Harvey Hornstein says they were a bit of a fad, a bit evangelical. "Some people had stopped thinking and were doing it just because it was new dialectic stuff that you didn't question." But when he and Mort were together at Teachers College, Mort encouraged Harvey to attend the NTL workshops, even though he had some initial misgivings about them. Harvey remained active in these workshops for nine years.

The first NTL, in 1947, was an extensive program of research and training, supported by the Office of Naval Research. The research group consisted of both Harvard and MIT students. The Harvard Department of Social Relations and MIT Research Center for Group Dynamics had a fairly close relationship and a number of their students were taking courses at MIT. Conversely, several MIT students were taking courses at Harvard, with the Harvard group, and Fred Bales was part of it. Henry Riecken and Shelley Korchin from Harvard, who were later important figures in social psychology, were at the workshop and almost all of the MIT students participated. However, there was a split between the researchers and trainers that reflected a split in social psychology — between people who were more involved in applications and training and organizational psychology, and those more oriented toward experimental research and what they saw as the development of theory. The trainers were naturally very gung-ho, enthusiastic, and non-critical of their training.

Ron Lippitt, who was a very creative man, although somewhat grandiose, and who tended to free-associate his ideas, almost saw these T-group meetings as the way to respond to the possibility of mass annihilation, but a lot of people, Mort included, were quite critical of this approach. Ron represented the more applied and somewhat looser thinking approach to social psychology and Leon Festinger represented the more theoretical, experimental and more systematic, critical approach. Lippitt and Festinger would have heated exchanges at the Research Center. "During these vigorous disputes, Lewin would be smiling benignly as he watched his intellectual offspring squabble."[16]

The PhD

The theoretical underpinning of the National Training Laboratory came out of the work that Lewin, Lippitt, and White did on autocratic, democratic, and laissez-faire groups in the late 1930s and on the notion of democratic leadership and group participation.

Lewin, influenced by Cassirer, a German philosopher of science, held that the idea of a group was not just a concept but could be studied through experiments and also applied to the way actual groups functioned, for example, to reduce prejudice or to train group leaders. Influenced by this viewpoint, Mort conducted experiments on issues such as cooperation and competition, trust and distrust.[17]

In this stimulating atmosphere Mort's ideas flourished. His doctoral dissertation was entitled "The Effects of Cooperation and Competition upon Group Process." He sees its intellectual roots as Lewin's theoretical interest in social interdependence and the "Marxist concern with two different systems of distributive justice: a cooperative, egalitarian and a competitive, meritocratic one." In addition, the writings of George Herbert Mead, an American philosopher and psychologist, affected his way of thinking about cooperation and its importance to civilized life.[18] But, as Mort says, it sprang initially from the very real issues of the time.

> My dissertation started off with an interest in the issues of war and peace (atomic bombs had been dropped on Hiroshima and Nagasaki shortly before I resumed my graduate studies), and with an image of the possible ways that

the nations composing the newly formed U.N. Security Council would interact. The atmosphere at the Center, still persisting after Lewin's premature death, led me to turn this social concern about the risk of nuclear war into a theoretically oriented, experimental investigation of the effects of cooperative and competitive processes. The specific problem that I was first interested in took on a more generalized form. It has been transformed into an attempt to understand the fundamental features of cooperative and competitive relations and the consequences of these different types of interdependencies in a way that would be generally applicable to the relations between individuals, groups or nations ... The intellectual atmosphere at the Center pushed its students to theory building. Lewin's favourite slogan was 'There is nothing so practical as a good theory.'[19]

Nobody, however, had really studied cooperation and competition from the point of view of the psychological processes that occurred during either situation, and the interpersonal relations that developed as a result. Mort formulated a theory on the nature of the differences between cooperation and competition and set up a complicated experiment using a Latin square design, with groups having problems in different sequences. At that time he was also teaching introductory psychology to a large group that could be broken down into groups of five. Half the groups were assigned to a cooperative condition and half to a competitive condition. He was able to use research assistants at the Group Dynamics Center to do systematic observations of the group and individual processes within the groups.

In those days, of course, everything was done by hand. There were no computers to do all these Latin square analyses of variances and correlations, and the analyses took weeks. Then Lydia typed it all and Mort turned in his dissertation just before the Center began the move to the University of Michigan in the summer of 1948. Mort defended his thesis in July 1948.

Just before the dissertation defence, an article by Ken Benne and Paul Sheats appeared in the *Journal of Social Issues* called the "Functional Roles of Group Members." It was based on material Mort had developed: the description of the kinds of task roles and social roles that individuals formed, and an observation scale that had been developed for it. When Mort confronted Benne and Sheats, they admitted that they had used his work, but they had provided no acknowledgment. Mort put a footnote to his publication of the dissertation in two articles in *Human Relations*[20], indicating that the Benne and Sheats article was based on his material. From then on he made sure that his name was on anything that he developed and that anybody who made any contribution to anything he was doing was fully acknowledged.

After completing his PhD Mort had a number of job interviews in Chicago, Connecticut, and New York. He decided on a career in New York, the city that he loved. In the first year, September 1948 to September 1949, he worked at the Commission on Community Interrelations of the American Jewish Congress and the New School for Social Research in New York. He had been recruited by Stuart Cook, who was head of a program at the American Jewish Congress that was studying prejudice and how to overcome it — a well-funded area in the time shortly after the atrocities of World War II. Its academic home was at the New School and it also functioned in office space rented by the American Jewish Congress. It derived its support from the Congress's Commission on Community Interrelations. Mort took an assistant professorship at the New School and was paid by the Commission.

When Stuart Cook's group moved to NYU in September 1949, Mort moved with them and took up a professorship, teaching there until 1956, and Stuart Cook became Chair of the NYU Department. While at NYU, Mort worked for a year with two clinicians who were involved in psychiatric diagnosis: Florence Halpern at Bellevue Hospital and Fred Brown at Mt Sinai. In 1954 he entered the psychoanalytic training program of the Post Graduate Center for Mental Health, which he did in addition to his regular job as a professor at NYU. Mort's time-consuming psychoanalytic training influenced his thinking on social psychology. This interest continued throughout his working life — he ran a practice until fairly recently. Mort used his experiences of intrapsychic and interpersonal conflicts in a clinical setting and applied them to his experimental work on conflicts between individuals and groups.

The SPSSI and Interracial Housing

During the period 1952 to 1954, Mort served as a member of the Society for the Psychological Study of Social Issues Committee on Civil Rights, chaired by Kenneth Clark, a distinguished African-American social psychologist, along with Stuart Cook, Isidor Chein, and Max Deutscher, among others. This committee provided a summary of research on the social-psychological effects of segregation to the civil rights lawyers who prepared the legal brief submitted to the US Supreme Court in the 1954 *Brown v the Board of Education* case that saw the end of segregated schooling. The Deutsch-Collins study on interracial housing was an important part of the research summary.

Mort's work on interracial housing, a study he conducted with Mary Evans Collins, was an examination of the effects of integration or segregation in various public housing developments in New York and Newark. The study had the cooperation of the New York and Newark Housing Authorities. It found that integrated and segregated housing did have different effects on the attitudes of the children and adults who lived in the housing projects. In brief, the attitudes of the White and Black tenants became more favorable to one another, and they had many more cooperative interactions with one another in the integrated setting as compared with the segregated setting. The attitudes appeared to generalize to members of the White and Black people not living in the projects. Integrated housing was clearly the way to go.

Louis Danzig, director of the Newark Housing Authority, used the results of the study to push for integrated housing in Newark, as did other housing authorities. In that era, the late 1940s and early 1950s, there was a rapid growth in public housing, and segregation had become a salient public issue. The study was widely quoted, within Newark and nationally. Mort also did another study, which was not published, of different public housing authorities right across the country — in Chicago, New York, Connecticut, and California — on patterns of intergroup relations for the Housing and Home Finance Administration of the US government.

As a result of the study, Mort came to be viewed as an "expert" on integration in housing and participated in many meetings and conferences with public officials and civil rights groups who were interested in developing a more integrated civil society.

SPSSI's involvement in the public housing debate was a reflection of the concern about how psychology was addressing social issues. There were many people in SPSSI, among them Gordon Allport, Gardner Murphy, David Krech, Goodwin Watson, Theodore Newcomb — the leading figures in social psychology who were active in the fight against prejudice and discrimination. Ross Stagner, another leading SPSSI figure, had earlier been interested in unions and industrial strife. At City College, Mort had been inspired by the involvement of people on the faculty in such issues, particularly Max Hertzman and Walter Scott Neff, who were among the founders of the Psychologists' League, a predecessor to SPSSI.

Mort says that earlier psychologists had been somewhat racist and did not challenge the racism of the times. For example, they accepted the skewed results of intelligence tests for immigrants (written in English), which had the effect of labeling many Jews as mentally inferior. He feels that it took some time for psychology to grow a conscience about racism.

Mort came up against this from the start. "When I was named the E.L. Thorndike Professor at Teachers College and I gave my inaugural address," he says with characteristic frankness, "I indicated my respect for Thorndike but I clearly dissociated myself from his racist views, which were fairly typical of the period in which he functioned as a psychologist. He was an eminent man but he didn't really understand the limitations of testing and the false conclusions that could be drawn."

SPSSI became, in a sense, the conscience of psychology. Until that time there had been individual voices but no organized group. While SPSSI was only one unit within the whole discipline or profession it was an important body because a lot of prestigious psychologists joined it, including Gardner Murphy, who was one of its early presidents. The important people associated with SPSSI gave the group more impact than its relatively small membership might suggest.

Donald Campbell, writing about the philosophy of science, spoke of such groups that were organized around what he called scientific "tribal leaders."[21] Mort borrowed the term to describe Lewin, who was an influential figure because he was one of the leaders of the Gestalt school. Lewin was pivotal in starting a direction in experimental social psychology as well as having a theoretical orientation to science.

In these early years Mort had a commitment, which he acknowledges as being strongly encouraged by Kurt Lewin, to produce rigorous science that was "socially relevant — tackling topics of concern to us as a society, and putting theories into practice." Many people who were interested in making the world a better place did not really try to anchor their ideas, proposals and actions in good theory and empirical research. Lewin was tough-minded, in Mort's opinion, because he had a profound view of theory and its importance as a basis of action. Lewin's slogan "there's nothing so practical as a good theory," was what Mort wanted to emphasize in this own work. Mort sees the split in social psychology between the tough-minded and the tender-hearted as unfortunate. He feels that there always has to be an intimate and two-way connection between theory and practice, and his *Handbook of Conflict Resolution*, published in 2000, has "Theory and Practice" as its subtitle. It is this emphasis of Lewin's that Mort has tried to emulate.

While Mort does not call himself a tribal leader, he does see himself as having had an impact through some of his published works. But his impact is also largely visible in the graduate students whose work bears the imprint of his ideas.

Mort emphasizes that "moral orientation," an important aspect of social psychology, has not been considered by most traditional social psychologists. There are not only cognitive and motivational components in social interactions, but also moral ones. To Mort, moral theory is no more abstract than motivational theory. It means what one ought to do in a given situation and what are the ought-nots, obligations, and taboos. These are areas, he says, that have mainly been neglected in psychology.

Bell Laboratories

Mort held the positions of assistant professor followed by associate professor at New York University from 1949 to 1956. Concerned about the possible consequences on funding of the government's suspicion of research in social science, particularly in areas such as interracial relations, he took a position at the Bell Telephone Laboratories.

Carl Hovland, a well-known Yale psychologist, had approached him at NYU and described a new group of researchers being created at Bell Laboratories and the kinds of resources that would be available. The support for the research would come directly from Bell. There was no need to raise money for travel, equipment, or wages. The salary would be good, Hovland said. Mort decided to accept the offer. Hovland was particularly interested in Mort because of his background in group dynamics and wondered what that might contribute to the functioning of the Bell system.

Bell Laboratories was a large separate unit within the larger system of the Bell Telephone Companies, which, with Western Electric, composed AT&T (American Telephone & Telegraph). Bell Labs did all the basic and applied research for the Bell companies (including the development of the transistor). It could also be said that information theory came out of Bell. They were already doing a lot of basic work on language and computers, and Hovland, who had been a consultant for AT&T's Personnel Department, convinced them that they ought to have a research unit in psychology, particularly in social psychology, that would keep them informed of what was going on in that field. Its job would be to research useful applications for the Bell system. Mort recalls that there were about 700,000 people working for the Bell system at that time. It seemed obvious that the people at Bell Labs could learn a lot from psychology. They were spending over $100 million a year in training and they had thousands of small-group meetings each week. They had problems of communication with their clients and among themselves, and negotiation problems with labor unions.

Bell was far-sighted in establishing the Bell Laboratories and supporting basic research and it paid off very well for them. Today it is Lucent Technology, the child of Bell Laboratories, that continues as a company whose research contributes to a number of different industries.

Mort went to Bell because he saw that he would have freedom to do the work he wanted. One of the results of this freedom was the co-edited book *Preventing World War III*, published in 1962 (see chapter 6).

During this time he conducted many studies as well as writing *Theories in Social Psychology* with Bob Krauss, whom he had hired as his research assistant. He invited Harold Gerard, who had worked with him at NYU, and later Seymour Rosenberg to join him at Bell. Alex Barelas was also asked by Hovland to join them, and he in turn invited Herb Jenkins, a Skinnerian psychologist working with pigeons, prompting a joke around the labs that they were going to substitute pigeons for the telephone. Then Alex had various problems at the labs and Herb took his position as director of his unit and persuaded Roger Shepard to join the group.

"It was an interesting group and we did have a lot of freedom," Mort says, "but there was always a pull from AT&T's Personnel Department, who really wanted us to work only on the problems they were interested in." A power struggle developed between Mort and his colleagues and the administrative head of their unit, who was a former member of AT&T. They were constantly subjected to high-level attention and had to put on what they called "dog and pony shows" for people such as the vice-president of personnel from AT&T, who would visit the little psychology unit to see what they were up to.

Because Mort and his group were different they stood out so much that a high level internal committee was appointed to assess their work. Luckily, when the committee was visiting it was announced that Mort and Bob Krauss had just received a prize from the American Association for the Advancement of Science for research they were doing on bargaining using an experimental activity called the Acme-Bolt Trucking game. The announcement helped to stifle any problems the committee might have had with the group.

The Acme-Bolt Trucking game arose out of Mort's driving experiences on the Italian Riviera and in Crete. On a road where you suddenly come up against another car and the road is too narrow to pass one another, one or the other has to yield. You have to back up to a point where the other can get through or the other has to back up. Mort found this an interesting change from the Prisoner's Dilemma game, another activity that he had been using to study conflict, because it made him think more about what was going on between the United States and the Soviet Union.

At Bell Laboratories Mort introduced barriers or gates that could be used in the game to prevent the other person going through after you had gone through. It was a threatening device, a sort of weapon.

The Acme-Bolt Trucking Game
—

There are two truckers from two trucking firms, Acme and Bolt (A and B). They each start at opposing points on a road, and there are two ways to get to their destination. One way is a short main route, which has a middle section that is only one lane wide and only one truck can go through it at a time. The other way of going to their destination is a long alternative route. They are being paid a certain amount of money for making each trip, minus the cost of the trip. The cost is in terms of the amount of time it takes to make the trip. If they take the long alternative route they will lose money on the trip. They could make money by taking the short route, or they could make money even if they were the second person to go through on the short route, but they would have to work out an arrangement. What Mort and his team did was simply give experimental participants that situation and study the conditions under which they would be able to make an arrangement to alternate the use of the short route — so that they would take turns in going through first on the short route.

When the AT&T vice-presidents came to visit, Mort sometimes invited them to play the game. Not infrequently they would sit on that one-lane road opposite one another for ten or fifteen minutes and, macho-style, refuse to yield.

Psychoanalysis

While at Bell Labs Mort was still doing psychoanalytic coursework at night and was also in analysis himself three times a week. On top of all this he saw patients for psychoanalysis. "I don't know how I did it," Mort admits. "You know, I had a young son who was then six years old. I was certainly busy."

The psychoanalytic training had started out as an interest before Mort became interested in social psychology. He saw the two as related and as enriching one another, not as separate. Practicing psychoanalysis was also a welcome supplement to his academic income. It was also a good way of keeping in touch with his inner feelings and thoughts, and of getting a slice of life different from the world he encountered as an experimental social psychologist.

He did his analysis over three years with Ernst Schactel, a highly intelligent and dignified man who had written a brilliant book called *Metamorphosis*. Mort knew the earlier work Schactel had done on the Rorschach tests and respected it. He found him a somewhat distant kind of figure, not a man who encouraged personal closeness. "I don't think he ever called me by my first name or encouraged me to call him by his. We called each other Dr Deutsch and Dr Schactel. He was very perceptive and had lots of wonderful insights, but he wasn't warm enough as an analyst for me. It would have been better if I'd had an analyst who was more emotionally expressive." Asya Kadis, with whom he later did group therapy, was a warm, embracing, expressive person. Mort smiles when he talks about her. "Perhaps I had some defenses against her, maybe she was too embracing. She was certainly a contrast to Ernst Schactel."

Columbia University Teachers College

By this time Mort was getting weary both of the special attention he was getting from senior management at Bell Labs and the long drive to and from New Jersey. He decided he had had enough and that he wanted to work back in the New York area. He had received an offer from Yale to head up the psychology program in a new school of management they were developing. There was another offer from Albert Einstein Medical School to join their psychiatry department, and then came an offer from Teachers College at Columbia University to head up their social psychology program.

"The offer from Teachers College was probably the least remunerative and offered the fewest facilities," says Mort, "but it seemed the most attractive. I didn't want to be in a psychiatric department working as a psychologist in a department of MDs while having a special status of full professor — that way I couldn't have had the authority and freedom to do what I wanted. So I accepted the offer from Teachers College." Mort was to teach at this college until after his "retirement" in 1990, becoming the E.L. Thorndike Professor of Psychology and Education at the College in 1982.

Teachers College lies across the street from the main campus of Columbia. In some ways it was seen as a sort of poor cousin within the Columbia family, and there were times when its student intake was of lower caliber than its more prestigious counterpart. Bob Krauss reflects on Mort's position at this somewhat impoverished teaching institution: "Teachers College, as an institution, doesn't draw the best students. They don't compare that well with our students at Columbia and some other first-rate institutions. Given that, the students that Mort has produced and attracted are really quite remarkable because he has turned out a good number of quite spectacular people." In joining such a place and staying there for so long, Mort was obviously not seeking status.

Teachers College has a long tradition of teaching and research in psychology. In the 1960s people felt that it was a little odd to have psychology in a college of education. "You had to keep explaining to your colleagues," says Barbara Bunker, "why your psychology was in the School of Education, because to most people psychology belonged in the Psychology Department in the main university. I had to explain to people how there could possibly be two social psychology programs in one university. I always explained it as an incredible richness of resources."

The Psychology Department at Columbia was for a long time narrowly focused on comparative psychology and psychophysics, whereas at Teachers College other areas had developed, particularly clinical psychology, developmental psychology, measurement and statistics, social psychology, and learning or educational psychology. The College expanded into the areas that were not really well developed at Columbia in the Graduate Faculties. Edward Lee Thorndike was there; people such as Carl Rogers obtained their PhDs from Teachers College and there were some excellent people in clinical psychology.

It was at this relatively humble institution that Mort continued his important contribution to psychology. His years at Teachers College were marked by turning out a succession of fine students whose carefully guided doctoral dissertations became the basis for remarkable careers. Harvey Hornstein, Mort's first student there, sought out Mort while he was still at Bell Labs, knowing that he was coming to Teachers College. When Mort went to meetings in Europe, while experiments were running, he placed Harvey in charge of supervising other students. Harvey was one of the first people to be added to the College faculty as the program developed, and he has been a central figure in the program ever since.

"My ambition when I came here," says Mort, "was to create a doctoral program in social psychology which intellectually would be equal with the best doctoral programs but which would also be tender-hearted — tough-minded and tender-hearted. In that sense there was competition with across the street. I wanted them to feel that our graduates would be equally valued as their graduates."

It was a busy but exhilarating time in Mort's life. These were the days of the student sit-in movement, followed by the civil rights movement. Mort was involved in the organization of the march on Washington during the Vietnam War. He became well known as a peacenik, speaking at various meetings and attending high-level conferences.

Mort thinks that in social psychology at that time some of the attitude was *scientistic* rather than *scientific* — more concerned with *proving* that you are scientific. He was not worried about appearing unscientific because he was just getting on with what he wanted to do. He believes that there has always been a kind of split between people who are doing research in areas more closely related to social issues as compared with people doing research related to technological issues. "When I was at the Bell Labs, I was at a 'hard' institution. It was scientific — there was no question that you were seen as being part of the scientific inner circle. But coming to a school of education, I knew, was going to put me in the category of 'soft' institution where the scientists would look with a suspicious eye at what I was doing. But I didn't care. I had at that time sufficient hard-science status to be able to deal with that."

Nevertheless, throughout Mort's career, people such as Stan Schachter and Leon Festinger, while they respected his intellectual, experimental, and theoretical work, were unsure of the other work he was doing. At a 1968 meeting sponsored by the Transnational Committee in Social Psychology of the Social Sciences Research Council in Czechoslovakia with people from Eastern Europe (just after the Communists had occupied Prague) Mort gave a paper on productive and destructive conflict and talked about what people in low-power oppressed groups can do in relation to high-power, oppressive groups. Leon raised the question "whither science?" and Mort said, "My view and your view of science are not the same." Mort's paper was transcribed and circulated widely in Czechoslovakia at the time and he became especially well regarded by Eastern European psychologists.

Mort's dissertation had provided models of both cooperative and competitive learning. That had not been intentional, because when he wrote it he had been more interested in world peace than in education. But his new teaching position gave him a convenient format to test his theories. When he was asked to write a paper for a journal of education he wrote about the educational implications of these theories.

Mort was attuned to issues such as trust and suspicion more than he might otherwise have been because of his work in psychoanalysis, so he did research in these two areas. This followed from his earlier work on cooperation; he was interested in the question of what would determine whether a person would have cooperative or competitive relationship with another, and trust and suspicion seemed very important. Through Hal Gerard, who was working with him at NYU, he met the game theorist Howard Raiffa and they talked about game theory and specifically about the famous Prisoner's Dilemma game. The game had been first developed by Ledyard Tucker at Princeton, who had been influenced by Von Neumann and Morgenstern's classic work *The Theory of Games and Economic Behavior*.

Mort was fascinated by the game and became the first psychologist to use it in his research. He saw it as a profound illustration of some of the basic issues of trust and suspicion, and it became a very valuable tool. His use of the game in the 1950s sparked off a lot of work with it in the next two decades and he was at the forefront of developing and using game situations in the lab for psychological research.

The Prisoner's Dilemma Game

The game in its simple form involves only two people, but it can involve any number of people. Mort describes this famous psychologists' puzzle. "Each person has a choice of pressing a green button or a red button. If you press a green button and I press a green button we both win, say a dollar, but if you press a green button and I press a red button, you lose two dollars and I win two dollars. Thus, for you to press the green button you have to trust that I won't press the red button. If we both press the red button, we both lose a dollar. If I press a green button and you press a red button it is symmetrical, so that you win two dollars and I lose two dollars. So the incentive for each player is to press the red button because they win more even if the other presses the green button. They win two dollars rather than one dollar or they lose less if the other presses the red button. If you press the red button and I press the green button, I lose two dollars, but if I press the red button when you are pressing the red button, I lose only one dollar, so I win more or lose less by pressing the red button, rather than the green. But if we both take that course of action, we both lose, and it is possible for us to both win by pressing the green button. To press the green button you have to trust me to press the green button and you have to be trustworthy. If you trust me to press the

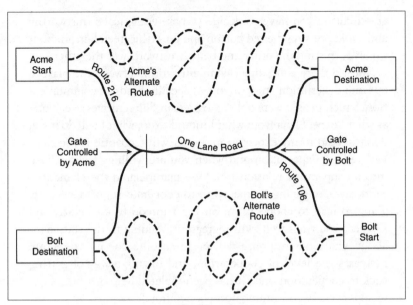

The AB game

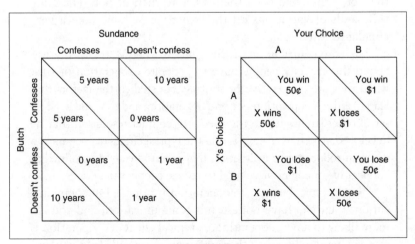

The PD game

green button you have to decide you are going to be trustworthy and avoid pressing the red button and press the green button. So it involves trusting the other and being trustworthy to the other."

Mostly there is no direct communication between the players, but one dissertation study involved specific kinds of communication, which people were able to express in different messages, such as what I expect from you; what I intend to do; what I will do if you don't live up to my expectation; how I will recognize if you have violated my expectation and when you are willing to come back into a cooperative relationship. "We manipulated the elements," Mort says, "so saying I expect you to cooperate is not necessarily going to lead to cooperation. Saying I intend to cooperate, and I expect you to as well, will increase it. Adding to the statement about what your response will be in case he doesn't cooperate increases the level of cooperation, and having a way of getting back to cooperation once it has been violated helps get out of the vicious cycle of continuing non-cooperation."

In general, people sat in separate cubicles and were asked to make their choices simultaneously, so they had to really trust without having much information. "Sometimes you had them meet and talk and then you had them in separate cubicles and you would see how that prior contact would influence things like that, or if they had been friends before then or not. There are thousands of variations on the experiment. It became a very popular research tool."

The core contribution of this game is what Mort's theory was about: the capacity people have to generate cooperation or trust when they are cooperative or trusting. He studied the factors that lead to either cooperation or non-cooperation, and that and a whole set of other studies led to the theory of conflict resolution that he developed, which in essence is that the typical effects of cooperation when introduced into a situation that is not already determined as cooperative or competitive tend to induce cooperation.

"So if a typical effect of cooperation is honest, full communication, then you have honest, full communication, and you are more likely to have cooperation. A typical effect of cooperation is that you tend to like the other and so on. A typical effect of cooperation is you see the differences between yourself and the other as being small, emphasizing the similarities in beliefs and attitudes. All these things enhance the likelihood that that situation will move toward a cooperative process and cooperative outcome. On the other hand, if you introduce threat, if you introduce deception, or strong differences in power and so on, these tend to produce a lack of trust and non-cooperation." This is the basic theory Mort developed from both games and from other experiments. The obviousness of it only emerged for him after a while.

"The Prisoner's Dilemma game," says Mort, "is a very good sort of representation of a lot of dilemmas like an arms race and disarmament. You will only choose to disarm if you think the other will cooperate and disarm. If you disarm and the other continues to arm secretly, then you're put in a severe disadvantage. On the other hand, you could exploit the other's cooperation, if he disarms, by arming. It's the same situation in a black market or in taxation: it's to your advantage to cheat on taxes as long as everyone else pays taxes, but if everybody cheats on taxes it's to everybody's disadvantage."

"So it represents a very interesting dilemma, but it also represents a dilemma for many simple theories of markets and the notion that if you simply pursue your own self-interest, the blind hand of the market will coordinate to everybody's mutual benefit. But if everyone chooses to maximize his or her gains and minimize his or her losses, pursuing self-interest, each and all will end up losing, when all could win. So it poses a dilemma for any theory of market economy. The market economy can only function if there's some common basis of trust. So in that sense, the game is a very interesting dilemma for any theory of social life based on selfish interest, and it was interesting to study. I did a lot of experiments with the Prisoner's Dilemma."

The work on what Mort calls the "initiation of cooperation" is very similar to work on conflict and negotiation and on trust and suspicion. When he moved to Bell Laboratories, Mort reformulated it as work on conflict, on bargaining and negotiation, but intellectually, he says, it's the same issue. Conflict, except for zero-sum or win-lose conflict, is typically a mixture of cooperation and competition, and the question became what determined whether a relationship would move in a cooperative or competitive direction. That same question can become what determines whether a conflict situation moves in a constructive, cooperative direction or in a destructive, competitive direction. It was an evolution of that line of research that began with Mort's initial research on the effects of cooperation-competition.

In 1985, partly in response to changes in the funding structure within academia, Mort ceased to conduct laboratory-based research and focused instead on writing, publishing prolifically. He presented papers at many conferences, most frequently on the themes of conflict or justice, and often as award addresses for the many honors he received.

Part Two

A Legacy

Chapter 3

Teacher and Mentor

"He's just a great human being"

"At the Center there was a deep belief in his students, that they would produce good work and that we had an obligation to think about the implications of our work for a larger world."

Perhaps no statement better encapsulates the success this remarkable teacher had in turning out fine students who went on to make their mark on their chosen fields.

This belief arose directly from Morton Deutsch's personal qualities. In the words of the same student, Michelle Fine, he had "a soul that seemed to have no bottom." He didn't shove his ideas down his students' throats because he had a genuine respect for others, and this created a space in which people could blossom. He could have this respect, she feels, because he had a positive view of himself. She thinks it was important that he also had a positive outlook on the world. He exuded an optimism that energized people and brought out the best in them — an educator in the original sense of the word. "He's one of the few guys at Teachers College that everyone likes. This is a dungeon, people hate each other here, and Mort is adored because he's done something profound about sustaining not just his own soul but the soul of an institution."

Susan Opotow recalls an incident that deeply moved her. "He was very gracious one year, and this was long after his retirement.

He came up to Boston to give an all-day talk at the University of Massachusetts and attend an evening dinner. It was a little bit much to ask, and I don't know how it got to be planned quite so ridiculously but he agreed to come, so it was my department that sponsored it. He flew up the night before and he spent the day with us and we flew back together."

"The students in my program were totally transported. Every room he was in was full. It was so gratifying, because students can be in the room with incredible people and not be touched at all. His generosity in doing this was extraordinary — coming virtually uncompensated, spending the day and just giving of himself. The gentleness and the intensity simultaneously were just so touching to me. I felt he came out of love. I felt he came out of love of the field, out of love of the next generation and out of love of people who really care about his work — people he doesn't know but feels are important. They all used words like 'treasure' about him."

What kind of a teacher is this man who evoked such strong feelings in those with whom he worked? Above all, he is a careful and respectful listener. He attends to other people and their ideas in a way in which most people are incapable. He is a man who relates to you apparently without the bundle of ego, neediness and hidden agendas that people so often carry. He can get angry but he doesn't show it. Whatever the cause, he relates to the world as someone who seems to have got beyond the human body of pain that drives so much behaviour.

Peter Coleman relates a small incident that illustrates Mort's unusual lack of ego. Mort took Peter out to lunch one day at a Middle Eastern restaurant up the street. Mort ordered and was served immediately, while Peter ordered something that took longer to prepare. Peter noticed out of the corner of his eye that Mort was waiting for him instead of going to the table and sitting down and eating. At that time he was certainly in a relationship of power over Peter — Mort was his sponsoring mentor and teacher. "But to Mort," Peter says, "I was a human being worth waiting for. It struck me that this deep respect for people, whoever they are, is part of the essence of Mort. He's just a great human being." Peter was the colleague who later co-edited with Mort the much-admired *Handbook of Conflict Resolution*.

Anecodotes such as Peter's show how Morton Deutsch embodies the very virtues he studied and promoted. David Johnson, Mort's second student at Teachers College after Harvey Hornstein, also acknowledges Mort's generosity because Mort allowed him the freedom to do what he wanted. The first two studies he did were on the impact of teaching Black history to Black children at a Freedom School in Harlem. One of the reasons David became so fond of Mort is that when he talked to him about what he wanted to do in his research, Mort said that while he was not interested himself — this wasn't what his research grant was focused on — if David wanted to do it, he should go and do it.

Mort gave his students the sense that they were being taken seriously, and that, says Bob Krauss, is an awful responsibility. He would really listen to what his students said, which was part of the painstaking approach he took to his own work. "He felt that he owed you the obligation of listening seriously to what you had to say, and that he also owed you the obligation of telling you exactly what he thought about it. If you were smart enough to understand what he was saying, it was no less devastating. You realized that he had just sort of disembowelled your idea. But that is a very good experience for a student to have."

In the classroom Mort's patience and large-heartedness were able to turn some indifferent students into first-class psychologists who produced excellent dissertations. He had a particularly good reputation as a mentor for doctoral students. "I worked with students who had some independence and some initiative," he says. "With such students I felt I could play a very important role in helping to extend their range. With most of them I was attempting to set reasonably high standards for what they were trying to accomplish, intellectually as well as methodologically. But really it was to have them take the bull by the horns, not have me do it for them. Occasionally, with some students who were really marginal, I had to do it for them, but with any student that I thought had any potential, I really wanted them to use their independence and initiative."

◈

Madeleine Heilman received her PhD in 1972 and runs the organizational psychology doctoral program at New York University. She recalls, with much amusement, her early days as Mort's student. "One of the first problems for people in the class was what to call him. The senior students seemed to call him Mort but the new students could not bring themselves to call him this. He was Dr Deutsch … if anybody was Dr, he was. After much whispering before class and saying, 'How're we going to call him Mort? What shall we call him?' and so on, we finally did call him Mort. I don't know what he'd have done if we'd called him Dr Deutsch. It would have probably astounded him."

When she applied for graduate school Madeleine was working in a research institute at City University. She had taken a year off after college and Claire Selltiz, one of the people she worked with, said, "Oh you *have* to go work with Mort Deutsch at Teachers College." Claire had done research with Mort on integration and housing projects. She recommended Mort as somebody who was broad-ranging, a psychologist's psychologist who really appreciated all aspects of psychology and was not afraid to think about the real world and apply what he knew.

Her first brush with him was over a paper she had written. When Mort returned the paper there was writing all over it. "I looked at it and thought 'Oh, I'm going to have to leave graduate school. I mean oh my God, this thing's *written all over!*' I read all the comments and I made an appointment to see him. He looked at my face — I must have looked absolutely terrified — and said, 'I only write on papers when there's a lot to say, when there's a lot of things to talk about.' And we had the most wonderful conversation."

"He really was so incredibly *insightful*. You'd go in to see Mort with an idea or the kernel of an idea and you'd leave having moved so far along. To this day he's so able to *frame ideas*, to play with them and turn them around in a way that makes you see something different that you'd never seen before. That was an electrifying experience for me, absolutely electrifying."

"I was terrified all the time. I was afraid to speak up in class. I never thought my ideas were very good. And he somehow allowed me to come out so that I started to feel very comfortable and confident in myself. He did this without ever sitting there and talking about it, just by working on my work and allowing me to know it was good. He really allowed me to go on in a way I never would have imagined when I started."

Mort was never ebullient, so like all his students, Madeleine had to learn to read what he was saying. She learned that little signs meant very positive responses. It wasn't his way to throw his arms around people and say "Fantastic!" She never saw real disapproval, but she started to know what the signs were — a nod of the head, a turning towards you. You really had to pick up the cues, and those of his students who worked directly with him were able to do that. He always spoke softly but did provide useful feedback. Negatives were framed as ways to improve ideas. Mort always said, "It's an interesting idea — let's see what we can do with it."

In his research group there were some pretty half-baked ideas that somehow turned into gems by the time Mort had finished with them. Mort didn't give people the answers. He'd allow them to think about it and let the ideas emerge. He was a wonderful mentor not only in generating ideas but also in getting people to do the most with what they had started. At that time there were a lot of senior faculty elsewhere in Teachers College who were very punitive, who would go to colloquia and watch people get eaten up. This never happened in Mort's program. It just wasn't the way people behaved around Mort.

Mort was always available to his students. No matter how busy he was — there was always time for students. He gave people the sense that giving time to his students was what he loved doing.

One of Madeleine's first studies, done with Lida Orzeck, was a study on deception. Lida and Madeleine analyzed the data and produced great stacks of printouts. They brought all this data into Mort's office and showed him the effects, interactions, and numerous complicated statistics. Mort just sat there quietly and let them finish. After a few uncomfortable moments, Mort asked, "But what happened?" Madeleine and Linda learned that there is always a core question which is the one you want to know the answer to; the rest is embroidery.

Madeleine thinks that one of the best things about Mort is his lack of arrogance. Mort used to teach a course about his days with Kurt Lewin. He'd talk about how they would all sit around talking, and how Lewin always had these tremendous insights. "We'd all sit there and look at each other. He had no cognizance that, for us, he was doing exactly the same thing that Lewin had done for him, and he would be surprised if we'd said that to him. There was always a kind of humility about that, and I wouldn't cast Mort as a very humble man. He is proud of his tremendous accomplishments. But there was never any arrogance about what he was doing and how important it was and how many lives he touched."

"That's what made him so endearing. When you got past being in awe, he wound up being a very endearing and supportive guy. He wasn't what I'd call warm and toasty, but he wasn't distant and cold either. Every time I've made a career move, I've come to see Mort, just to talk about it, because I always feel that if I don't have that conversation I might really miss something very important."

Mort was a caring, intellectually rigorous mentor. He gave his students a wide berth, giving them what might be called an intellectual invitation. Madeleine needed somebody to give her the space to carve out some work that she cared about and help her not make a fool of herself. "You could tell if you looked in his eyes — if they were twinkling he thought what you were saying was smart and he would, with very few words, bump you into a new corner of reading. I was always both terrified and thrilled to have conversations with him."

The first legacy for Madeleine is the intellectual breadth of her work at Teachers College and the sense of a seamless connection between her political and academic life. The second is the structure of the work groups. They created a space with a mentor and peers in which ideas simply grew. Mort invited his students to think in interdisciplinary ways about topics where they could have theoretical and practical input. "I remember sitting around presenting our work. I don't remember it being high comfort. I do remember it being rigorous and compelling. Mort is not a very directive facilitator and people often didn't know where to go, but we produced amazing work and to this day I use research groups; it's a primary way in which I do my work."

❧❧

Michelle Fine hailed from a Jewish working-class family, which she describes as being "high on love but low on books." She is involved in the women's movement, particularly reproductive rights and violence against women. She went to Teachers College in 1976 and found the experience electrifying. "I got to join another genetic line from Kurt Lewin and Mort Deutsch with a bunch of siblings I was more than happy to share with — a line of Jewish intellectuals and a series of progressive scholars. I understood the power of being able to talk about Marx and Freud and laboratory experimentation in the same sentence."

Michelle's dissertation was titled "Options to Injustices." She was interested in how roles in groups influenced views of injustice. Mort was then writing about a Marxist version of victims knowing more about injustice than perpetrators. Michelle was interested in the victim–non-victim perpetrator relationship — who was more likely to claim injustice? From her work with battered women it was clear to her that if women knew about shelters they were more likely to say, "This is unfair. I don't have to take this." But she had also done work in communities where there were no shelters and no opportunities to leave, and women often said, "This is what men do; this is marriage. It isn't fair or unfair, it's just what happens in marriage."

"Mort was really willing to go places with me. I remember bringing him drafts and he would say, 'That's very interesting but is there a difference? You have to have access to the option, or can you just know that?' So then I had to add other cells, about knowledge of injustice, knowledge or options compared to access."

Michelle describes her occasional visits to Mort's office: "There's a profound sense of a space to be invited into. Year after year I'd be invited into this sacred space with a cover story of intellectual work. If you were lucky there was a deeper kind of emotional connection that was only obvious through eyes, not words. That again for me was both compelling and frightening because there's a kind of forcing you to look hard at yourself, feeling a set of emotions in a very raw way — an invitation to be present. That's why I keep coming back to the eyes. His eyes always gave me an enormous amount of invitation, of comfort, of yearning for more. Because he's a man of few words, people often felt that as disapproval. I always read it as this kind of invitation — a scary one. It was as though the intellectual stuff came easily and the intimacy was what was backstage, but they didn't really feel separate to me. I feel like I owe him my intellectual life and my capacity to mentor others."

Mort's care was not limited to his students. Michelle remembers his concern for Dorothy, the secretary at the college. Dorothy was a woman who had a tough life — she had health and family problems and she just adored him. It would have been easy for Mort to say, this is too much work — I need a secretary who's around. But he never faltered. He stood by her again and again.

ॐ

Len Solomon, who studied with Mort at NYU, remembers him as being a great teacher. Mort was extremely patient and was always well prepared. He would give students a good amount of discussion opportunity and also build practicum assignments into his courses. He created networks of friendly, cooperative relationships among the students working with him. He gave them plenty of room to develop their own ideas and design their research, and yet they all seemed to fit, however loosely, under his umbrella.

Mort's style of government was somewhere between laissez-faire and gentle guidance and direction. "You never knew you were governed," says Len, "because he was so unobtrusive, so mild and indirect in his suggestions." Sandra Sandy says that Mort gave his students a lot of creative leeway to pick their own direction, then, once they had decided what was good for them, he was very supportive.

Mort's own account of this is characteristically modest. "I'm not a dramatic teacher. There are teachers who were much better at dramatizing what they're talking about. I'm a teacher who's very much interested in the ideas I'm talking about. In the more formal lecture courses I would try to get students to partic- ipate by asking questions, and having other students be free to respond to the questions, but in general I would try to get my ideas across every session, to lecture in one way or another. In the seminars it was much more give and take. This depends on the nature of the student group; some student groups are very lively, others are like a lump of clay, and it takes work to mould them into something. What I enjoy most is having an interac- tion about ideas and that's what I try to encourage, not always successfully. I don't think I'm a particularly good course teacher, particularly for students who are not that interested in the subject matter to begin with. If the students are really interested in ideas, then I think I appeal to them, but a lot of students taking basic courses are not that much interested in ideas; they want to be entertained as they're being enlightened."

When Mort needed to criticize a student paper he did it in such a way that the student responded well. "Jeff Rubin would have told you quite openly," Mort says, "because this was a positive quality of his, that I turned back his first essay in the theories course. It was on the war in Vietnam. It was a very well-written paper, but it was more heart — it was more tender-hearted than tough-minded. I said, 'Look, if I had to grade it now I couldn't pass it, for the reason that you're advocating the position, and it's not based upon psychology. What you have to do is develop your position using psychological ideas and principles.' And as was characteristic of Jeff, he accepted the critique, and within a week he turned back a really superb paper that did what I asked him to do."

Mort admits having to occasionally chastize a student. "I remember one student whom I don't really want to identify by name — he's very prominent now. We had a Black woman as secretary, Jacki Ferguson, who was the mother of us all. She was a very warm, embracing woman — always had food or cookies or something on the secretarial table. Once she told me she had been insulted by one of the students by a kind of racial slur. I talked to the student and I made it clear that that sort of thing wasn't acceptable, and that I wouldn't tolerate it in this program. I did that in private, rather than before the group."

In his early career Mort was one of the most productive profes-sors at New York University, not only in the research he generated but also in the number of students who did their dissertations with him. At Bell Laboratories he had a similar style in spite of the fact that he was working under a corporate structure. He had a gift for understanding that the best research was done when it was driven by curiosity, and that the issue of application to real-world problems would grow out of quality research.

Sandra Sandy says that Mort seems to remain a mentor to his students forever. "We never quite seem to get away from him; we always come back and ask him for advice. He really is so amazing in this field, and just amazing as a human being who really does nurture and support students. You still need to bounce your ideas off someone and he is the best person I know to bounce things off. He will give you interesting insights and then come up with something that is exactly what you need. He is very good at problem-solving."

Barbara Bunker agrees that Mort gave people space and freedom. "The nice thing about Mort was that he always was a person who recognized people's different abilities. He didn't try to make everybody identical to him. He didn't want to turn out clones. I can remember him saying to me, 'Barbara, if you don't want to do any more laboratory research, why are you doing it?' I said, 'Mort, I think I have to,' and he said, 'Why do you have to? I can't imagine why you have to. You have so many other talents. Do what you like to do.' He was very helpful, very freeing about developing who you really are rather than trying to do what the system tells you is what you should do to become famous."

Mort had a lot of women students, and he really encouraged them at a time when it wasn't all that common to have women students or to encourage them. He wisely steered them away from embarrassment over non-performance that can dent a woman's confidence. He would say "Look, don't be afraid of expressing a bad idea. This is a place to get rid of bad ideas". His message comes as an enormous relief to anyone who is lacking in confidence: "It's nothing to be ashamed of," he would say, "we all have bad ideas."

From a feminist perspective he was good news. He had the conscious attitude, he says, that women had equal rights to any place in society and in science, and certainly in psychology. He recognized that many women were not as assertive as men were in seminars, and tried to encourage them to be more assertive. Male–female conflicts were discussed in his classes, and readings were given in this area. When he first came to Teachers College he taught a course in the social psychology of mental health, and gender conflict issues were a popular part.

❧❧

Peter Coleman has been a particularly close colleague of Mort's over several years and greatly admires his intellectual prowess. "I've seen him at meetings and conferences where there's a stimulating and complex discussion that gets into a bit of conflict, or maybe we're trying to come to a decision, or come to understand some phenomenon. I've watched Mort capture the essence of the thing. He'll sort of get underneath the conversation and say, 'There are essentially three dimensions here, and if you look at this issue and you look at the other one, and then again at the third one, this is how they are related to each other.' It brings such clarity to the room, and so it's often a sharing process. This is a roomful of people who think about these things a lot, but he has the ability to step back and see basic issues and basic relationships. Obviously that's part of his theoretical mind, but he can get that clarity in the heat of discussion and see the context and the issues and what's lying underneath."

"He can do that in personal matters as much as in theoretical things. There's a capacity for perspective that I can only call a deep kind of wisdom. It's a bit like what Mozart said, that music is the silence between the notes. I've got used to watching what Mort doesn't say. In my young eagerness I'd go into a meeting and go after every question and every contradiction. I'd know that Mort was right with me but he'd choose his words and they'd be just right. He had a canny sense of what the right thing was to say — who's involved, what's happening with them — and he could do this on several levels at once. It's a lucidity he hasn't lost, an acumen that's as sharp as ever."

Bob Krauss thinks that Mort is the best critic of any psychologist he's ever known. "He can read a piece of work that really isn't in his own area, and he can make very cogent comments on it that often reveal either the shallowness or the parochialism of your own thinking." He agrees that it is unusual to find this acute critical sense in an individual who also has an ever-present fund of ideas for experimentation. Mort would apply this to his teaching, giving relentless criticism of his students' work while at the same time deeply respecting their ideas and efforts.

Dolores Mei, one of Mort's former PhD students, sees him as an interesting combination of logical and creative thinker. "I think his deliberate manner of thinking and expressing himself, his way of building an argument, is very powerful, and one that I've tried to model on a much smaller scale in my own work."

Another former student, Ivan Lansberg, says Mort was phenomenally gifted at being able to take what they were reading in the New *York Times* every day and bring it into the classroom. He would take it apart using sociological concepts. "That was a real lesson. Mort was also renowned for his work on the sociology of science and that was very influential to me in the sense that he was able to bridge natural sciences like chemistry and biology and mathematics and link them to a social process that led to taking a look at Kuhn's ideas on the history of paradigms and revolutions in science. He looked at it from a sociological point of view and brought it to life, because you were able to see how the social process of science impacted on the actual process of discovery."

Harvey Hornstein remembers Mort's ability to get at the essence of a problem. "In thinking about theory and thinking about social problems or sitting at a colloquium listening to someone present, Mort was always able to go to the heart of the matter, to lift it out and display it in its simplicity. That's always been interesting to me because when you take out the essence there is a simplicity to it. It's only when it's embedded in the social problem that it's seen as this complex mishmash of issues."

Barbara Bunker has vivid memories of Mort in the classroom. "You had to learn not to finish Mort's sentences, because he would [pause] wait a while before he [pause] said anything; he had a pace that was just very different from most people. As a graduate student you wanted to hear what he had to say, but when he left that huge silence people would tend to finish his sentences, and then they wouldn't hear what he had to say, so they had to learn how to hang on to themselves and allow him to speak at the pace that he felt like speaking."

Despite a quietness that is almost sombre, Barbara says that he has an impish quality. "He loves the arts," she says, "he loves to laugh — there's this great joy in him."

Mort has an unusually soft voice and had to work at improving his delivery in lectures. He also experienced constant anxiety lecturing formally before a large group, and yet he didn't over-prepare his lectures. Like his mentor, Kurt Lewin, he is best in small groups, interacting with issues as they come up out of discussion, although he could give good prepared speeches under certain circumstances where he felt confident. He thinks this anxiety goes back to some speech problems he had when he was quite young. He had a bit of a stammer for which he had speech therapy. As an adult he took further speech therapy to help him with his lecturing. "I've learnt to speak more loudly," he says, "but it requires a conscious effort."

To his students this manifested as a reticence that some found difficult. In seminars he would only talk occasionally and what he said was usually brilliant, so people really paid attention. When he didn't say enough, students would think that they were failing and that he wasn't telling them. Some people would interpret his wriggling his eyebrow as a sign of disaster.

Mort's style of working with students sometimes drove them wild. One group of students called a meeting with Mort and told him that they needed more feedback about how things were going. With his usual humility he said, "Look, I will try to do this. But you should assume that if I'm not actively talking about something things are okay. I understand that you need to hear that things are good more often, but don't make the assumption that some disaster has happened just because I'm quiet about things. I'm assuming that you're working hard and that things are going along, and that if I don't hear from you and you don't hear from me, your work is proceeding in a satisfactory way. You shouldn't ask me every ten minutes to come in and pat you on the back and say that things are fine, you're doing well." His style was simply not to give a lot of positive feedback to people, but after that, for a long time he did give more feedback.

"It's not that I don't get or can't express strong feeling," Mort says, "but I don't try to undermine the person or devalue the person in the process, so it's not just a crude expression of feelings or a condemnation. It's an attempt to say something strongly but affirmatively, to let them know there are things that can be done to improve the situation. I think that has been a lifelong trait of mine. I remember that when I was applying for admission to the Postgraduate Centre for Mental Health I asked Marie ("Mitzi") Jahoda to write a letter of recommendation for me and she wrote that I don't get angry and I thought that it wasn't the best letter. I think she did have ambivalent feelings about me. But it's true. I don't lose my temper or express a temper — I temper my expressions. I get exuberant and joyful but I'm probably not as typically expressive as many people are."

Mort is indeed capable of anger but has the capacity to keep it under tight control. At a meeting one day, another psychologist, who had behaved really badly, accused Mort of something unethical. Mort said, with evident calm, "Well, I think we ought to talk about this and understand why you feel that way. I don't think that I did behave that way." His controlled manner was belied only by profuse sweating under his arms.

Susan Opotow heard other people complain about their supervisors — they gave too much direction, too little, it was never the right amount. A lot of people said Mort was too remote. In Susan's case she was in heaven because he left her alone. When she needed help she could go and ask for it. He would just think about the problem with her and they would present it in the work groups. Most of the thinking together was done in a group setting. But it was primarily in that setting that she could develop her own ideas. She didn't want to go to graduate school to become the clone of the teacher.

"I see the heart of my research as being justice and conflict theory as applied mostly to schooling, environment and large divisive social issues such as affirmative action. I deconstruct the justice arguments and use them as a kind of lab for my thinking. So I do things quite differently than Mort does in terms of how I go about my thinking and the kinds of variables I look at and the kind of development. But he was just the kind of intellectual parent that I needed, somebody who allowed me full rein — and not out of confidence in me but just because that's how he is. When my dissertation was finished it was a really solid body of work and I've always trusted him because of that. I trusted his intellect. I trust who he is as a teacher. So when he suggests that I do something, I do it. It's kind of an unquestioning faith that I don't think I would give to anybody else. I trust him as you would a Zen master."

Mort's lack of personal flamboyance also showed up in his writing. He wrote in a very terse, dry manner, according to Barbara Bunker.

"His style wasn't reader-friendly; you had to work at it, and it felt like you were labouring through the paragraphs. He told us that he'd had to do an enormous amount of work on his writing, and over the years his writing has become a lot easier to read. I remember that he wrote a paper we used to refer to as the water-hose paper, which opened with a vignette about two kids fighting over a water-hose. Everybody sort of said, 'Oh, can't he get a better example than this? I mean, this isn't a very exciting example.' Even now, his writing isn't much fun to read; you still have to work at reading Mort's stuff."

Mort acknowledges that as you write more and more, you get more practiced, more skilled. "I think what I've aimed for is a writing which is clear but subtle, in the sense that it can be read at different levels. So that if you're not a social psychologist, nor a social scientist, you might be able to understand what is being said, though of course you'll get more out of it if you know the area. I don't know if I've achieved it but that's been my aim. When I edited the *Handbook of Conflict Resolution*, I told the contributors that I would like them to write so that the book is easily readable by non-social scientists but is also credible to experts in their area."

Carol Liebman, a mediation expert, confirms that it is both readable and credible. Mort was delighted when Madeleine Hornstein's mother, at the age of eighty-nine, read the first couple of chapters and said she enjoyed it!

It had taken him years to achieve this accessible style. One of the first articles drawn from his dissertation, a theoretical piece on cooperation and competition, was written in a heavy Germanic style. He says he was still under the influence of Gestalt writing, which tended to be obtuse.

"When I worked with Mitzi Jahoda on the first edition of the research methods book, she put up a little slogan on my blackboard: 'You don't have to write complex, difficult sentences to be a scientist,' or something, I forget the exact phrase. And that did a nice job in deflating my pompous image of the Gestalt theorist scientist. But I think the most important influence later was Gary Boring. He was a very distinguished Harvard psychologist who edited a series for Basic Books, which included the one I was writing, *Theories in Social Psychology*. He obviously went over it sentence by sentence. He would type his comments and they were very helpful. He helped me to write more clearly."

Mort passed his writing skills on to his students. Madeleine Heilman says that when she first came to Teachers College she wrote in a heavy and ponderous manner. Somehow she thought that to be a scholar she had to write long, complex sentences. On one occasion when she handed something in to Mort, he said, "Writing is a skill and it can be learned. We don't necessarily mean writing a novel here, but writing can be learned."

"He'd turn a paper of mine around overnight, not for the ideas but for the writing, and I'd get it and work on it for the next few days. I'd bring it to him late at night, he'd read it overnight and I'd get it back in the morning. He made me work on my writing until I really learned what had to be done. Ever since then I've never had a problem with writing. He really forced me to recognize that you can say complex things in a clear and simple way. He wouldn't put you down but he'd say 'You're doing a disservice to your ideas.' I always remember that. I sometimes say that to my own students — 'You're burying your ideas, nobody can even figure out what they are.'"

Barbara Bunker was in one of the first classes where he hired an editor from Teachers College Press to edit dissertations. "He said to us quite openly, 'You all need to be better writers than you are, and one way I can help you is pay for you out of the program to at least get this experience with an editor.' That was my first experience with an editor, and it was quite revelatory to me."

Many of Mort's books were collaborative works. Bob Krauss recalls that Mort very generously made him co-author of *Theories in Social Psychology*, even though Mort had done most of the writing. Bob, however, did the rewriting, since Mort was known as an indifferent stylist. "He would write something and I would collaborate, or I would work it over, and it was very good, because we would work out a lot of things that were unclear in both our minds."

❧

Someone who has taught at one institution for thirty years would have to have made an impact. Mort's colleagues and students think Mort's impact was considerable. "Mort's presence here has raised the standard of scholarship," says Harvey Hornstein, "not just in our program of social psychology, but throughout psychology. In the college as a whole, his presence made everyone very conscious of the ways in which they were working on ideas and the ways in which they were working with students."

"When Mort came he introduced the ideas of research groups, which formed around individual faculty members, and this became a major way for us to train our students. It became the envy of the college. In psychology it was sometimes imitated and the idea was that you were in a continuous tutorial during graduate student days here. People in social psychology, and to some extent people in other areas of psychology, were regarded as a very well trained and talented group within the college. There were those who didn't like us and saw us as unduly privileged. But Mort did raise the standard."

Universities and colleges can be difficult places. Mort's colleagues found his cool and generous sanity a refuge that was always available. "I think he also raised the organization in a social way," says Harvey. "People throughout the college have said to me on a number of occasions how judicious he is. There is a Solomon-like character to his observations and his judgments and his participation in decision-making, which percolated down to all of us. He'd insist that we become sane and judicious, and of course that necessarily had a consequence within the college and certainly within psychology. As Director of the Division for nine years, it was very clear to me that he was having that kind of impact in psychology. Whenever there was a need to deal with matters that were disputed or sensitive, we always pushed to involve Mort, not to get his political weight but to get his measured wisdom. It uplifted us and it certainly did good things to our scholarship."

In 1963 Barbara Bunker was looking around for a suitable graduate school. She was thirty-three and felt that she'd like to be in New York, where she had spent her early years. "I went to NYU for an interview, because I thought they might have an interesting program, and the Head of the Psychology Department, Isadore Chein, talked to me in great detail about my interests. He said 'Barbara, we'd be glad to have you here as a graduate student, but in truth I think you'd be happiest at Teachers College with Mort Deutsch.'"

"I remember very vividly my first conversation with Mort because he started talking to me about conflict resolution and the program they had going. I didn't know anything about conflict resolution and what I said to Mort must have made that pretty obvious, but he was very generous. He didn't get upset about the fact that I was trying to sound knowledgeable when I wasn't. I had a good feeling about him, and I began to think that Teachers College was the right place because there would be substantial training as well as substantial application."

"I had heard of Kurt Lewin and the National Training Laboratory but I didn't really know what I was in for. I was quite shocked when I started running Prisoner's Dilemma studies. That was a very new way of thinking. Graduate school for me was a very useful education in thinking carefully and precisely about very complicated issues at a level that I hadn't experienced before."

Barbara remembers going to lunch regularly with Mort and the other students at an Inter-Faith Center near the Hudson River. In these pleasant surroundings they would talk about what was happening in current affairs that day. Mort would guide the discussion, which would always turn into questions such as, What does social psychology have to say about this? What relevance do we have to this issue? What should we be studying? What should we be doing?

"We had a consistent pattern," Barbara says, "of discussing doing something about social problems not by acting but by understanding and getting some theoretical handle on them so that when we did take action it was smart action. We all learnt really big values from Mort at those lunches."

In the teaching structure Mort set up, as with Kurt Lewin, the real education took place in work groups, which were informational discussions among students. When David Johnson was at Teachers College the groups weren't formalized. "Students were expected to hang around the lab all day, study, work, and prepare for tests, but the real training program was in the informal discussions we had. Doing research, helping other students do research, talking about our ideas with each other — that was the real training, the real education."

"I don't know that I invented the idea of work groups," says Mort, "but when I came here [to Teachers College] in 1963 I started them immediately. I felt that the apprentice-training model was the best model for doctoral students; that is, to have a group of apprentices working with me who could stimulate one another, who could learn from one another, and who could also stimulate me as I shared some of my ideas with them."

"With Lewin there would be seminars in which all the graduate students and faculty would participate. There weren't that many students then and there weren't that many faculty, so it was a group of twelve, thirteen, maybe fifteen people. These weren't quite the same as our work groups but you could come in and talk about what you were doing and that might be the topic. Lewin was the guiding light, of course."

"The students would work in a number of ways. Sometimes the experiment would be designed by me or by the group under my direction, and they would run the subjects. Later, when they were more advanced, they would be designing their own dissertation, and other students would help them run subjects. So it was a cooperative activity where the students would help one another. I didn't plan it that way. I just went ahead and assumed that's what we'd do. We would work together in a cooperative way. It would be the norm that students could call on one another to help them run experiments."

"The groups served a double purpose. We needed students trained in research and wanted to give them experience, but we also wanted to promote our own research activities. In my case I did have grants so I had certain objectives to accomplish, so the students would be working with me on grant-related activities."

Barbara found that the most exciting teaching at the college was in Mort's work groups. "They were really fun, a place to get rid of your bad ideas. So the idea was not that you had to be competitive and act smart about things you hadn't read, but that you should talk about what you're thinking in order to find out whether it's really full of holes; if you don't talk you'll never know whether your ideas have credence or not. Mort set a very supportive and also very high-level demand for careful thinking, and he wouldn't let you get away with anything. He couldn't tolerate shoddiness. It was tough, but it was also loving and supportive. The people across the street [at Columbia's main campus] were wonderful fun, but I almost couldn't stand going to the colloquia. People would get up and reel off study after study, and it was just sort of 'look at how great I am.' It just turned me off. I didn't hate what was being talked about but I did hate the atmosphere, the way they did their business."

Mort was rigorous and demanding about content. There was substantial but very focused reading. "It wasn't all over the place," says Barbara. "You'd have a particular set of chapters or articles to read for a particular seminar, then he'd begin the discussion with open-ended questions. It wouldn't be like 'Show me what you know,' it would be 'What do you think about the following issue?' And then he would come in to shape the discussion from time to time, but he didn't tramp all over the landscape and make his presence so felt that you couldn't move. It wasn't clear where our discussions would go and sometimes very exciting things would emerge; sometimes it was kind of boring and not too great, but he'd work hard to see what could be brought out of that discussion."

"The T-group I was in, of about twelve students, was a bonding experience. It opened up a lot of issues, and it created, particularly for students, the capacity to really talk to each other in a way they never had before. When we went back to Columbia I remember that one outcome of it was that all work on the Prisoner's Dilemma game almost stopped for about a week or two because people were so into interpersonal this and that. I can remember Mort coming out of his office one morning, and saying 'That's enough. It's time to get back to work.'"

"He was supportive but he was also very focused on his research and his academic responsibilities. And he was very good about not letting a lot of things seduce him into other kinds of activities. He wasn't one of these people who was so politically concerned that he could hardly get his research done. He spent a lot of time in the lab and a lot of time training us."

Mort's clinical experience and practice interacted in an unusual way with his research activity. Barbara remembers that if she inadvertently said something at conferences about Mort taking some concept from his practice, or from something that happened, and applying it to some other situation, she would get raised eyebrows from the audience, as if to say, "This is not the way we do psychology." "Mort certainly taught all of us to think that way, and I think most of us have ended up appreciating that the world is complex. We'd be in a seminar and all of a sudden he'd come in at a different level. He'd make a comment about what happened last week in his practice, and wasn't that interesting. It was just occurring to him that probably this was a principle that applied to the situation we'd just been talking about. When you work in that kind of environment you start thinking that way."

"I didn't realize how unusual this was until Peter Gumpert, a graduate student who later became a faculty member, came into the lab one day and said, 'Do you realize that the way Mort thinks about this is not the way most psychologists think?' I was quite surprised, and I realized that Mort's approach was really somewhat different from most of the people I was actually reading."

"Kurt Lewin was very visible to me, partly because Mort talked about him a lot, partly because I identified myself as someone in that tradition. Mort would make analytic comments from time to time about Freud and his views, and I think there were even some seminars on various psychoanlytic theories. He would bring Freud's ideas into relevant spots, in other words we'd be talking about some conflict, particularly intra-psychic conflict. I don't recall his talking much about Marx. Marx certainly influenced who he was, but that wasn't a name that came up much at all, and of course this was right after the fifties when the threat of communism hung over all of us. People didn't talk a lot about their politics; we were still pretty raw from that time when if you said you thought Marx had something to say you could end up in jail."

❧

Harvey Hornstein was at Columbia before Mort arrived and stayed in the same department as Mort for thirty-one years. His dissertation, which was finished in 1964, was on the effects of different magnitudes of threat on negotiation and bargaining. The bargaining game was similar to one developed by Siegal and Fouraker[1] and looked at the ways in which different magnitudes of threat reflected the outcomes of those situations. There was a clear line from the work of Morton Deutsch and Bob Krauss to Harvey's dissertation.

Mort was working at the Bell Laboratories when Harvey was planning his dissertation research. "I was very interested in Mort's work on cooperation and competition and knew I wanted to work in that general area. When I talked to the person who was then head of the program, Kenneth Herald, he told me to contact Morton Deutsch at Bell Labs. I did and we met in November 1962, at his house."

Harvey laughs at the recollection. "He was very generous, and he needed to be because the idea I had was terrible. I really don't think I had been very well trained to that point, though I knew the literature pretty well. I was a good statistician. In fact, I taught statistics about a year later. The field had gone way beyond me at the time I was there, and I knew Mort's work, but my ideas were awful. He was very gentle and talked about them, and he raised questions and encouraged me to pursue them and so gave me some general ideas about where that pursuit might take me. When I left him I felt simultaneously disappointed and uplifted."

"I'd been doing work on altruism, and in the summer of 1965 there was to be a conference in Belgium on altruism and aggression. I could have gone. I was also invited to go to the National Training Laboratory at Bethel in Maine. I had been awarded a National Institute of Mental Health, Applied Behavioural Science Scholarship, which would let me go to Bethel for free, stay there for six or eight weeks and be trained to do T-groups and to design experiential workshops and things of that sort."

"Anyway, I spoke to Mort about these two possibilities and he didn't discourage me from doing either one but he certainly encouraged going to NTL and developing those skills. I know he had misgivings and questions about that kind of practice, but nonetheless he thought it was worthwhile. There was always that kind of open-mindedness with Mort at the helm. All the doctoral students, even the faculty, felt very free to explore and experiment with ideas and different ways of practice. I remained active in NTL for a few years after that and eventually brought Mort back into NTL activity. Mort joined with a fellow named Steve Ruma and they actually trained people who were professionals and were planning to move into the field of experiential training and consultation."

Like Harvey and so many others, Eric Marcus, one of Mort's students in the early 1980s, found Mort very supportive. "I guess this is because he always started from wherever I was at and pushed it to the next level. I never got the sense that he was throwing his superior knowledge at me. The defense of my dissertation always stands out for me. Mort asked me questions which I knew that he knew that I knew the answers to. I couldn't figure out why he was asking me these questions — we'd talked about this stuff — and I asked him afterwards. I said, 'Mort, why did you ask me those questions?' and he said, 'I wanted to give you an opportunity to show that you knew this stuff.' I felt that was a pretty neat way of doing things."

"Mort is one person who I see as a truly great man. He was generous with his ideas and with encouraging people to develop their own ideas. He was always looking at a synthesis of other people's ideas to stimulate his own thinking. To me he was someone who never — this was after I'd been in the business world for several years — tried to steal credit for something of somebody else's work. He was always very eager and willing to kind of share the wealth — not monetary wealth, intellectual wealth."

An experience that affected Ivan Lansberg was when Mort handed him a box of articles on justice that he had been collecting. There were articles on the philosophy, psychology and legal aspects of justice. "When I decided to enter his work group he called me to his office and basically gave the box to me and said, 'Once you read all of this and try and make sense of it, come back and talk to me.' This was like diving into the Pacific Ocean or something — justice is a big topic. It gave me a sense that you could look at an issue from many vantage points, and there was something to be learned, no matter which discipline you latched onto. So often our discipline boxes us in; it limits our capacity to be able to borrow ideas or transfer knowledge from one field to the other."

"Parallel to this I was developing, quite on my own, an interest in psychoanalytic ideas. Mort had the capacity to be able to look at issues from that vantage point, which is unusual in a social psychologist. Often the clinical way of thinking was in opposition to a more situationally-based approach to behavior, so he was able to talk about behavior and social and psychological issues from multiple levels of analysis almost in the same breath. He could look at the psychodynamics of justice, at the situational issues that come with justice, and then at the macro sociological and philosophical issues. He was perfect, you know, exactly what I wanted, and gave me an appreciation for a more eclectic approach for looking at this issue and not boxing myself in prematurely."

Ivan's first project with Mort was looking at the relationships between different kinds of social processes and distributive systems. Mort was very committed to the notion of multiple methodologies and thought up some unorthodox research paradigms. "Mort taught me that a lot of the criticism people have of social psychology is that the lab experiments with undergraduates don't represent the world. He was always telling us that you never go from a lab experiment to the world. You go to your theory, and from your theory to the world. So the issue is not about replicating the world in the lab, it's about forming a piece of your theory and then having some empirical basis on which you can then justify going to the world."

Bob Krauss sees Mort as a force of an unusual kind within Teachers College. "He was a moral leader, and they are very rare in academia. You get a lot of people who flaunt their superior morality and take the moral high ground on this or that, but somebody who is just quietly himself, who has distinguished himself in his own field, but still is willing to stick his neck out on moral issues — I think that's rare."

Mort had a kind of calm inner wisdom. "You get a lot of smart people in universities," says Bob, "but wisdom is not a common commodity, in my experience; it's a sort of unanalyzed term. Mort's wisdom was a combination of being knowledgeable and the balance created by being willing to take a long view of things, to view things from other people's perspectives, to take a lot into account. This is not a gift that everybody has. I've known people who were extraordinarily smart. I mean who were really, really good — better psychologists than Mort in some respects — but not as wise."

Mort has a world-view that is integrated, Bob says. "I can understand things in their individuality, but it's hard to put them all together. Most of us exercise local understandings, and Mort's view of psychology has always been this high-level integrated view and I think his outlook on the world is similar. There are both positive and negative sides to this. I think that sometimes he's taken this long view of psychology, and it's so long that he misses some of the details. Mort has very little curiosity of that sort. He's much more interested in making things fit together, and very often in doing that I think he's likely to slight the details of things, even get them wrong."

Many researchers are driven by a childlike sense of wonder and inquiry, but Mort's starting point is mostly something quite different. He often refers to some basic tenet such as the need to make a social contribution, and many think that this goes back to his experience in the airforce during the war. Although he was politically active before the war, the actual experience of bombing people sobered him. The war set in motion his lifelong concern with big questions like resolving conflict and how you achieve justice. The playful curiosity that appears in many scientists was not part of his motivation.

Along with this moral seriousness there was a good deal of moral courage. He did not hesitate to make administrative decisions that the bureaucrats might not have liked. Bob Krauss recalls that when he and Mort were at Bell Laboratories, "the AT&T vice-presidents would come in wearing their dark suits and starched shirts, and we'd have these dog and pony shows. We'd talk about our research and they'd ask questions, and it was a sort of a ritual that nobody attributed much to. One time one of the vice-presidents made some patronizing comment to Mort, but Mort wouldn't take it. He said, very politely and very directly, 'Well, you're wrong, you simply don't understand,' and proceeded to explain to him what he didn't understand. And the funny thing was, you know, that for all the collegial atmosphere, this was a very structured organization, and one did not talk to a vice-president that way."

On a more personal level, Mort was famous for some endearing shortcomings. Bob says that Mort is the least mechanical person he's ever known. "His technical competence extends maybe to a pencil sharpener. One of my first experiences with Mort at Bell was running an experiment with him. I was running the experiment and he was observing it. We were trying to get the procedure down and I had arranged a tape recorder so that we could listen to it afterwards. We had finished and I was sort of thinking over the subject and he said, 'Is there anything I can do?' I said, 'Why don't you rewind the tape?' — really more to give him something to do. A few minutes later I looked up and there he was and — this was open reel tape — both his hands were struggling with the tape. He said, 'Well, what do I do now?' and I said, 'Mort, you just sit down and don't do anything.'"

Chapter 4

Theorist First and Foremost

"A direct bearing on human relations"

Mort's theoretical work can be seen as falling into five overlapping phases. Phase 1 was the study of the effects of cooperation and competition, which was initiated in his doctoral dissertation at MIT and reflected in his work on Interracial Housing at NYU. In Phase 2 he reframed the research on cooperation–competition at Bell Laboratories as research on conflicts and bargaining. Phase 3 included his work on distributive justice. In Phase 4 he founded the International Center for Cooperation and Conflict Resolution, while Phase 5 includes his current work on oppression and how to overcome it.

This chapter presents some of Mort's important theoretical contributions from these phases of his life. They include his theory of cooperation and competition, his theory of what determines whether a conflict will take a constructive or a destructive course, his "crude law of social relations," his work on justice, his use of conflict resolution in education, and current thoughts on conflict and oppression in a global context. In his many writings Mort has also presented valuable integrative summaries of the work of others. Some of these summaries are presented here without especially referring to the work of those scholars. Mort, in his own writings, fully acknowledges others' work.[1]

Morton Deutsch in Context

Morton Deutsch is one of the early generation of social psychologists whose work was motivated and primed by deep human values. According to Barbara Bunker: "They were the first generation of the non-religious, committed to social issues in a way that their fathers might have been committed to organized religion. They had this passion about social science." In that sense, Mort was a man of his times, fired by the great political movements of his youth and hopeful about the possibilities of bringing justice to a world marked by incessant conflict. And it may be, though he has never said as much, that his Jewish background, with its emphasis on justice, may have also influenced him.

Barbara met Mort in the early 1960s, the turbulent days of the sit-ins and civil rights marches. "He is deeply committed," she says, "not just to peace, but to issues around fairness and justice, and I assume that's partly the Jewish background and the kinds of issues that being Jewish confronts you with."

Mort's career was fashioned in the early days of social psychology, when the term itself was new. The interest in social psychology was evidence of a new consciousness about social issues. Today, however, social psychology is about interrelationships, what Barbara calls "people stuff."

"Modern social psychology," says Harvey Hornstein, "with its concerns about cognition, social cognition and so on, is much more interested in formulating theoretical principles that have helped to describe and explain the dynamics of individual experience in social settings. It's much less concerned with explaining the dynamics of the group. Mort has always worked at that other level of social issues. Some of his work has looked at individual experience in social settings, but generally speaking his work has dealt with the broader level of an issue and a broader range of issues. He's always drawn his research concerns from the arena of social problems."

Of the advent of social psychology Mort has written:

> It is a child of psychology and sociology, having been conceived in the ambivalent mood of optimism and despair which has characterized the Scientific Age. The rapidly expanding knowledge, the increasing confidence in scientific methods, the ever quickening technological change with its resulting opportunities and social problems, the development of new social organizations and of social planning, the social turmoil, the repeated disruption of communities and social traditions — all these helped to create both the need for social psychology and the awareness of the possibility that scientific methods might be applied to the understanding of social behavior.[2]

Turmoil and conflict were inherent in the theories of Darwin, Marx and Freud. In one way or another, all of them saw competitive struggle as an integral part of human nature. The century that was then unfolding certainly gave credence to such notions. Social Darwinism, which Mort regarded as a vulgarization of Darwin's ideas, took this inherent conflict further and provided an intellectual rationale for racism, sexism, class superiority, and war. Although social Darwinism was not so fashionable after the 1920s, its effects were felt for a long time afterwards. Such values led straight to Nazism, and it was this complex of attitudes that Mort's work in effect confronted. He was very critical of constructivist doctrines that posited innate motives of "selfishness", "aggressiveness", "cruelty" and "conquering others" as well as doctrines of innate group differences in intellectual abilities. He favored the view that evolution had created human beings who were quite plastic and who could develop a wide range of behaviors or abilities, and who could adapt to as well as create a wide range of environments. Mort believed that people had the capacity to be kind as well as cruel, peaceful as well as warlike, friendly as well as hostile. The important question was what determined which form human behavior would take.

Mort explains the psychological way of accounting for phenomena such as war and group hostility that arose after the decline of social Darwinism:

> The "psychological" mode attempts to explain such phenomena … in terms of the perceptions, beliefs, values, ideology, motivations, and other psychological states and characteristics that individual men and women have acquired as a result of their experiences … The "socio-political-economic" mode, in contrast, seeks an explanation in terms of such social, economic, and political factors as levels of armaments, objective conflicts in economic and political interests, and the like.[3]

Partisans of these two modes regard their particular mode as the cause of the opposing one when in fact the two modes are complementary rather than contradictory.

This early empirical orientation to social psychology led to many studies, some of which investigated cooperation and competition. Mort sees these as the precursors of the empirical social psychological study of conflict but he thinks that they were methodologically flawed and limited in scope:

> He saw that the purpose of most of the early research in the field on social interactions was directed at showing how competition, rather than cooperation, increased motivation. Thus the research that related to communication processes, problem-solving methods, interpersonal attitudes and attitudes towards the self, work or the group, were guided by the American ideology that competition rather than cooperation promotes greater motivation and productivity.

Conflict was therefore a field ripe for research, a task which Mort enthusiastically set himself to address.

From the 1920s, Kurt Lewin and his students conducted research that had had a powerful influence on social psychology. Mort says that Lewin's field theory, "with its dynamic concepts of tension systems, 'driving' and 'restraining' forces, 'own' and 'induced' forces, valences, level of aspiration, power fields, interdependence, and overlapping situations, created a new vocabulary for thinking about conflict and cooperation–competition."

In 1931 Lewin published a theoretical discussion of three basic types of intrapsychic psychological conflict: approach–approach (the individual stands between two positive valences of approximately equal strength), avoidance–avoidance (the individual stands between two negative valences of approximately equal strength), and approach–avoidance (the individual is exposed to opposing forces deriving from a negative and a positive valence.[4] Clark Hull and N.E. Miller elaborated Lewin's analysis and numerous experimental studies supported it. Thus, when Mort started at Lewin's research center at MIT, the work on conflict had already begun.

Mort says that:

> even more of my thinking was indebted to the ideas which were 'in the air' at the MIT Research Center for Group Dynamics. Ways of characterizing and explaining group processes and group functioning ... were under constant discussion among the students and faculty ... Thus, it was quite natural that when I settled on cooperation–competition as the topic of my doctoral dissertation, I should employ the Lewinian dynamic emphasis on goals and how they are interrelated as my key theoretical wedge into this topic. Even more importantly, the preoccupation with understanding group processes at the Center pressed me to formulate my ideas about cooperation and competition so that they would be relevant to the psychological and interpersonal processes occurring within and between groups.[5]

In summing up Kurt Lewin, Mort describes himself. If any student ever successfully emulated his teacher, it would have to be Morton Deutsch:

> Lewin was not only an original, tough-minded theorist and researcher with a profound interest in the philosophy and methodology of science; he was also a tender-hearted psychologist who was deeply involved with developing psychological knowledge that would be relevant to important human concerns. Lewin was both tough-minded and tender-hearted; he provided a scientific role model that I

have tried to emulate. Like Lewin, I have wanted my theory and research to be relevant to important social issues but I also wanted my work to be scientifically rigorous and tough-minded. As a student, I was drawn to both the tough-mindedness of Leon Festinger's work and to the direct social relevance of [Ron] Lippitt's approach and did not feel the need to identify with one and to derogate the other.[6]

Mort thinks that Lewin's early death in 1947 precipitated an undesirable split between theory, represented by Festinger, and practice, represented by Lippitt. Mort believes as passionately as his mentor that the two are intimately linked.

Major Questions Addressed by Social Psychological Research on Conflict

1. **What are the conditions which give rise to a constructive or destructive process of conflict resolution?**

   In terms of bargaining and negotiation, the emphasis is on determining the circumstances which enable the conflicting parties to arrive at a mutually satisfactory agreement that maximizes their joint outcomes. In a sense, this first question arises from a focus on the cooperative potential inherent in conflict.

2. **What are the circumstances, strategies, and tactics that lead one party to do better than another in a conflict situation?**

   The emphasis is on how one can wage conflict, or bargain, in order to win or at least do better than one's adversary. This second question emerges from a focus on the competitive features of a conflict situation.

3. **What determines the nature of the agreement between conflicting parties if they are able to reach an agreement?**

   Here the concern is with the cognitive and normative factors that lead people to conceive a possible agreement and to perceive it as a salient possibility for reaching a stable agreement: an agreement which each of the conflicting parties will see as "just" under the circumstances. This third question is a more recent one and has been addressed under the heading of research on the social psychology of equity and justice.

---

4. How can third parties be used to prevent conflicts from becoming destructive or to help deadlocked or embittered negotiators move toward a more constructive management of their conflicts?

This fourth question has been reflected in studies of mediation and strategies of de-escalating conflicts.

5. How can people be educated to manage their conflicts more constructively?

This has been a concern of consultants working with leaders in industry and government and also with those who have responsibility for educating the children in our schools.

6. How and when to intervene in prolonged, intractable conflicts?

Much of the literature in conflict resolution has been preventive rather than remedial in its emphasis. It is concerned with understanding the conditions that foster productive rather than destructive conflict (as in point 1) or developing knowledge about the circumstances that lead to intractable, destructive conflict, in the hope of preventing such conflict. More recently, the reality that many protracted, destructive conflicts exist in the world has induced some scholars to focus their attention on appropriate interventions.

7. How are we to understand why ethnic, religious, and identity conflicts frequently take an intractable, destructive course?

With the end of the Cold War, there appears to be a proliferation of such conflicts. In the past ten years, interest in such conflicts has been renewed. Attention has been given to what causes such conflict but also what can be done after the typical atrocities of such conflict to bring about reconciliation and reconstruction.

8. How applicable to other cultural contexts are the theories related to conflict that have largely been developed in the United States and Western Europe?

In recent years, there has been much discussion in the literature of the differences that exist in how people from varying cultural backgrounds deal with negotiations and, more generally, manage conflict.[7]

The Theory of Cooperation and Competition

There is no better way to explain the gist of Mort's theory than to give a summary of the first two chapters of the book he co-edited with Peter Coleman, *The Handbook of Conflict Resolution*. Occasional passages from Mort's other publications have been worked into this section.

As initially presented by Morton Deutsch and elaborated by David and Roger Johnson, the theory of cooperation and competition comprises two basic ideas: the type of *interdependence among goals* of the people involved in a given situation; and the *type of action* taken by the people involved.

Two basic types of interdependence among goals were identified: positive (where the goals are linked in such a way that if one person attains his or her goal the other person is also likely to do so); and negative (where if one person attains his or her goal the other is unlikely to do so). Hence, negative interdependence among goals may be thought of as an either/or situation: if one person attains his or her goals then the other cannot.

Mort posited two types of actions: "effective actions" are those that can be seen as enablers (they improve the actor's chance of attaining the goal); "bungling actions" are those that can be seen as inhibitors (they lessen the chances of attaining the goal). People's goals may be linked for a variety of reasons:

> [P]ositive interdependence can result from people liking one another, being rewarded in terms of their joint achievement, needing to share a resource or overcome an obstacle together, holding common membership or identification with a group whose fate is important to them, being unable to achieve their task goals unless they divide up the work, being influenced by personality and cultural orientation, being bound together because they are treated this way by a common enemy or an authority, and so on. Similarly, with regard to negative interdependence, it can result from people disliking one another; or from being rewarded in such a way that the more the other gets of the reward, the less one gets, and so on.[8]

As well as these positive and negative interdependencies, there can also be a lack of interdependencies in a relationship. For instance, the fate or activities of one person may be of no consequence to the other person, directly or indirectly. Where people are independent of one another, no conflict arises. Conflict assumes that some form of interdependency exists.

In addition, the degree of interdependence in a relationship may be asymmetrical. For example, where person A has considerable impact on person B, but B's actions have little or no impact on A, A is more dependent on B than B is on A. Because of the asymmetry, one person has more power and influence in the relationship than the other.

Mort combined the types of interdependencies and actions to propose how they affect three basic social psychological process: "substitutability," "attitudes," and "inducibility". He suggested that these three concepts were crucial for understanding the social and psychological processes involved in creating the major effects of cooperation and competition.

Substitutability refers to how one person's actions can satisfy another person's intentions. This is central to the functioning of society as we know it: we rely on others to do certain activities for us (e.g., a plumber to fix our drains and an architect to design our house). So substitutability refers to accepting the activities of others to fulfil our needs. *Negative substitutability* refers to a conscious rejection and an effort to counteract the effects of another's activities.

Attitudes refer to our predisposition to respond to certain aspects of our environment evaluatively — favorably or unfavorably. Humans have an innate tendency to be attracted to the beneficial and repelled by the harmful. It is from this innate tendency that the potential for cooperation and love, or competition and hate, develops. Hence the basic orientation of cooperation implies positive attitudes (we are for each other), whereas competition implies negative attitudes (we are against each other).

Inducibility (openness to influence) refers to the readiness to accept another's influence to do what he or she wants. *Negative inducibility* refers to a readiness to obstruct or reject fulfilment of what the other wants — inducibility is the complement of substitutability. Person A is willing to be helpful to person C, whose actions are helpful to person A, but not to person D whose actions are harmful to person A. Person A may reject the request to help person D, and if possible may interfere with person D's harmful actions if they occur.

Mort's theory therefore predicts that person A, who is in a positively interdependent relationship with person B, who bungles, will view person B's bungling negatively because the bungling is not a substitute for the effective actions person A intended. An example would be a husband and wife who both stand to gain from the other's success. In such a relationship, each spouse can be expected to help the other to be successful and to discourage the other from self-defeating behavior. However, if the relationship between persons A and B is negatively interdependent, as it would be in a tennis match, then the opponent person B's bungling substitutes for effective action for person A, whereas person B's effective actions are viewed negatively by person A.

The theory of cooperation and competition makes certain predictions about different aspects of intrapersonal, interpersonal, intragroup, and intergroup processes from the predictions about substitutability, attitudes, and inducibility. Thus, assuming that the individual actions in a group are more often effective than bungling, cooperative relations are positively interdependent where the goals of predominantly all members of the party are involved.

The competitive process stimulates the mindset that the solution to the conflict can only be imposed by one side on the other, which in turn leads to the use of coercive tactics such as psychological threats and violence. The scope of the conflict is expanded through the quest for superiority and control; it is no longer a confined issue in time and space, but rather grows to be one of power or moral principle. This escalation increases the motivational significance to the participants to make a limited defeat less acceptable and more humiliating than a mutual disaster.

As the conflict intensifies, it perpetuates itself by the processes of autistic hostility, self-fulfilling prophecies, and unwitting commitments.

Autistic hostility involves breaking contact and communication with the other because of my hostility toward the other. This perpetuates the hostility as there is no opportunity to learn that it may be based on misunderstandings or misjudgments, or to learn that the other has changed for the better.

Self-fulfilling prophecies are those processes where a person's hostile behavior is based on the false assumption that the other has done or is preparing to do something harmful to them. This assumption is reinforced when it leads oneself to engage in hostile behavior toward another which then provokes the other to act with hostility toward oneself. As both sides engage in such hostile self-fulfilling prophecies, the conflict escalates and each becomes hostile toward the other, and this in turn generates mutual suspicion. The problem is that each side tends to be unaware of how it, as well as the other, have contributed to this destructive process.

Unwitting commitments mean committing to rigid positions and potentially negative attitudes and perceptions, beliefs, and defenses during the course of the intensifying conflict. Thus, during an escalated conflict one may commit to the belief that another is evil and intends to take advantage of them and to the conviction that one needs to be vigilant and prepared to defend oneself against the danger the other poses to one's interests. Thus, the person invests in defending themselves alongside attacking the other. It is then hard to give up a grudge or to disarm without feeling vulnerable, as well as to relinquish the emotional charge that being mobilized and vigilant adds to the conflict.

The apparently insoluble conflicts between nation-states in parts of the world today are good examples of these three points. Current examples are the relationship between India and Pakistan, where each is suspicious of the other's nuclear capabilities, and North Korea and the United States, where the latter has named North Korea as part of an "axis of evil" and North Korea views the United States with suspicion.

These ideas have stimulated much research[9] which shows that cooperative processes (as compared with competitive ones) lead to greater group productivity, more favorable interpersonal relations, better psychological health, higher self-esteem, and greater learning.

Studies have also shown that more constructive conflict resolution results from cooperative than from competitive processes. This is of central theoretical and practical significance for understanding the nature of the processes involved in conflict. It indicates that constructive processes of conflict resolution are similar to cooperative processes of problem-solving, and that destructive processes of conflict resolution are similar to competitive processes.

An Escalating Conflict

In conversation, Mort gives an example of how a small personal conflict can escalate into something involving larger and larger groups:

"You and your husband are looking at television and you want to watch one program and he wants to watch another, and as you start discussing it it becomes a conflict, not about one person at this specific time and date who wants program 1 or program 2, but it expands to: 'You are the kind of person who always wants your way', 'You come from a kind of family who always wants their way,' 'Your ethnic group is one that wants to be the chosen people' and so on. You can see how it can escalate from a little thing that's happening here and now to something that involves the other person as a person, the other person as a family member and so on.

"If, to take a bigger example, the Cuban missile crisis was defined as a crisis involving a contest between the free world and the communist world, it would be very difficult to resolve, but if it were viewed as a conflict about where seventy-two weapons systems would be located, then it would become much easier to resolve. I think it's often people inexperienced in conflict who tend to frame their difference in excessively large terms, so that it becomes more difficult to resolve."

Mort distinguishes three types of conflict: *zero-sum* or win-lose conflict, in which what one person gains the other loses; *cooperative conflict*, in which both parties can gain or lose together; and the *mixed-motive conflict* where one party can gain and the other lose, or both parties can gain, or both parties can lose. The mixed motives refer to the mixture of cooperative and competitive interests each person has toward the other. Mort thinks that most forms of conflict are such a mixture. Knowing what type of conflict it is helps in understanding what processes are involved in producing good or bad outcomes. Although there are many ways of defining the outcomes of a conflict (e.g., satisfaction–dissatisfaction), it is plausible that cooperative-constructive processes of conflict resolution lead to good outcomes, such as mutual benefits and satisfaction, strengthening relationships, and positive psychological effects, while competitive-destructive processes lead to material losses and dissatisfaction, worsening relationships, and negative psychological effects for at least one party (if it is a win-lose situation) or for both parties (if it is lose-lose).

Mort describes destructive conflict in this way:

> Destructive conflict is characterized by a tendency to expand and escalate ... As a result, such conflict often becomes independent of its initiating causes and is likely to continue after these causes have become irrelevant or have been forgotten. Expansion occurs along the various dimensions of conflict: the size and number of the immediate issues involved, the number of motives and participants implicated on each side of the issue, the size and number of the principles and precedents that are perceived to be at stake, the costs that the participants are willing to bear in relation to the conflict, the number of norms of moral conduct from which behavior toward the other side is exempted, and the intensity of negative attitudes toward the other side. Paralleling the expansion of the scope of conflict is an increasing reliance on a strategy of power and on the tactics of threat, coercion, and deception. Correspondingly, there is a shift away from a strategy of persuasion and from the tactics of conciliation, minimization of differences, and enhancement of mutual understanding and goodwill.[10]

He points out that using the terms "competition" and "conflict" interchangeably is confusing and wrong. "Although competition produces conflict," he says, "not all instances of conflict reflect competition. In conflict that is derived from competition, the incompatible action reflects incompatible goals. However, conflict may occur even when there is no incompatibility of goals." For example, a husband and wife are in conflict about how to treat their son's mosquito bites. Their goals are the same but their methods are in conflict. So "conflict can occur in a cooperative or a competitive context, and the processes of conflict resolution that are likely to be displayed will be strongly influenced by the context within which the conflict occurs."[11]

Competition is not by definition negative. It can vary from destructive to constructive. On a competition continuum we might have unfair, unregulated competition lying at the destructive, negative end of the continuum; fair, regulated competition residing near the middle of the continuum; and constructive competition lying at the positive end of the continuum.

Constructive competition typically results in both the winner and the loser benefiting, as when two equally matched tennis players are more interested in having a good time than in winning or losing. It is a process that involves using competition in order to reach a good outcome for each of the competitors. Constructive competition typically occurs in a cooperative context and is often enjoyable for both winners and losers because they experience the pleasure of stretching themselves to their limits. However, if the emphasis is mainly on winning, the competition is likely to be harmful to the loser. Competition is often used to evaluate and rank people according to their capabilities. When this is done to improve group outcomes from which all benefit, it is likely to be constructive; when it is done to make invidious distinctions among the competitors, it is likely to be destructive.

Competition is therefore a useful social mechanism where a process of selection needs to occur to determine who has the highest capabilities. In this cooperative context it is deemed positive. However, competition can be destructive when it is not embedded in cooperation or regulated by fair rules.

The interdependency of parties in conflict is illuminated especially clearly by game theory. Mort has written that

> it has been [the] core emphasis [of game theory] that the parties in conflict have interdependent interests, that their fates are woven together," and that is what has made

it so valuable to social psychologists. Game theory, he says, "helped buttress a viewpoint that I had developed prior to my acquaintance with [it] — namely, that conflicts were typically mixtures of cooperative and competitive processes and that the course of a conflict would be determined by the nature of the mixture. This emphasis on the cooperative elements involved in conflict ran counter to the then dominant view of conflict as a competitive struggle.[12]

What gives rise to cooperative or competitive processes? Based on many research studies, Mort formulated what he calls Deutsch's Crude Law of Social Relations.

Deutsch's Crude Law of Social Relations

The Crude Law is that the characteristic processes and effects elicited by a given type of social relationship (cooperative or competitive) also tend to elicit that type of social relationship.

> Thus, cooperation induces and is induced by a perceived similarity in beliefs and attitudes; a readiness to be helpful; openness in communication; trusting and friendly attitudes; sensitivity to common interests and de-emphasis of opposed interests; an orientation toward enhancing mutual power rather than power differences. Similarly, competition induces and is induced by the use of tactics of coercion, threat or deception; attempts to enhance the power differences between oneself and the other; poor communication; minimization of the awareness of similarities in values and increased sensitivity to opposed interests; suspicious and hostile attitudes; the importance, rigidity, and size of the issues in conflict.[13]

If you know the effects of cooperative and competitive processes you can identify the conditions that generally elicit such processes, and you can identify whether a conflict is taking a cooperative, constructive or competitive, destructive course.

Mort called this law crude because "it expresses surface similarities between effects and causes; the basic relationships are genotypical [fundamental] rather than phenotypical [observable manifestations]."[14] The "surface effects" of cooperation and competition are based on the underlying type of interdependencies (positive or negative), the type of action (effective or bungling), the basic social psychological processes involved in the theory (substitutability, attitudes, and inducibility), and the social medium and social context within which these processes are expressed. The communication of a positive attitude, therefore, is dependent on the social context; for instance, a person would typically avoid expressing their positivity in a manner that was humiliating. Different cultures may give opposing meaning to the same surface behavior; for example, smiling when describing a tragic occurrence has an entirely different meaning in Japanese and American cultures.

Similarly, the extent to which any typical effect of cooperation or competition initiates a cooperative or competitive process is caused by the inferred genotype regarding the type of interdependencies and the type of outcome. For instance, seeing similar values in someone else makes a positive link between you and the other person possible (interdependency), but when this similarity translates into a quest for scarce resources only available to one person, a negative link is likely.

So, in reciprocal fashion, the effects of a relationship tend to induce that relationship. Two of the typical effects of a cooperative relationship are positive attitude and perceived similarities: positive attitudes result from and also cause perceived similarities.

Characteristics of Cooperative and Competitive Relations
ॐ

Cooperative relations (those in which the goals of the parties involved are predominantly positively interdependent), as compared with competitive relations, show more of these positive characteristics:

1. **Effective communication** is exhibited. Ideas are verbalized, and group members are attentive to one another, accepting of the ideas of other members, and being influenced by them. They have fewer difficulties in communicating with or understanding others.

2. **Friendliness, helpfulness, and less obstructiveness** is expressed in the discussions. Members are more satisfied with the group and its solutions

and favorably impressed by the contributions of the other group members. In addition, members of the cooperative groups rate themselves as having a strong desire to win the respect of their colleagues and in obligation to the other members.

3. **Coordination of effort, divisions of labor, orientation to task achievement, orderliness in discussion, and high productivity** are manifested in the cooperative groups (if the group task requires effective communication, coordination of effort, division of labor, or sharing of resources).

4. **Feeling of agreement with the ideas of others and a sense of basic similarity in beliefs and values,** as well as confidence in one's own ideas and in the value that other members attach to those ideas, are obtained in the cooperative groups.

5. **Willingness to enhance the other's power** (for example, the other's knowledge, skills, resources) to accomplish his or her goals increases. As the other's capabilities are strengthened, I am strengthened; they are of value to me as well as to the other. Similarly, the other is enhanced by my enhancement and benefits from my growing capabilities and power.

6. **Defining conflicting interests as a mutual problem to be solved by collaborative effort** facilitates recognizing the legitimacy of each other's interests and the necessity to search for a solution responsive to the needs of all. It tends to limit rather than expand the scope of conflicting interests. Attempts to influence the other tend to be confined to processes of persuasion.

In contrast, **competitive resolutions** have the opposite effect:

1. Communication is impaired as the conflicting parties seek to gain advantage by misleading the other through use of false promises, ingratiation tactics, and disinformation. It is reduced and seen as futile as they recognize that they cannot trust one another's communications to be honest or informative.

2. Obstructiveness and lack of helpfulness lead to mutual negative attitudes and suspicion of one another's intentions. Each person's perceptions of the other tend to focus on the person's negative qualities and to ignore the positive.

3. The parties to the process are unable to divide their work, duplicating one another's efforts such that they become mirror images; if they do divide the work, they feel the need to check what the other is doing continually.

4. The repeated experience of disagreement and critical rejection of ideas reduces confidence in oneself as well as the other.

5. The conflicting parties seek to enhance their own power and to reduce the power of the other. Any increase in the power of the other is seen as threatening.[15]

Mort's theory of conflict resolution equates a constructive process of conflict resolution with cooperative problem-solving processes (the conflict is a mutual problem that is to be solved collaboratively). Conversely, it equates destructive processes of conflict resolution with competitive processes (the conflicting parties struggle to determine who is the winner and who is the loser). Such cooperative-constructive processes are fostered by the typical *effects* of cooperation.

The theory of cooperation and competition is a well-verified one that allows insights into what can give rise to constructive and destructive processes. It is intended to serve not as a practitioner's cookbook but as a framework for understanding the processes involved in conflict and how to intervene. It should be noted that understanding and intervening require specific knowledge about conflicting parties, their social contexts, their aspirations, for example, their conflict orientations, and their social norms.

Although of central importance, cooperation–competition is only one factor influencing the course of conflict. Other factors affect conflict, such as power and influence, group problem-solving, social perception and cognition, intrapsychic conflict, and personality characteristics. Rather than relying on a single theory, a practitioner should use a mosaic of theories relevant to the specific situation. The symptoms or difficulties in one situation may, for example, require dealing with the theme of power, while another situation may require focus on an understanding of preferences and expectations.

The most important implication of the cooperation–competition theory for understanding conflict is that cooperation or a win-win orientation facilitates constructive resolution, while a competitive or a win-lose orientation hinders it.

> In a constructive process, the different parties seek to understand one another's needs and concerns (through empathic communication and listening) as a basis for diagnosing their mutual problem, and then they creatively search for new options for dealing with the conflict that can lead to mutual gain. If no option for mutual gain can be discovered, they seek to agree upon a mutually acceptable fair rule or procedure for deciding how the conflict will be resolved.[16]

A cooperative orientation is developed and maintained by social support from friends, co-workers, employers, the media, or the community generally. Managers in social systems, such as parents, school principals and CEOs need to accept that developing a win-win orientation requires more than just education of their subordinates. It involves educating themselves and other key people in the system so that their actions model and support this orientation. It also means changing incentives such as grades, salaries and bonuses, in order that the system does not foster or perpetuate win-lose relationships among the people involved.

The second most important implication of Mort's theory involves the cooperative processes involved in constructive conflict resolution. A fundamental process is reframing or redefining the conflict as a mutual problem to be resolved by joint cooperative efforts. This engenders cooperation even if the conflicting parties' goals are at first seen to be unattainable by both parties. It assumes that whatever the solution, it is acceptable to both parties and is considered to be just by both parties.

Conflicting parties are therefore more likely to succeed in this reframing if they follow the norms of cooperative behavior, which include respectful, responsible, honest, caring behavior toward friends or fellow group members. Yet, in the heat of conflict people tend to violate these norms. If you find yourself personally attacking the other person, Mort would say to stop, apologize and explain what made you angry enough to want to belittle and hurt the other person. If the other person starts to attack you personally, interrupt them, explain why you are interrupting and try to resume in a mutually respectful manner.

Getting to know your "hot buttons", the sore spots that are likely to evoke strong emotions when pressed, is a good idea. It is also important to know how you react when they are pressed, so that you can control your reactions. It also helps to know the other person's hot buttons in order to avoid provoking disruptive emotions in them.

Norms of Cooperation and
Constructive Conflict Resolution

The norms of cooperation and constructive conflict resolution reflect some basic values that can be shared by all the people concerned.

Reciprocity. The maxim "Do unto others as you would have others do unto you" requires each party to treat the other with the fairness it would normally expect if in the other's position. Reciprocity applies to how we should behave toward one another if we are to avoid a destructive conflict or motivate constructive management of the conflict.

Human Equality. This norm implies that all human beings are equally entitled to just and respectful treatment, with consideration for their needs, and to basic liberties, such as freedom of conscience, thought, and expression as well as freedom from coercion. It does not imply that people necessarily have the same status, privileges, power, needs, or wealth, but that such differences should not be the consequences of one person's violation of the other's entitlement.

Shared Community. Implicit in constructive conflict resolution is a mutual recognition of being a part of a broader community that members wish to preserve, sharing some key values and norms.

Fallibility. Reasonable people understand and accept that their own judgment as well as the judgment of others may be fallible.

Non-violence. Non-violence implies that coercive tactics (physical violence to the person or property, and psychological abuse) are not employed by either party to obtain agreement or consent.

LEFT: Mort, in July 1922, with his first girlfriend, Pauline.

RIGHT: Kurt Lewin (Fall 1945), Morton Deutsch's mentor, at MIT.

LEFT: Mort in summer of 1960 with his second son, Nicholas.

ABOVE: Mort with his wife Lydia, in Summer 1980 — his last girlfriend.

ABOVE: Mort and Lydia, 1982, taken after his inaugural lecture as EL Thorndike Professor.

ABOVE: Mort with two of his three brothers, John (seated) and Henry (standing), taken about 1972.

ABOVE: Spring 1986. Mort with his two sons and two of his grandsons (Tony's sons). From left to right: Anthony, Michael, Mort, David and Nicholas.

LEFT: Mort holding his grandson, Sanders, at his briss on January 8, 2001. Sanders is Nick Deutsch and Lisa Matzers's second son

ABOVE: 1951 Meeting of Council of the Society for the Psychological Study of Social Issues
at the Community of Michigan in Ann Arbor, Michigan.
Front row (left to right): Morton Deutsch, Brewster Smith, Jeanne Watson, Kenneth Clark.
Rear: Urie Bronfenbrenner, Herbert Kelman, Nevitt Sanford, Abraham Maslow,
Gardner Murphy, Milton Rokeach, Robert Chin, S.I. Hayakawa, Theodore Newcomb.

LEFT: Mort giving his inaugural lecture
as EL Thorndike Professor of
Psychology and Education at
Teachers College.

ABOVE: Harvey Hornstein's retirement party in the late 1990s. Left to right: Kathy Garner, Lida Orzeck, Morton Deutsch, Kenneth Kressel, Noel Tichy, Madeline Heilman, Harvey Hornstein (all, except Mort, graduates of the Doctoral Program in Social Psychology at Teachers College).

ABOVE: Spring 1997, Yosemite Conference. Left to right: Robert V. Levine, Elliot Aronson, Harold Gerard, Aroldo Rodrigues, Robert Zajonc, Albert Pepitone, Leonard Berkowitz, Philip Zimbardo, Harold Kelley, Morton Deutsch and Bertram Raven.

LEFT: Winter 2001. Mort receiving an award from the CPR Institute of Dispute Resolution (a distinguished group of lawyers interested in dispute resolution) for his book (co-written with Peter T. Coleman), *The Handbook of Conflict Resolution: Theory and Practice.*

ABOVE: 2002. Social Interdependence Theory Conference, Fifth Annual Silverwind Farm Summit, sponsored by Cooperative Learning Institute, held at the Silver Wind House Farm of David and Linda Johnson.
Seated (left to right): Laurie Stevahn, Norman Miller, Peter Coleman and Morton Deutsch. Standing: Dean Tjosvold, Roger Johnson, David Johnson and Frank Murray.

ABOVE: Mort and the author at lunch in New York in 2000, discussing the book.

ॐ

Knowledge and Skills Integral to
Constructive Conflict Resolution
—

The attitudes, norms, and values that foster cooperation are necessary but are not sufficient for promoting constructive conflict resolution. Knowledge and skills are also important. Knowledge of theory gives a person some direction in approaching novel situations. Skills are also vitally important in successful cooperative problem-solving. There are three main skills that are useful to the participants in conflict as well as to the mediators, conciliators, and counsellors who are called upon for assistance.

Rapport-Building. Rapport-building means establishing an effective working relationship. Desirable skills here are breaking the ice, reducing fears, tensions, and suspicion, overcoming resistance to negotiation, establishing a framework for civil discourse and interaction, and fostering realistic hope and optimism. Before negotiations begin, it is sensible to get the adversaries to meet informally in order to get to know each other as human beings who share mutual interests and goals.

Cooperative Conflict Resolution Skills. Cooperative conflict resolution skills develop and maintain a cooperative conflict resolution process among the parties throughout the conflict. These skills include identifying the type of conflict in which the parties are involved, reframing the issues so the conflict is seen as a mutual problem to be resolved cooperatively, active listening and responsive communication, respecting the other, acknowedging the other's situation and position, identifying shared interests and similarities, and being non-violent and non-abusive in interactions.

Group Process and Decision-Making Skills. Group process and decision-making skills include those relevant to group processes, leadership, and effective group discussions — the setting of goals and standards, monitoring progress toward goals, eliciting, clarifying, coordinating, summarizing, and integrating the contributions of parties, and maintaining group cohesion. They also include problem-solving and decision-making skills such as identifying and diagnosing the problem, acquiring the information necessary for devising solutions, creating or identifying several alternative solutions, choosing criteria for evaluating the alternatives, selecting the alternative that optimizes the results on the chosen criteria, and implementing the decision by appropriate action.

People are not novices in dealing with conflict. From their life experiences they have developed some component skills, but most may not be aware that they have such skills or know how and when to use them. People's reactions to conflict are usually ingrained and stem from knowledge, preconceptions, attitudes and behavior learned during childhood. Many people's pre-existing orientation to conflict reflects what is prevalent in their culture, and earlier experiences.

Before people can acquire competence in conflict resolution, they must become aware of their attitudes and typical behaviors. They can develop awareness and motivation by comparing themselves to a good model. The goal is to internalize the model by guided, repeated practice and feedback. Once the model is internalized, recurrence of old patterns of behavior will feel awkward because they deviate from the model that has been internalized.

Without competence in the skills, having a cooperative orientation and knowledge of conflict processes is often insufficient to set up a cooperative process of conflict resolution. Similarly, having the skills is not enough without the cooperative orientation and motive to apply the skills, or without the knowledge of how to apply them in various social and cultural contexts.

Deutsch's Twelve Commandments of Conflict Resolution

ಶಿಇಞಿ

1. Know what type of conflict you are involved in.

2. Become aware of the causes and consequences of violence and of the alternatives to violence, even when you are very angry.

3. Face conflict rather than avoid it.

---

4. Respect yourself and your interests, respect the other and his or her interests.

5. Distinguish clearly between "interests" and "positions".

6. Explore your interests and the other's interests to identify the common and compatible interests that you both share.

7. Define the conflicting interests between yourself and the other as a mutual problem to be solved cooperatively.

8. In communicating with the other, listen attentively and speak so as to be understood: this requires the active attempt to take the perspective of the other and to check continually your success in doing so.

9. Be alert to the natural tendencies to bias, misperceptions, misjudgments, and stereotyped thinking that commonly occur in yourself as well as the other during heated conflict.

10. Develop skills for dealing with difficult conflicts so that you are not helpless nor hopeless when confronting those who are more powerful, those who don't want to engage in constructive conflict resolution, or those who use dirty tricks.

11. Know yourself and how you typically respond in different sorts of conflict situations, of which there are six dimensions:

    (a) Conflict avoidance versus excessive involvement in conflict (denial, repression, postponement of facing the conflict, compared with a tendency to seek out conflict in order to show one is not afraid of it)

    (b) Hard versus soft (a tough, aggressive, unyielding response, out of fear of being considered soft compared with being unassertive so as not to be considered hostile or presumptuous)

    (c) Rigid versus loose (seeking to control the situation by inflexible rules, feeling threatened by any deviation compared with being averse to anything that seems formal, limiting, controlling, or constricting)

    (d) Intellectual versus emotional (suppressing all emotion compared with the belief that only feelings are real)

    (e) Escalating versus minimizing (experiencing the conflict as involving oneself, family, ethnic group, precedence for all time, etc., compared with refusing to recognize the importance of the conflict)

    (f) Compulsively revealing versus compulsively concealing (needing to show whatever you thinks about the other, compared with feeling you cannot show real feelings or thoughts without damaging the relationship).

12. Finally, throughout conflict, you should remain a moral person (i.e., a person who is caring and just) and should consider the other as a member of one's moral community (i.e., as someone who is entitled to care and justice).[17]

✀✀

The Theory of Justice and Conflict

Justice and conflict are closely connected: injustice breeds conflict and destructive conflict gives rise to injustice. Preventing such conflict necessitates reducing the gross social injustices that characterize much of the social world. Reducing these in turn requires that societal institutions recognize and live by the values underlying constructive conflict resolution.

Many philosophers, social scientists, and psychologists have contributed to the theory of social justice. Morton Deutsch's main contribution, as well as a summary of the contribution of others, is found in his book, *Distributive Justice: A Social Psychological Perspective*, his second chapter to the *Handbook of Conflict Resolution*, and his paper on oppression and conflict. Several kinds of justice are usually distinguished.

Distributive Justice

Distributive justice is concerned with what leads you to feel you received a *fair outcome*. The problems surrounding this pervade both social and intimate relations. They arise when something of value is scarce, or when something with a negative value cannot be avoided by all. For example, all hospital staff cannot take leave at Christmas time.

Many principles have been formulated for distributing scarce resources. They are mainly variants of three key principles: equity, equality, and need.

- The *equity* principle is that people should receive benefits in proportion to their contribution — those who contribute more receiving more than those who contribute less (used by economics-oriented groups).

- The *equality* principle is that all members of a group should share its benefits equally (used by solidarity-oriented groups).

- The *need* principle is that those who need more of a benefit should get more than those who need it less (used by caring-oriented groups).

In any situation, the three principles may be in conflict. In addition, the principles of distributive justice may be favored differently among individuals, groups, social classes, and cultures.

Theory and research suggest that the principles are usually prominent in different social contexts. Equity is most prominent where economic productivity is the goal. Equality is most prominent where social harmony is primary. Need is most prominent when the goal is encouraging personal development and personal welfare. Often all three goals are important, in which case they can be applied in a manner that is either mutually supportive or mutually contradictory.

An example of a mutually supportive application is a football player helping the team to win by an unusually skilful feat. He is honored by teammates and others in such a way that everyone is left feeling good rather than demeaned by his being honored. His being honored does not imply that he has won something and they have lost something. In a mutually contradictory application, on the other hand, the honoring ceremony could be held in a way that suggests that he is a better player and entitled to superior treatment, in which case the social harmony and cohesiveness of the team would be impaired.

Whether or not you see a judgment as leading to a fair outcome is determined both by the distributive justice principles employed and by whether your outcome is comparable with outcomes received by people like you in similar situations, for example your fellow workers. The theory of relative deprivation developed by such writers as Walter Garrison Runciman, Fay Crosby, and Robert Folger indicates that the sense of deprivation or injustice arises if there is comparative imbalance. Two types of relative deprivation are distinguished: egotistical *deprivation* occurs when I feel disadvantaged relative to others; fraternal *deprivation* occurs when I feel that my group is disadvantaged relative to other groups.

A sense of deprivation occurs when there is a perceived discrepancy between what I get and what I believe I am entitled to (assuming that I want what I am entitled to). Deprivation is *relative* in that it is determined by past and present comparisons with others, and by future expectations.

Procedural Justice

Procedural justice is concerned with *fair treatment* in the decisions that determine the outcome, for example, in procedures. Research indicates that fairness of procedures has greater impact than fair outcomes. Fair procedures are psychologically important for many reasons:

- They give rise to fair outcomes in the present as well as the future.
- In situations where "fair outcomes" are ambiguous, fair procedures are perceived as a guarantee that the outcome is fair.
- People are less committed to authorities, organizations, social policies, and so on if the procedures associated with them are seen to be unfair.
- Feelings of affirmation arise when the procedures they are subjected to treat them with the respect and dignity they feel is their due.
- Procedural fairness leads to greater acceptance of disappointing outcomes.

The values that are associated with procedural justice are as follows:

- Procedures should generate relevant, unbiased, accurate, consistent, reliable, competent, and valid information and decisions.
- Procedures should generate polite, dignified, and respectful behavior when the decisions are made and carried out.
- Those directly affected by the decisions should have voice representation in the decisions.

Fair procedures, therefore, are expected to generate good information for use in decision-making. They give a voice to those affected by these decisions and they promote considerate treatment of those affected by those making and carrying out the decisions.

A Sense of Justice

A sense of justice centers on what factors determine whether a circumstance is experienced as an injustice. Some people are insensitive to injustice and so seem unaware of it. The factors that influence the sense of injustice are as follows:

Victims and Victimizers. Here there is differential sensitivity or awareness according to differential gains and power. Those who benefit from injustice are often — intentionally or otherwise — its perpetrators or perpetuators. The *victimizers* typically hold the power (e.g., set the terms of relationships, establish definitions of justice), gain from exploitative actions, and find reassurance in social definitions of justice and social institutions.

Awareness of Injustice. The awareness of injustice leads to unpleasant emotions such as rage, guilt, or helplessness to change social situations. The victims or the disadvantaged are more aware of injustice and may feel anger and resentment. They are less likely to be insensitive to injustice because they are at the receiving end. Similarly, they are less likely to feel committed to official definitions of justice because they don't take part in creating them. Positive emotions, on the other hand, are felt by those who engage in effective actions to eliminate injustice, whether for the disadvantaged or advantaged.

Positive Self-Conception. Maintaining a positive self-conception results in opposing reactions from victimizers and victims in situations where the victimizers do not hold power over the victims, but by projecting blame onto the victims they can feel blameless and hence maintain a positive self-conception. In contrast, the victims, who feel pain or harm from an outcome, need to believe that they were not responsible for the outcome in order to feel positive about themselves. Victims may also deny or minimize the injustice they are suffering, but this is less likely to occur where similar victims are willing to acknowledge and protest their own victimization. Maintaining positive self-regard is not universal.

"Identification With the Aggressor". *"Identification with the aggressor"* (Freud, 1937) is another factor. Victims control dangerous feelings of injustice and outrage toward the victimizers by denying these feelings and internalizing the derogatory attitudes of the victimizers. The victimizers gain a sense of empowerment by attacking the victims, on whom the victimizers project the "bad" characteristics the victimizers possess and have suppressed because of the fear of being attacked by someone who has the power to harm them.

Nothing can be done to repair an injustice unless a *sense of injustice* is activated in both victims and the victimizers. There are several ways this can be done:

- falsifying sanctioned ideologies, myths and prejudices that "justify" the injustices
- exposing victims and victimizers to new ideologies, models and reference groups that support realistic hope about the possibility of eliminating injustice
- managing resistance and anxiety by becoming aware of the value systems that support the change and of models of successful change
- managing resistance and anxiety by obtaining social support from individuals and groups who support the change
- making the group an effective force for social change: within the group, enhance cohesiveness, trust, effective organization among members supporting change; outside the group, build allies, political and economic strength as well as bargaining power.

Retributive and Reparative Justice

Retributive and reparative justice concerns our response to the violation of moral or ethical norms and how to repair the moral community that has been violated. It concerns the attitudes and behaviors of people in response to the breaking of moral rules. Injustice to me or to others involves me not only personally and individually but also as a member of a moral community whose norms are being violated. It evokes the obligation to restore justice.

Once moral rules are violated, their validity is re-established by seeking redress from the violator (confession, an apology, restitution) and community actions to deal with the violator (punishment, incarceration, reconciliation). Retribution can serve a number of functions:

- Since a moral code is typically weakened by its violation, one of the most important roles of retribution is to reassert the continuing strength and validity of the code.

- Retribution can serve as a cathartic function for members of the moral community who have been offended and angered by the violation.

- Punishment of the violator may have a deterrent effect on future violation.

- Retribution may take the form of reduction of resources or opportunities so that the offender will no longer engage in the immoral behavior.

- Retribution in the form of restitution may help the victim recover from loss and damage.

It should be noted that there are considerable variations among cultures and subcultures with regard to moral or ethical rules and the response to their violation. Cultural ignorance or ethnocentrism will give rise to misunderstandings, and so may result in the violation of such a rule.

Moral Inclusion and Exclusion

The scope of justice concerns moral inclusion and exclusion — who is included and not excluded in the moral community and who is thought not to be entitled to fair outcomes and treatment. For example, in some countries religious heretics, sexual deviants, and slaves are not entitled to fair outcomes and fair treatment because they are excluded from the moral community. "Marginalization," a lesser form of moral exclusion, often leads to abusive treatment of those considered to be socially inferior, for example, women, minority groups, and subordinates.

Three central psychological questions arise with regard to moral exclusion:

1. What *social conditions* lead an individual or group to exclude others from their community?

2. What *psychological mechanisms* enable otherwise moral individuals to commit atrocities against other individuals?

3. What determines *which individuals or groups* are likely to be excluded from the moral community?

Social Conditions

Studies have shown that the following social conditions may lead to otherwise non-violent people developing hatred and other alienating emotions that allow them to dehumanize and kill their victims.

- the emergence of, or increase in, difficult life conditions, with a corresponding increase in the sense of relative deprivation

- an unstable political regime whose power may be under challenge — scapegoating may be used by those in power to deflect criticisms and attack potential rivals

- a claim for superiority — national, racial, gender, class, cultural, religious, or genetic — that justifies treating others as inferior

- the cultural sanctioning of violence as a result of past wars, the media, or the availability of weapons

- little sense of human relatedness or social bonding with the potential victims because there is little sense of positive contact or cooperation between them

- authoritarian social institutions, where non-conformity and open dissent against violence sanctioned by authority are inhibited

- the absence of an active group of observers of violence inside or outside the society who serve as a constant reminder of its injustice and immorality.

Psychological Mechanisms

People who commit atrocities against others employ the following psychological mechanisms:

- appeal to a higher moral justification for killing
- rationalize by relabeling the behavior as being more morally acceptable
- minimize the behavior by saying it is not harmful
- deny personal responsibility for the behavior
- blame the victims
- isolate themselves emotionally to the human consequences
- desensitize themselves to the human consequences.

Selection of Targets for Exclusion

We are most likely to delegitimize others whom we sense as a threat to anything important to us (religion, economic group, family, moral values, institutions). If harm was experienced at the hands of the other in the past, we readily interpret the other's ambiguous behavior as threatening. We exploit others, take advantage of them, or otherwise treat them unfairly because of their deviance from normative standards of appearance or behavior. The powerful can exclude others more openly, whereas the weak can do this only covertly. The targets are therefore more likely to be those with relatively little power.

Suppressed inner conflicts also encourage individuals to seek out external enemies. The kinds of internal needs for which a hostile external relationship can be an outlet are:

- an acceptable excuse for internal problems
- a distraction so that internal problems appear less prominent
- an opportunity to express hostility arising from the internal conflict
- the projection of disliked aspects of the victimizer onto the victim, and an attack on those aspects.

The general tendency is to select for projection those who are weaker, those with whom there is a history of enmity, and those who symbolically represent the weaker side of an internal conflict.

If it has a dangerous undertone, conflict can serve to counteract negative personal feelings such as aimlessness, boredom, and a lack of focus. It can be an addictive stimulant masking underlying depression. Or it may allow important parts of a person such as attitudes or skills to be expressed and valued because the relations with the present adversary resemble earlier conflictual relations. For example, a supervisor may remind you of a parent with whom you have had a troubled relationship.

The Implications of Mort's Theory of Justice for Understanding Conflict

There are several interrelated implications of Mort's theory of justice for understanding conflict:

- Perceived injustice is a frequent source of conflict.
- If the processes or outcomes of conflict are perceived to be unjust, the resolution of conflict is likely to be unstable and give rise to further conflict.
- A conflict may exist about what is "just."
- "Justifying" as a negotiation technique is likely to escalate the conflict unless the other agrees that he or she has been unjust and takes responsibility for remedying it.

Injustice as the Source of Conflict

When a child who divides a piece of cake into two takes the larger piece, the other child sees it as an injustice. A clear procedural way to avoid such an injustice would be for the one who divides the cake not to get first choice of portion. There is also final-offer arbitration for parties who cannot resolve conflict by themselves. The aim is to create an incentive for making fair offers. Each party agrees to binding arbitration and secretly informs the arbitrator of his or her last and best offer for an agreement; the arbitrator then selects what seems to be the fairest bid.

Injustice in the Course of Conflict Resolution

Unfair procedures employed in resolving conflict undermine confidence in the institutions that establish and implement policies and rules on conflict (e.g., I feel that elections are not conducted fairly). Trust in organizations, groups and interpersonal relations is also undermined if, when conflict occurs, I am abused, not given the opportunity to raise my concerns or treated as inferior. Possible responses to unjust procedures are alienation, withdrawal of commitment, anger, and aggression. Depending on the perceived possibilities, a person may become overtly or covertly active in trying to change the situations that give rise to injustice.

Conflict About What Is Just

Many conflicts are about which principles of justice should be applied, or how they should be implemented. For example, in a dispute about affirmative action, the question might be whether employees from an ethnic minority should be selected because of their merit alone or so as to reflect the ethnic diversity in the population. There is a clash, therefore, between two selection procedures, both of which are based on a reasonable principle of justice. The solution is to turn the conflict into a win-win situation, where the conflict is seen as a mutual problem to be resolved cooperatively.

"Justifying" as a Negotiation Tactic

"Justice" can be used as a tactical weapon during negotiations to claim the higher moral ground for yourself. This implies greater morality for your position as compared to the other's. This form of justifying typically has several effects. It hardens your position and makes it inflexible as you become morally committed to it; it leads to blaming, and implicit denigration of the other as morally inferior; and it produces a similar effect in the other and escalates the conflict into a conflict about morality. As a result the parties lose sight of the actual interests underlying their positions, and the conflict becomes a win-lose one that does not advance the cause of either side. Whatever justifying takes place, it should give full recognition to the other's equal moral status.

Implications for Training

Several important implications arise from the theory of justice for training in constructive conflict resolution:

- Knowledge of the intimate connection between conflict and injustice has to be imparted.

- Training should enlarge the scope of the individual's moral community so that he or she perceives that all people are entitled to care and justice.

- The empathic capacity of the individual should be increased so that he or she can sense and experience in some measure the injustice that victims experience.

- Insight needs to be gained into the processes involved in forgiveness and reconciliation.

- Training should develop skills in inventing productive, conflict-resolving combinations of justice principles when these appear to be in conflict.

Knowledge of Systematic Forms of Injustice in Society

Some injustices are committed by individuals with full awareness. Others arise from unwitting participation in a system that has established traditions, structures, procedures, norms, or rules that determine behavior. Injustices of this kind are difficult to recognize because they are embedded in a system in which a person is enmeshed, and so are taken for granted.

Types of Injustice

Awareness can be raised by taking the type of injustices listed earlier (distributive, procedural, retributive, and morally exclusive) and using them to probe the system, looking for structural sources of injustice.

Enlarging the Scope of Your Moral Community

A good place to start is to become aware of your own social identities (national, racial, ethnic etc.). Explore what characteristics you attribute to each identity, for example being American, or White, or Catholic, or female, and what you attribute to contrasting identities such as being Russian or Black. Recognize which of these identities claim an implicit moral superiority and greater privilege in contrast to people who have different identities. Reverse roles, so that you hold an identity that is frequently viewed as morally inferior and less entitled. Act this out, subtly, but realistically.

A moral community can expand or contract in response to temporary events. Research shows that people are more likely to trust a stranger after hearing "good news" about him or others (acts of heroism, altruism, helpfulness) and more likely to be suspicious after hearing "bad news".

Increasing Empathy

Empathy allows you to imagine how other people feel and to put yourself their shoes. It is a core component of helpful responsiveness to another and is more readily aroused by people with whom we identify. Empathy is inhibited by excluding others from your moral community, by dehumanizing them, and by making them into enemies. Empathy can occur at different levels: knowing what the other is feeling; feeling in some measure what the other is feeling; understanding why the other is feeling the way they do, including their wants and fears; understanding the other's perspective and frame of reference.

Forgiveness and Reconciliation

After protracted, violent conflicts in which the parties have inflicted grievous harm upon each other, the parties may still have to live and work together in the same communities (e.g., civil wars, ethnic conflicts, and family disputes). Forgiveness can be defined as giving up rage, the desire for vengeance, and a grudge toward those who have inflicted grievous harm on you, your loved ones, or the groups with whom you identify. It implies willingness to accept people so that they are entitled to care and justice.

A well-developed psychological and psychiatric literature deals with posttraumatic stress disorders, which are the psychological consequences of having been subjected or exposed to grievous harm. Forgiveness and reconciliation may be difficult to achieve at more than a superficial level unless the disorder is substantially relieved. Even so, forgiveness and reconciliation may be an important factor in relieving posttraumatic disorders.

There are two distinct but interrelated approaches to achieving forgiveness. One centers on the victim, the other on the relationship between victim and victimizer. The focus on victims, in addition to providing relief from posttraumatic stress, seeks to help victims recognize the human qualities they have in common with victimizers. Reconciliation goes beyond forgiveness, by accepting the other into your moral community and establishing or re-establishing a positive cooperative relationship.

Issues Related to Establishing Cooperative Relations After Destructive Conflict

1. Mutual security — real security from physical danger requires that both sides have mutual security as their goal.

2. Mutual respect — each side must treat each other with the respect, courtesy, and consideration normatively expected in civil society.

3. Humanization of the other — both sides need to experience one another in everyday contexts that enable them to see one another as human beings who are more like themselves than not. This is the antidote for the demonizing that characterizes bitter and protracted conflict such as ethnic or religious strife.

4. Fair rules for managing conflict — it is important to anticipate that conflicts will occur and to develop beforehand the fair rules and other resources for managing conflicts constructively and justly.

5. Curbing the extremists on both sides — parties need to cooperate in curbing extremism on their own sides and restraining actions that stimulate and justify extremist elements on the other side.

6. Gradual development of mutual trust and cooperation — in the early stages it is important that cooperative endeavors be successful. This requires careful selection of the opportunities and tasks for cooperation so that they are clearly achievable as well as meaningful and significant.

Inventing Solutions

In trying to resolve any problem constructively, it is helpful to be able to discover or invent alternative solutions that go beyond win-lose outcomes.

The relationship between conflict and justice is two-directional — injustice breeds conflict, and destructive conflict gives rise to injustice. As well as training, preventing destructive conflict requires reducing the gross injustices that characterize much of our social world.

Conflict Resolution in Education

Schools are especially important as sites of conflict. As Mort and Susan Opotow point out, a school is the center of a student's social life. "Differences in ethnicity, gender, age, affluence or poverty, skills, and disabilities can be a fertile ground for conflict as well as an opportunity for growth".[18]

"It has been increasingly recognized," they say, "that schools have to change in basic ways if we are to educate children so that they are for rather than against one another, so that they develop the ability to cope with their conflicts constructively rather than destructively and are prepared to live in a peaceful world."

This means establishing, throughout the school system, cooperative learning, training in conflict resolution, the constructive use of controversy in teaching subject matters, and the creation of dispute resolution centers. "By the time they become adults, students will have developed the attitudes, knowledge, and skills that will enable them to cooperate with others in constructively resolving the inevitable conflicts that will occur among friends, neighbors, colleagues, and within families, ethnic groups, communities, and nations."

The starting point is cooperative learning. Johnson, Johnson and Holubec[19] recognize five key elements of this:

- positive interdependence, where students see that it is to their advantage if other students learn well and that it is to their disadvantage if others do poorly

- face-to-face interaction, in which students can express their positive interdependence in behavior
- individual accountability of each member of the cooperative learning group to one another
- interpersonal and small-group skills
- provision of the time and procedures for processing or analyzing how well students' learning groups are functioning and what can be done to improve how they work together.

The numerous studies that have been done show very encouraging results:

> Students develop a considerably greater commitment, helpfulness, and caring for each other regardless of differences in ability level, ethnic background, gender, social class, or physical disability. They develop more skill in taking the perspective of others, emotionally as well as cognitively. They develop greater self-esteem and a greater sense of being valued by their classmates. They develop more positive attitudes toward learning, school, and their teachers. They usually learn more in the subjects they study by cooperative learning, and they acquire more of the skills and attitudes that are conducive to effective collaboration with others.[20]

Putting cooperative learning into practice, however, is far from simple. New skills are required in teaching, monitoring and curriculum development as well as conflict resolution. While the contents of training programs vary with the age and background of the students, there are common elements.

A mediator is called in when the conflict is too difficult for the parties to resolve by themselves. Johnson and Johnson (2002) summarize what school mediators are expected to do:

> The procedure for mediation consists of a series of steps. First, you end hostilities. Break up fights and cool down students. Second, you ensure that both people are committed to the mediation process. To ensure that both persons are committed to the mediation process and are ready to negotiate in good faith, the mediator introduces

the process of mediation, sets the ground rules, and introduces him- or herself. Third, you help the two people negotiate with each other successfully. This includes taking the
two persons through the negotiation sequence of (a)
jointly defining the conflict by both persons stating what
they want and how they feel, (b) exchanging reasons, (c)
reversing perspectives so that each person is able to present
the other's position and feelings to the other's satisfaction,
(d) inventing at least three options for mutual benefit, and
(e) reaching a wise agreement and shaking hands. Fourth,
you formalize the agreement. The agreement is solidified
into a contract. Disputants must agree to abide by their
final decision, and in many ways the mediator becomes
"the keeper of the contract."[21]

There are also ways of using a technique Mort calls constructive
controversy to teach various subjects. Deutsch and Opotow set out
the discussion rules that students are instructed to follow during
the controversy:

> (a) be critical of ideas, not people; (b) focus on making the
> best possible decision, not on winning; (c) encourage
> everyone to participate; (d) listen to everyone's ideas, even
> if you do not agree; (e) restate what someone has said if it is
> not clear; (f) bring out the ideas and facts supporting both
> sides and then try to put them together in a way that makes
> sense; (g) try to understand both sides of the issue; and (h)
> change your mind if the evidence clearly indicates that you
> should do so.[22]

Mort has always emphasized that conflict is an important and
pervasive aspect of life and should be enjoyed:

> Conflict is like sex; it is an important and pervasive aspect
> of life. It should be enjoyed and should occur with a
> reasonable degree of frequency, and after a conflict is over
> the people involved should feel better than they did
> before. This is most likely to happen if the people
> involved are mutually respectful and mutually responsive
> to each other's needs.
> Some psychiatrists and social scientists have given
> conflict a bad reputation by linking it with psychopathology,

social disorder, and war. Conflict can be dysfunctional, but it also can be productive. It has many positive functions, including preventing stagnation and stimulating interest and curiosity ... It is the medium through which problems can be aired and solutions developed. It is the root of personal and social change. The practical and scientific issue is not how to eliminate or prevent conflict but rather how to have lively controversy rather than deadly quarrels.[23]

Seventh-graders describe the way that conflict can enliven their lives

"I think fights are important because next time they'll think twice before messing with you because they know you'll defend yourself."

"Without conflicts and fights you will never find out who you are and what type of person you like and what you want out of life."

"You can find out how another person reacts to certain things. You can find out more about persons. Sometimes even the fights help you establish a relationship with somebody."

"I'm not gonna say that it was all her fault. Because it might have been something else that I had done to her already and maybe with that on top of it she said 'Forget it.' I don't know. Maybe it might have been something else that I had already done and never realized that I did."

"Everybody's looking at you; when you lose everybody puts their backs to you."[24]

"The Bridge Between Ideas and Applications is Theory"

Mort always insisted that theory came first, recognizing that theory was where his personal contribution lay. But as he readily acknowledges, all the theory in the world will do nothing to make the world a better place unless it is applied to specific situations. His work and that of the practitioners were therefore complementary.

Theory was the bridge between the idea in the mind of the researcher and the action of the practitioner. Mort's contribution has been to formulate ideas into sound theories by solid research and so make them available to the practitioner.

Several of Mort's doctoral students went on to become well-respected psychologists, following his emphasis on rigorous science and research methodology in their respective areas. These people include Adrienne Asch, Susan Boardman, Bert Brown, Barbara Bunker, Peter Coleman, Rebecca C. Curtis, Michelle Fine, Marha Gephart, Madeleine Heilman, Harvey Hornstein, David Johnson, Charles M. Judd Jr, Robert Krauss, Kenneth Kressel, Ivan Lansberg, Roy Lewicki, Harold Proshansky, Susan Opotow Jeffrey Rubin, Sandra Sandy, Leonard Solomon, Janice Steil, David Johnson, Harold Yuker, and Eben Weitzman.

Many of them went on to explore topics that Mort had not addressed but that were close to his heart. Harvey Hornstein did research on altruism, particularly in organizational settings; Barbara Bunker on education and leadership, Charles Judd on education and social relations; Michelle Fine on gender, class and race; and Bruce Tuckman in education.[25]

Janice Steil worked on the distribution of power in families, Susan Opotow's work is done against the background of an interest in organizational psychology, and Roy Lewicki has written a book on organizational justice. Ken Sole does a lot of work with organizational people but is also interested in issues of diversity, prejudice, discrimination, and fair treatment. Roy Lewicki and Jeffrey Rubin published many books on negotiation and mediation. Bert Brown focused on bargaining and negotiation, Yakov Epstein on the effects of crowding, and Kenneth Kressel on mediation.

Michelle Fine and Adrienne Asch followed another theme in Mort's work by looking at the social psychological process in involving people from disadvantaged groups. Harold Yuker and Adrienne Asch looked at attitudes to people with disabilities, and Lois Biener and Madeline Heilman focused on gender issues. Some students contributed to the clinical area, such as Rebecca Curtis and Joyce Anne Slochower.

The Handbook of Conflict Resolution has found its way into multidisciplinary study circles. Its contents give a good idea of the wide field to which the theory gives rise. Its twenty-seven chapters cover interpersonal and intergroup processes, which include Mort's own theories in the first two chapters (summarized earlier in this chapter) and essays on trust, power, communication, and conflict; intrapsychic processes such as judgmental biases, anger, and retaliation; personal differences in conflict; creativity and change; intractable conflict; culture and conflict; and three models of practice in teaching, mediation, and managing conflict through large-group methods. Dean Pruitt has said that this book is "a feast of new ideas and perspectives on conflict resolution. It is based on solid theory and research, yet it is eminently practical — a true Lewinian synthesis."

At Teachers College, says Barbara Bunker, Mort set his students straight on the apparent tension between those who emphasized theory and those who emphasized application. Most people thought that the theoretical, hard-nosed stuff was better than the soft, applied stuff. Even though his own emphasis was so thoroughly on theory, Mort never tolerated that notion. He was always very supportive of students and would not allow put-downs of ideas simply because they were different. He would just say, "It's more complex, it's more difficult to understand." He wouldn't let people make derogatory remarks about application as though it were something you would only do if you couldn't make it in the work of hotshot theoretical thinkers, and he constantly confronted people and forced them to think about application. But if all they wanted to think about was application he would confront them and make them think about theory.

You could say that Mort was interested *theoretically* in application. He did not feel he needed to apply his theories himself, but he was delighted for his students to do it. Barbara did not see him as being anti-application at all. "What he didn't do," she says, "was go around the country and try to mediate conflicts". Mort was very good at setting boundaries and saying "I'll do this, but not that, this is where I am," without putting down other people's choices."

The four major fields where Mort's theories have found application are education, law, business and organizations (key students are Harvey Hornstein, Ken Sole, Roy Lewicki, and Barbara Bunker), and international relations (Jeffrey Rubin). Mort co-edited the book

Preventing World War III, participated in many conferences, wrote a number of papers on international relations and is well-known by people working in this area (e.g., Ronald Fisher, Robert Jervis, David Ham, the people at George Mason University, Harvard University, and the University of Colorado).

The International Center for Cooperation and Conflict Resolution

Throughout his career Mort remained committed to producing work that was socially relevant and applying such work to social problems. He felt that education was a crucially important area and in 1986 established the International Centre for Cooperation and Conflict Resolution (ICCCR), based at Teachers College, which is committed to developing cooperative learning and constructive conflict resolution in schools.

Mort founded the center several years before he retired. It took a lot of work and bureaucratic wrangling but the result was the organization that Mort had envisioned many years earlier. He appointed Ellen Raider as Training Director, and Sandra Sandy and Sue Boardman as co-Research Directors. They were paid from external grants for research on training rather than from the College's funds. The President of the College provided funds to run the first workshop.

Mort hired Ellen Raider because he needed someone with practical skills to complement his own emphasis on theory. Ellen had come from the corporate world and had done a lot of work in international negotiation. After years spent teaching developing nations' governments and multinationals how to work better collaboratively, she felt that to have a real impact she needed to get to children. She turned to education. Mort's offer was just what she needed — "It seemed like a match made in heaven." Mort taught the theory courses and Ellen the practicum courses. "He is such a low-key kind of guy," she says. "He allowed me the space to do my practitioner thing. I think I helped put the Center on the map."

The first activity of the Center was the workshop for school superintendents in and around New York City, which involved a series of mini-seminars that illustrated the Center's objectives. The seminars included such topics as cooperative learning, conflict resolution, the use of constructive controversy, mediation, peace education, and research. The leaders of the seminars included David and Roger Johnson of the University of Minnesota, the Training Director of the San Francisco Community Board, the Director of the Victims' Service Agency in New York City, and Betty Reardon and Mort from Teachers College. As a result of this workshop the Center received an invitation from a wealthy suburban school district to teach cooperative learning and conflict resolution, as well as conduct research on the effects of the training. However, when the district's Board of Education saw the questionnaires, which included measures of social skills, social relations, and psychological adjustment, they refused to allow the questionnaires to be administered. The team had to withdraw. Mental health at that time was seen as an explosive, dangerous topic.

The W.T. Grant Foundation, which was supporting the project, readily agreed to change the site of the study to an inner-city alternative high school. Ellen Raider, who knew the principal of the school, obtained permission to conduct the study in this quite different setting. However, they also needed to obtain permission from the various administrative layers of the New York City school system, as well as from the school's teachers at each of its four campuses. Consent was obtained from the various levels of administration at all but one of the campuses. The fourth was in a period of considerable turmoil and wanted to postpone the study (which Mort could not afford to do).

"It was a long and difficult project in many ways," says Mort. "Teachers there were really overworked, they had terrible working conditions, and many of them were working with troubled adolescents. The students were kids who had dropped out of high school previously and had come back. They were from underprivileged backgrounds: mostly Blacks and Hispanics, a few Asians and few Whites. They had a high turnover rate. A lot of them didn't have great literacy, but we managed."

Prior theory and research predicted the results — the children who had been exposed to the training had better self-esteem, were less victimized, less depressed, had greater control over their lives, and actually performed better academically. Being able to measure depression in the pupils was a minor triumph on its own.

"I wanted to get more than the usual superficial measures — Did you like it? Have you learned something? Did the teachers like it? We got some extremely valuable measures. The value of the study was that it was the first one done in this kind of setting, with this kind of duration. And this was a difficult school, a difficult environment, and to have some indication of positive results which were consistent with the theory and consistent with the other research results gave strong support to the message that this was a worthwhile thing to be engaged in."

The project was a significant win for Mort and his team and led to a contract with the New York City Board of Education to train two staff from every high school in the area in techniques of conflict resolution. Within two years, most of the 150 high schools that took part had established mediation centers in their schools. The training was done under Ellen Raider's direction.

Ellen's passion is social justice, and she is vastly inspired by Mort and his writings on the subject. "Mort is a man who has lived and written about his convictions, and stood by his writings and what's important to him, and he has inspired me to do the same. We tease each other about what effects change in the world. He has certainly effected change because he has created a whole field that has a direct bearing on human relations. I am not a researcher, nor am I a writer, so my way of changing has to be in the activist mode. I hope I can contribute in the activist mode what he has done through theory and writing."

She is concerned with issues of power — of whites over blacks, of men over women, of straight people over gays. "I have a conflict between myself as a conflict resolver and mediator and myself as an advocate. I spent years building up the conflict resolution part of me, but the school situations in New York City are so horrible and racism is so strong that I feel there is work to do for the next ten years of my life. I want to do more advocacy work and it's been a tension within me. Mort and I have started a new seminar on

oppression and we have been talking about how to look at oppression and how to change the situations where there are haves and
have-nots."

Peter Coleman succeeded Mort as Director of the Centre. He
found it interesting being intellectually parented by both Mort and
Ellen. Following Mort's belief in the synthesis between theory and
practice, Peter says that there was a fair amount of tension and
energy at the Center around the issue of theory versus practice,
which really forged the dual emphasis the Center has. There are a
lot of other places that have an emphasis on practice, but theory
centers with a practical orientation are rare.

What they were trying to develop at the Center is what Peter
calls the "pedagogy of reform." Conflict resolution had previously
been on the periphery of education, a sort of icing on the cake.
Those at the Center wanted to work out how these ideas and
approaches could be institutionalized into the core of education so
that it became part of how intellectual problems were solved in
classrooms, how disciplinary problems were resolved, how
teachers managed their workload, and how the administration
addressed parent issues. Conflict resolution processes would
become a key force in reforming schools to better address the
needs of the population.

"We made a decision a few years ago to stop doing what we
called 'service', because we're not really set up as a service shop,
but I do think that ultimately this is the applied area and we don't
want to lose that connection. That's why we are developing our
trainers and why we're doing systemic intervention, which entails
training, consultancy, coaching and mediating disputes as they
emerge — perhaps facilitating the change process systemically, and
that's a set of skills that's broader than training. It's all part of
changing how people think about things. If schools develop the
skills and the approaches of conflict resolution it has the potential
to really affect the culture of schools."

When tensions and problems arose over who was to replace
Mort as Director of the Center, Mort responded by being open and

honest with everyone. "I was looking forward to stopping teaching but the college would only appoint a junior person. The Chair of the Department wanted Keith Allred, who came here partly because of my work and was very interested in taking the director-ship of the Center. He had little interest in education and was more interested in negotiation in business settings. He was a very bright, nice guy. I liked him, but I didn't think he was going to be the best person to help develop the Center the way Ellen and I wanted it to develop." Mort solved the problem by suggesting that Keith be co-director with Peter Coleman, his own choice, but fortunately Keith received a job offer from Harvard and Peter became Director.

Mort's Personal Handling of Conflict

Considering Mort's academic and personal interest in conflict, how does he deal with conflict in his own life? Harvey Hornstein compares his own approach to conflict with Mort's.

"In the late 1960s, when there was a lot of political action at Columbia's main campus, a doctoral student called King Collins got involved in the radical student movement. He wanted to liberate Teachers College, including my secretary's mimeograph machine! On one occasion King wanted to use the machine to make flyers while I was out of the office. He was abusive and intim-idating and succeeded in scaring the hell out of my staff. I returned the place was a mess — my secretary was in tears."

"I just said calmly, 'Ask King to come and see me.' When King arrived he immediately proclaimed, 'I have every right to do this, I'm liberating this machine for the people.' I responded, 'Calm down, King, come into my office and we'll talk about this.' King came in and I shut the door behind him. As soon as the door closed I threw King to the floor and took a martial arts stance over him [Harvey had a black belt in karate] and said, 'If you ever intimidate my staff again I will find you and I will kill you.'"

The same man appeared in one of Mort's lectures, Harvey recalls. King entered the lecture theatre and announced that he wanted to liberate the curriculum. He wanted the course to focus on democracy and free speech, and to throw the "social psychology propaganda" out. According to Harvey, Mort paused for a moment then said, "So my understanding is that you have a deep belief in democracy?"

"Yes," said King, "I do." And Mort said, "So, based on that I would presume that you would be open to a democratic vote as to how the course should proceed." "Of course I would," said King. The class voted for him to leave and for Mort to go ahead. "That," says Harvey with relish, "is some difference in strategy."

Academic life certainly provides many opportunities for conflict over ideas and how they are expressed. Peer review and peer debate are expected when work is placed in the public domain. When the work is overtly value-laden, however, the criticisms often come more strongly and readily. Mort describes how he handled conflict over his academic work.

"Michel Plon, a French social psychologist, wrote a critical article about conflict resolution attacking me and my work because he considered me to be the most progressive of American social psychologists — he was writing from a Leftist perspective. I felt great enjoyment in responding, because it just took me back to my City College days where there were a lot of polemics in the lunchroom alcove. If you were interested in the political issues of the day you developed some skills in polemical argument. I don't use them very much now but I did enjoy using them against Michel because I thought he really didn't know what he was talking about."

There have certainly been challenges to Mort's ideas. Mort's work with the Acme-Bolt game and the effects of threat on bargaining was seen as a challenge to deterrence theory. Jerry Shure, who worked at one of the defense institutes, published an article criticizing Mort's experiments with the game, as did one of Harold Kelley's students. "I was a challenger to the deterrence approach to international relations. I was saying that all kinds of misunderstandings grow out of the use of threats as potential ways of preventing war, which prompted a lively discussion."

Jerry Shure, Hall Kelley, and Mort were part of a "conflict study group" supported by the Office of Naval Research, which was comprised of European as well as American social psychologists. They met twice a year, which gave Jerry, Hal and Mort many opportunities to discuss their differences in a friendly, cordial setting. "I don't recall whether or not we ever came to agree," Mort says. The trio also participated in a conference on "Strategic Interaction" which included Thomas Schelling, Albert Wohlstetter, and Anatol Rapaport. "I remember these three names because 'Kip' Weinberger, who later became the Secretary of Defense in the Reagan administration, invited us to participate in the debate on Vietnam on a radio program that he hosted. Rapaport and I were vigorous opponents of the war while Schelling and Wohlstetter were equally vigorous supporters of it. Weinberger was a good moderator."

Other critics of Mort's work included Erika Apfelbaum, a French social psychologist, who criticized American social psychology from the New Left, and Serge Muscovici and Henri Tarjfel who criticized American social psychology and Mort's approach to psychology as "the psychology of the nice guy." Muscovici and Tarjfel thought that Mort's emphasis on cooperative processes was naïve, as though he had no awareness of the evil that was in the world. "I always thought I was aware of evil," Mort says. "I was just trying to prevent it."

Mort on International Relations

As one of the founders of the scientific study of conflict resolution, Morton Deutsch is an obvious man to ask about the current intractable world problems. In the early 1960s the nagging question was the Cold War with the Soviet Union. Mort wrote a conference paper called "On Changing the Devil".

He says "the notion was that you had to think of the Soviet Union, if it were a devil, whether it was a *corrigible* devil or an *incorrigible* devil. If you thought it was incorrigible then, given that it had enough H-bombs, there was really nothing that could be done to change and improve the world situation. On the other hand, if you thought it was corrigible, there were certain kinds of possibilities, and even if it were incorrigible and you made the mistake of thinking it was corrigible, you were better off taking that perspective, because you were lost if it were incorrigible. So I developed that notion — it was a kind of game theory notion and I talked about how to deal with a corrigible devil."

When he contemplates the continuing conflict in the Middle East, Mort sees each side as having made basic mistakes. The Palestinians under Arafat made the mistake of trying to use force to improve their bargaining position, and Israel made the mistake of responding to the Palestinian use of force with their own excessive use of force. The result was the escalation of the conflict.

Under what conditions can you establish readiness for intervention in this situation? Mort thinks that the Palestinians made a significant error when they turned away from the best offer that Ehud Barak was apparently willing to accept from US President Bill Clinton at the failed 2000 Camp David peace summit. They would have been much better off to try to agree, at that point, and then see how the situation improved as cooperation developed between the two sides. Now, as then, it is a question of both sides cooperating to curb their own extremists.

In a powerful application of his conflict resolution theory, Mort says that it is important to understand that each side needs to feel secure, to feel that they are treated civilly without being humiliated by the other side. Each side can expect that there will be future conflict, so they have to develop agreed mechanisms to manage such conflict. They also have to understand that trust is going to be developed very slowly, and that it usually has to be guaranteed by an external party. Cooperation, likewise, has to progress in small steps that are likely to succeed and are also significant in terms of their benefit to each side.

"I'm afraid there are too many people in the world in leadership positions," he says, "who still think that the way to deal with conflict, particularly if there has been some hostility, is only through force. What Ariel Sharon is doing now by escalating conflict is not going lead to any long-term peace." The hope is that both sides, after a certain amount of mutual damage and mutual harm, get so weary with the conflict that they realize that their only option is to really try to negotiate a peace. Mort quotes the political scientist Zartman when he describes this situation as a "hurting stalemate" — one that's so hurtful to each side that they feel it's no longer sensible to continue hurting one another.

Mort thinks the situation in the Middle East became more open to possibilities of peace when the other Middle Eastern nations realized that Israel could not be simply wished out of existence or conquered, and they no longer had the surplus of oil money that allowed them to feel they could go on undermining Israel as a way of protecting their own governments from internal uprisings. On its part, Israel came to the realization after the war with Lebanon that, despite being the most powerful military nation in the area, it had inflicted so many costs on itself, from a humanistic and economic point of view, that it too became more ready for genuine peace. The problem, during this long hostility, was that extremist groups developed on both sides and were partly supported by outside forces. Extremist groups Hamas and Hezbollah, for example, have been supported by Iran and Iraq and other nations not interested in peace with Israel. Similarly, some religious Christian fundamentalist and Orthodox Jewish groups are supporting the radical Right in Israel, feeling that Israel should never yield any of the territory it occupies because it is sacred land. As in other protracted conflicts, such as in Northern Ireland, the problem always lies in curbing the extremists.

Mort is especially lucid when he discusses the crucial question of the part played by membership of an ethnic group in international or civil conflict. He says the bonds arising out of family or ethnic status are generally unalterable and have a huge social significance. They pervade people's makeup, affecting their thoughts and actions. And "membership in such groups typically excludes membership in other groups of a similar type. That is, if you are Black, you are not also White; if you are male, you are not also female; if you are Jewish, you are not also Christian."

> Suppose that one is emotionally attached to one's identify as a Jew, woman or Black, but that it results in systematic oppression and discrimination and places one at distinct disadvantage in obtaining many kinds of opportunities and rewards. How one copes with this situation will be largely determined by whether one views the disadvantages to be just or unjust. If those who are disadvantaged by their

group identity accept their disadvantages as being warranted, they are unlikely to challenge and conflict with those who are profiting from their relatively advantaged positions. The sense of being treated unjustly because of one's membership in a group to which one is strongly attached and bound is the energizer for much intergroup conflict. The sense of injustice is felt particularly intensely in interracial, interethnic, and intersex conflicts because of the centrality of these group identities to the individual's self-esteem. When women or Blacks or Jews are devalued as a group, those who are identified and identify with the groups also are personally devalued.[26]

Each side has to be aware of the internal problems of the other side, and help the other side with those internal problems. Mort points out that the way each side phrases its messages is really important — extremists on the other side should not be given any ammunition by the way you interact with them. He thinks people are aware that this is the real danger to peace processes. He also points out that it is much less costly and much more effective to try to anticipate the problems and to develop the kinds of institutions that can deal with them before they get to the crisis stage. Most nations of the world are not willing to bear those costs in a way that is adequate to the problem that is involved in the crisis.

In response to George W. Bush's program of missile defense, Mort says, "It seems to me a very dangerous expansion, without real justification at this point. The whole notion of missile defense is absurd for a number of reasons. One is that even if the technology gets to the point where a missile can knock down another missile, that assumes that the other missile is not using defensive tactics, and it's likely that it's going to be easier to develop defensive tactics to prevent the bullet hitting another bullet."

"That's one thing, and even if you were successful in overcoming the defence, you still have the reality that any group that wants to inflict severe damage on the United States could put H-bombs in ships in the harbors of New York, San Francisco, Los Angeles, and blow them up. There are other ways of smuggling in atomic weapons than through missiles, so it's not a perfect defense against atomic weapons in any case. It's simply an enormous expenditure that will increase military competition and increase the dangers to the world without increasing its security. So I feel the only people it will benefit is the armaments industry. With the billions of dollars that would be spent, you could do so much to improve the world and make it more peaceful. It's just the wrong way to go."

"I think there are positive things happening. There is an increasing awareness of the need to develop strategies that help prevent, mediate, arbitrate, and educate about conflict. Yet there is poverty and despair among many minority groups, and the availability of destructive weapons and the tendency for demagogues to try to use discontent for their own power-based motives is growing faster than the positive factors."

"My general feeling is that it's a race. It's a race on a lot of things. A while ago, on the Internet, I was looking at some stuff on global warming increasing, and its effect on potential health problems. There are a lot of groups pressing for awareness of the global environment and for changes that will decrease pollution, decrease the rapidity of the increase in warming and so on. Who's going to win this race?"

In spite of the huge scale of world problems, Mort is optimistic. He believes that the answer lies partly in education, because however many billions of dollars people have or however much coercive power they wield, they will be affected as well, in the long term, if they don't help to control these adverse forces, whether they be political or environmental. It is matter of helping people to understand where their true interests lie. He thinks that there are increasing numbers of ordinary people and their leaders who are becoming aware of the issues. Leaders, however, often have too short a vision in terms of time — they are looking toward the next election rather than working at a constructive long-term perspective.

Asked about Huntington's thesis, which asserts that conflicts in the future are going to be fought along religious lines, Mort says he thinks the religious issue is no different from any other prolonged ethnic conflict. Like many, he holds that fanaticism is driven by poverty, alienation, and injustice, and that the way to combat fanaticism is to work on improving these conditions. In situations that do not allow the real expression of need, people are likely to develop rebellious and potentially violent reactions. In Iran, however, he thinks that the religious groups are starting to lose their power — recent election results indicate that people are starting to feel that fanaticism is interfering with economic growth and internal freedoms. Mort does not see a religious battle arising between Muslims and Christians. He feels the differences can be worked out.

In the context of globalization, Mort thinks technology may help start a conciliation process. Because of the anti-globalization protests, organizations such as the International Monetary Fund and the World Bank have become more aware that when they make loans to various regimes they have to monitor the effects of those loans to make sure that the money assists impoverished people, not just to a handful of the rich or western banks. Globalization is potentially of value but it has to be monitored and supervised.

Mort thinks that the United Nations has been much more effective in its developmental policies than its military interventions. He believes that the nations of the world are generally not willing to put up the money and other resources necessary to coerce the "bad actors" in the world. The UN, he thinks, has done better when it has tried to relieve famine and disease, and when it has tried to build community sanitation and provide economic development aid. It has not been so good at stopping war and destruction.

—

Unfinished Business

Mort is now in his eighties but his work continues unabated. He is currently working with a group of researchers at Columbia on social justice.

The principles and observations derived from his earliest work continue to challenge the teaching of current and future researchers.

Back in 1982 Mort published a paper entitled "Interdependence and psychological orientation."[27] In it he tried to put "cooperation and competition" into a broader context which included some of the other main dimension of social interdependence. In doing so he attempted to characterize the nature of psychological orientation which enables us to act appropriately in different types of social situations. It was an early attempt to sketch out what a more complete theory of interdependence would look like and also to indicate a way of characterizing personal dispositions that would be a useful link to social interdependence.

He refers to psychological orientation as a more or less consistent complex set of cognitive, motivational, and moral orientations to a given situation which serve to guide a person's response and behaviors in a given situation.

In addition to the psychological orientation he identifies the five types of interdependence, namely *cooperative-competitive* (also termed pro/con, love/hate etc.), *power distribution* ("equal versus unequal"), *task-oriented versus social-emotional* (e.g., emotionally involved/detached), *formal versus informal* (e.g., relations with a bureaucracy or social club), and *intensity or importance versus superficiality*. He makes the point that distinct types of psychological orientations are associated with distinct types of interdependence. There is a bidirectionality implied in the relationship where "the psychological orientation may induce or be induced by a given relationship."

He points out that implicit in this view is the further assumption that each person has the capability to utilize the various psychological orientations and their associated cognitive, motivational, and moral orientations. Although individuals may differ in their readiness and ability to use the different orientations as a result of their cultural backgrounds, their personal histories and their genetic endowments, people participate in diverse social relationships in complex societies; and these varied social relations require and, hence, induce different psychological orientations. Thus, my basic assumption is an evolutionary one; namely, to cope with the psychological requirements of assorted types of social relations, people have developed the capacity to utilize psychological orientations as they are necessary in different situations.

In the paper he outlined these ideas in considerable detail. The fabric of relations is a complex one, with an ongoing interplay between personal and situational factors. Several studies were tested in Deutsch's laboratory and by many other researchers. For example, Charles Judd (1978) found that competition led to decreased perceived similarity between the positions of two parties in a conflict relationship and cooperation had the opposite effect. Another study reported in the chapter by William Wenck in 1981 involved a three-person task in which the group's outcome was determined by the activities of the three persons. He found that the "equality" groups (where the group's outcome is shared equally by all its members) were more productive than the "equity groups" (where the group's outcome is distributed to the individuals in proportion to their respective contributions to the group); these in turn were more productive than the "winner take all" groups (where whoever contributes the most to the group receives the total outcome or reward received by the group).

The ideas presented provide the stimulus for a further lifetime of research. Mort and his students made a start on this but clearly the task remains to be completed by others.

Chapter 5

The Legacy
of Morton Deutsch

"A commitment to make the world a better place"

Neither Mort nor Kurt Lewin could have predicted the far-reaching effects that their casual breakfast meeting in 1945 would have for the future of conflict resolution. Mort's bent toward the study of social phenomena was well suited to Lewin's research program. The young man's aspirations and inclinations exactly matched Lewin's concern about the future of democracy.

The meeting started a chain of influence that stretches from Lewin, through Deutsch, to the work of his students, onward to some of their students, and thence to books, theories, and practices worldwide where the name of Deutsch is not even known. It is like a stone cast into a pond whose ripples never end.

One of Mort's students, Madeleine Heilman, says, "His influence has been vast because what he works on implications on almost every arena, and it's not by accident. That's the way he thinks about the world, so it has effects on kids at school, on people in therapy, on married couples who are having problems, and on units within organizations that are at each other's throats. Mort was one of the first people to work in the area of justice in the way that he did and that's a huge area in organizational psychology now: procedural justice, distributive justice, the whole issue of authority and respect, interactional justice. A lot of those ideas can also be traced back to Mort. He is not always given credit for them, but I was around when some of those ideas were developed and I know that they come from him."

Lewin was the founder of group dynamics, a field of study that evolved out of many developments and disciplines within the social sciences. In the midst of the darkness of World War II, Lewin had said at an SPSSI meeting: "There is no hope for creating a better world without a deeper scientific insight into the function of leadership and culture, and of other essentials of group life." That deeper insight manifested itself in the next three decades by hundreds of research studies on group dynamics. Mort recounts it this way:

> Toward the end of the 1930s, under the enthusiastic but gentle leadership of Kurt Lewin, modern experimental social psychology began to flourish. Lewin and his students demonstrated that it is possible to create and study groups in the experimental laboratory that have important features in common with real-life groups. In doing so, they stimulated an interest in social psychological experimentation and attracted many experimentalists to work in this area.[1]

Lewin's intention was to train group leaders and members how to work together in a group situation to achieve a democratic way of doing things. With his students he conducted research that very clearly opened the way for Mort's own work on cooperation and competition. With Ron Lippitt and Ralph White, in the late 1930s, Lewin experimented with groups of 10- and 11-year-old children who had as a leader an adult who behaved democratically, autocratically, or in a laissez-faire manner. The results were predictable but dramatic: when the leader was out of the room, the children who had the autocratic leader exhibited antisocial behavior and were less productive than the children who had the democratic leader.

Other studies on group dynamics included the effects of fear and frustration on organized versus unorganized groups and determining whether the behavior of leaders of youth groups could be modified by training. Lewin and other researchers explored group decision procedures as a means of improving industrial production and changing eating habits related to wartime food shortages.

After World War II, there was general agreement that a better understanding was needed of how democratic organizations could be made to function more effectively. The health of a democratic society was seen to depend on the effectiveness of its component groups — the family, community groups, and church groups, for example.

The notion that the scientific method could be used to improve this group life gained popularity. People began to see that it could be applied to such important social phenomena as leadership, decision-making, and productivity.[2]

These laboratory studies opened the way for a host of others. It proved that social problems could be studied scientifically in a way that had real implications for the strengthening of democracy. David and Roger Johnson comment:

> The drive to strengthen democracy by using the scientific method to strengthen groups resulted in two movements within psychology. The first was the scientific study of group dynamics. Social psychologists (a newly arrived group of specialists) began to conduct studies of group discussion, group productivity, attitude change, and leadership. They developed experimental methods of studying group dynamics, hoping thereby to find ways of strengthening democracy. Concurrently, the second movement began deriving methods for training leaders and group members in the social skills they would need in order to promote the effective functioning of democratic groups.[3]

Thus the symbiosis of research and practice was there from the beginning. According to Lewin, both theorists and practitioners were in the same business of examining reality:

> Practitioners identify significant problems to be solved, theorists develop a valid view of reality that contains the keys for solving the problems, and practitioners apply the theory. Practitioners keep theorists in contact with social reality, and theorists provide practitioners with a deeper understanding of the social problems that confront them.[4]

Morton Deutsch's twin convictions that research had to be founded on theory but that its application was crucial is an obvious legacy from Lewin.

Beyond Lewin

Morton Deutsch took the torch from Kurt Lewin and applied it to a wide field that would cover diverse methods of mediation and conflict resolution. If democracy was to be strengthened, what could be more important than discovering the mainsprings of conflict in people's behavior, and devising methods of training them so that the dangerous consequences of conflict could be averted?

In 1995 Barbara Bunker and Jeff Rubin felt "impelled" to collate and edit a book entitled *Conflict, Cooperation and Justice: Essays Inspired by the Work of Morton Deutsch*. Written to celebrate Mort's seventieth birthday, it presents cutting-edge research and theory on topics that have been prominent in the long career of their mentor. "Morton's ideas," they say, "will continue to provoke, comfort, and persuade for many generations to come."[5] For these former students this book illustrates the continuing relevance of Mort's work.

Barbara says that, "the sense of esteem and pleasure at having Mort around still, and acknowledging the sort of person he's been in our lives, is a comment on how he was as a mentor and a professor to us. There are people who are enamored of their professors for a variety of reasons, but for us the idea that we should do something to celebrate Mort's seventieth birthday was pleasurable. We just liked the idea, and I don't know how often that happens in academia. The fact that we have stayed connected enough that we could have had an idea like that and carry it through — you could read something into that about people acknowledging a debt they feel about being very well trained, and about having a relationship you don't have to work at but is a pleasure to maintain — is a kind of commentary on the sort of person that Mort is."

The legacy is not always obvious. According to Peter Coleman, it is often hard to trace the effect of Mort's ideas because there are other researchers that have been addressing the issues of cooperation and competition for a long time, such as George Herbert Mead, who Mort acknowledges as having influenced him, and Mary Parker Follet.

But while there are certainly other areas of influence, what Mort did pre-eminently for the field was to root these issues in systematic research and theory. People now talk a lot about mediation and win-win outcomes, but Mort was one of the first people to do rigorous social psychological research on these issues. As Peter puts it "I think that his ideas are all over this stuff and that the respect people have for him is because of the rigor with which he conducted his work and the depth and clarity of his theoretical thinking. He's really seen as one of the founding conceptual thinkers of this area. International researchers like John Burton and other folks have influenced similar types of issues, but they've often brought Mort in as being the seminal theoretical person in this area. When I go to something in the Justice Department I hear a lot of familiar ideas. I don't think many of the people there directly connect them to Morton Deutsch."

Mort is proud that he has been a leader of leaders — that he has intellectually fathered people who have gone on to make substantial contributions to the field. His influence has been passed onto other people who have become leaders and who have also produced a new generation of thinkers and researchers. For example, people such as David and Roger Johnson have been really crucial in education; their work in cooperative learning, constructive controversy and conflict resolution in schools has had profound and far-reaching effects on educational practice.

The tendency to forget to acknowledge Morton Deutsch arises from his own modest and generous nature. When he asked Peter Coleman to become director of the International Center for Cooperation and Conflict Resolution (ICCCR) in 1997, Mort made it very clear that he wanted Peter to do his own thing with the job. "I certainly hope I've influenced you," he said, "but whatever influence I've had, my hope is that you'll do with this place not what I would do or what Ellen Raider or anyone else would do, but what you would do. I hope that you see the potential and create a center and a life's work that is really about you and not about me."

Peter says, "I remember thinking that that was an extremely generous thing to say. This is a Center that obviously has a lot of meaning for him, into which he's put a lot of energy and ideas. In fact I think the Center in some sense embodies his ideas. But he trusted and respected me enough to give me free rein."

Bob Krauss is a professor in the Psychology Department at Columbia and works in communication, mainly through language. As a graduate student he worked as Mort's research assistant at Bell Laboratories. He found the collaboration a productive and congenial one because they complemented each other. Mort's focus on theory was balanced by Bob's capacity for experimental design, and this made for a positive tension between them. Mort's quiet demeanor was also balanced by his colleague's impulsive outspokenness.

Bob thinks that Mort is a major figure in social psychology. "If you look at what's happened in social psychology over the past forty or fifty years, you see that in the first part of the century social psychology was at the interface of sociology and psychology. It acted as the bridge between the study of the individual and the study of society, and the focus was on social interaction."

"After the 1960s there was always a tension between sociology and psychology. Social psychology split into two. There was *sociological* social psychology, which was located in sociology departments, and *psychological* social psychology, which became more individualistic and reductionistic. What was studied in the 1970s, 1980s and 1990s was increasingly the individual processes that have social consequences.

"Mort's focus has always been on genuinely interactive phenomena, so he fits into the sociological branch of social psychology. The other thing that sets him apart from the individual focus of the psychological branch is that he moved into an area that is multidisciplinary, and so his most important contribution is reflected in areas outside psychology, such as education and the law."

However, Bob says that the frequency with which Mort's name is referred to in social psychology has diminished considerably since his retirement because social psychologists have gone after "other game." He sees this to some extent as Mort's own doing. "I think that in a sense he created the conditions in which these other fields could prosper on their own. Mort's very general and very theoretical approach has a strength, but it also has a shortcoming, and that is that if I'm trying to negotiate with some damn union and I want them to, say, set a point at which you can no longer drop a course of study, I'm going to need more than theory to persuade them. It's easy to conceptualize such a thing in Mort's terms, but it's very hard to prescribe a solution. And of course the people in the field want solutions to the specific problems they encounter." Mort's emphasis on theory, he says, just isn't fashionable these days; it doesn't fit the present utilitarian ethos: "If you do psychotherapy, very soon you stop thinking about Freudian theory and start thinking about the specific problems that your patients present."

He nevertheless acknowledges the need for a true collaboration between theory and practice, something that Mort facilitated. "Technique falls from an understanding of how something works, the ability to look at a problem and say *this* is what's important about this problem, *this* is how it's different from this other problem. One of the problems with psychology is that not enough of it is applied, or it's applied badly."

"One of the good things about Bell Laboratories as an institution was that it had great reverence for science because it realized it could make lots of money from science, so that you were allowed to do a great deal of unfettered intellectual exploration. But there was also a requirement that you had to say, well, what can we learn from it? Tell us why we would want to know this? Is there any reason for knowing this rather than something else?"

Bob Krauss also joins the many voices acknowledging that one of the remarkable things about Mort was that he was able to produce students who were not carved in his image. "Many of the very best psychologists I know tend to churn out students whose work merely reflects the master, and I think that Mort's best students have gone on to take his ideas and to conceptualize them in ways that are appropriate for the things they're interested in."

Mort's legacy, then, has been twofold: the development of his work through the students he trained at New York University and Teachers College, and the application of his theories in fields as significant as education, the law, business and international relations.

David Johnson: Education

Education is particularly linked to the name of David Johnson, perhaps the best known of Mort's students. He is certainly the most prolific. A professor at the University of Minnesota, he has published over fifty books and over 400 papers. With his brother Roger, he systematically developed the whole field of cooperative learning, not only by using the theory but also by doing research demonstrating its significance and value. He also set up training institutions and worked with teachers; he has trained over a 100,000 people.

David met Mort by chance in the context of a shared interest in the peace movement. He had become involved in the civil rights movement in the early 1960s. One of the things he realized, working in civil rights, was that no one knew how to resolve conflicts or how to change attitudes. He had intended to study at Columbia under Goodwin Watson, but Watson retired early and Morton Deutsch replaced him. By then David knew about Mort's work on cooperation and competition.

"My whole life changed when Mort arrived at Columbia. The training he gave me involved hard-core experimental research and social psychological training. New York University had some activists, but nobody in Mort's league. And then much of Mort's work, while very theoretical, was aimed at making the world a better place. His famous paper called 'On Producing Change in an Adversary[6]' asks how you move an adversary from a competitive to a cooperative relationship. His theories and the Lewinian tradition of concern about theory validated research. You apply the practice and then the practice shows you where the theory is inadequate, so you reconceptionalize, you do new research, you modify the practical procedures and that leads you back to reconceptionalizing. That cycle is so important and I learned it all from Mort."

David knew Mort was one of the outstanding social psychologists in the country in the 1960s. Leon Festinger and Stan Shachter were still active, and there were a lot of prominent social psychologists working. Now he affirms that Morton Deutsch is the greatest living social psychologist in the world. "He was famous for his theory on cooperation-competition and for his work in trust and distrust. He was famous for seeing that the Prisoner's Dilemma game would be a perfect opportunity for the study of trust and distrust. So on theoretical and methodological grounds, Mort was known as one of the top people. The ideas he has dealt with are at the heart of human existence."

"Mort's theoretical brilliance comes along maybe two or three times a century. If you look at psychology in the late 1800s to early 1900s, there was Freud, there was Adler, there was Jung — a whole series of people working on the same general notions. Freud made all the difference in the world. When you look at the psychological community of the last half of the twentieth century, you've got B.F. Skinner, whose work will certainly last for a long time, and that's about it. But when you start talking about the major social psychologists like Jones, Tjosvold, Kelley, Campbell, you wonder whose work will be known fifty years from now. I think it's a good bet Mort's will, while these other people won't, and one reason is because Mort's work has had applications in so many fields", says David.

According to David, the basic premise of social interdependence theory, which is what Mort's work would be called now, is that how you structure the goals in a situation determines the interaction patterns, and those interaction patterns determine outcomes. There are three ways to structure goals: cooperative, competitive, and individualistic. With each you get a different interaction pattern. David has used this basic assumption in education: a teacher can create quite different types of classrooms by structuring learning goals in those three ways.

Mort's work, he says, is based primarily on social psychology relationship variables, not personal variables. By relationship variables he means that conflict is not a personality characteristic but something that happens between people. So is trust. These are relationship variables of events that happen between and among people, not within people. He recalls that Mort always said that people were multifaceted and that the same person could be looked at in a number of different ways. The same applies to the interpersonal conflicts with which an individual is engaged.

David says that Mort always focused on what he called powerful variables, such as cooperation, conflict, and distributive justice. With these variables it does not really matter if people are male, female, extrovert, introvert — it is the power of the situation that dominates. And these variables are true under almost every condition.

Mort would look at something such as cognitive dissonance, which occurs only after a decision is made that is important to the individual, and he would say "that's too narrow a focus, you want cooperation." If you look at cooperation and conflict as a whole, they operate in almost every situation, while cognitive dissonance operates in only a small percentage of situations. Mort would look for big, broad, powerful variables to work on. David and his brother, Roger, took his theory and made it into a set of teaching practices.

One of Mort's main ideas that is very underestimated by those working in the field, David says, is that the context controls the behavior. If the context is cooperative versus competitive versus individualistic, that really controls the behavior. If you are going to reduce prejudice you need personal contact. If this is competitive or individualistic it will just make things worse. It is only when the context is cooperative that you have a chance of reducing prejudice and stereotyping.

Almost all of David's work is based on Mort's research. He entered graduate school wanting to work on the civil rights movement and reducing racism, but he took Mort's framework of cooperation and competition and then developed theories around controversy; his work on integrating negotiation is influenced by Mort's work on conflict.

"My idea isn't to promote Mort, but to make the world a better place. Mort wouldn't want me to promote him. He'd figure I had better things to do than try to build him up. But I was, and am, very serious that whatever you say about education, cooperative learning comes up. And if someone tracks my work in cooperative learning they would run straight into Mort, because he did the basic theory," says David.

"While we've rarely had the same causes," says David, "there's a basic ethos that comes from Mort. Mort was very concerned about world peace, and the peace movement of the late 1940s and the 1950s. I came out of the civil rights movement, but there's always been a commitment on his part to using his work to make the world a better place, or to increase the chances of world peace. He did much of his work with that intent in mind, but he's left it up to others to apply the findings. He developed the theory and the theory validated his research, but he was hoping that other people would come along and apply it. And in education I've applied his work pretty correctly."

David went to a college of education at the University of Minnesota in 1966 and put all his energy into what Mort would call "a very grandiose scheme, which was essentially that I wanted to change the socialization patterns of all American youths to eliminate racism." His idea was to train teachers in procedures that would create massive attitude shifts among students which would mean that racism would be eliminated.

"I had no illusions of being successful," David says, "but I wanted to try." He began training teachers in the use of small groups in classrooms. He was involved with the National Training Laboratory, which trained small groups in experiential learning. His brother Roger was at that time part of the inquiry science movement in the United States and was doing his doctorate at Berkeley in science education and reading.

"Whenever we would get together and talk I would keep saying, 'Well, inquiry won't work unless teachers know how to run groups.' Roger was quick to recognize that, and by a series of flukes he started working at Minnesota in 1969 and the two of us got together doing research on cooperative learning. We began formalizing the training in group dynamics, inquiry, and experiential learning that we were doing collectively, and we conflated it into one movement which was cooperative learning, and then we started doing field research on its impact in the classroom."

"We started reviewing the literature on cooperation and competition. It was all scattered until Roger and I pulled it together. Where there were gaps in the literature, Roger and I would do these studies to fill them in. No one had put it together for educators, and we did. It's hard for me to imagine that there will ever be an educational text or instructional methods book written that will not mention cooperation and cooperative learning from now on."

"One of the things Mort used to say was that he knew his theory on cooperation and competition had great relevance to the world, but he didn't know how to apply it himself. I was sitting there, deeply immersed in the civil rights movement, saying I wanted to know how to establish cooperation among diverse populations. When I started I just wanted to know how to do it. I didn't care about the research or theory, but I quickly found that nobody knew how to do it. And so I had to become a researcher and a theorist to figure it out."

David started applying Mort's cooperation–competition to classroom learning. The best way he knew how to resolve prejudice and discrimination was to get minority and majority students to work together in a cooperative group over a period of time. It was not until the 1970s that he and his brother and several other groups of people really started focusing research on desegregated classrooms, relationships between majority and minority kids, and relationships between handicapped and non-handicapped students — a wide variety of arenas in which they clearly demonstrated many times that working cooperatively reduces stereotypes, prejudice, and discrimination. He admits that there is the difficulty of generalizing the findings from one setting to another.

He laughs about the grandeur of his vision. "My agenda was racism. The plan was to establish cooperative classrooms, cooperative schools, then for twelve years to teach every child how to manage conflicts so they became very good at conflict resolution. The third focus was going to be on teaching coping skills, how to deal with stress and adversity. I was going to spend eight years establishing cooperative learning in every school in the United States, then another five or six years establishing conflict resolution training in all the schools in North America, and then I'd go on to coping skills, and then we'd have this, then I'd see what's next ... Well, it didn't exactly go that way. Here I am, thirty-five years later, still trying to establish cooperative learning in schools, still trying to establish conflict resolution training in all the schools, and I haven't gotten to coping skills yet."

"With the exception of our work on academic controversy and constructive controversy, which comes out of a different literature, I have basically taken Mort's theories and tried to apply, extend, and refine them. I never saw the need to develop an independent conceptualization of cooperation-competition, because Mort's is so good. If you look at my work you can see it's all based on Mort's work. Every time I say what cooperation or conflict is you can see that it's Mort's conceptualization."

"I was never one of Mort's favorite students. Harvey was one, and so was Jakov Epstein. There were a number of students that Mort saw as very promising. I wasn't in that group. I was on my own agenda, and Mort supported me and let me be. But a few years after, I said to Mort when I get through there will be no book written on education that doesn't have these words all over them: 'This is Morton Deutsch's theory of cooperation-competition.'"

A true student of Morton Deutsch, David Johnson insists that ideas and studies need some conceptual backing if they are to make an impact. "If you go back to a basic Lewinian position, you have to have a clear conceptualization of theory. You have to do research to validate or disconfirm, refine the theory, and out of that comes informed practice. Most people in applied areas try to get to the informed practice with no theory or research."

On the other hand, theory alone is not enough. What is needed is validated research. This involves creating a procedure that can be put into operation. The practitioner has to ask: "How do you use this? What are the practical steps?" Then the practitioner can go to others and say with confidence, "Here's what you do" and present a procedure that will work. John Dewey, the pragmatist philosopher and Teachers College professor who formulated a theory of learning through experience, is an example of someone who had a framework but whose procedures were not clear enough. When Dewey died his project method died with him.

David's (and Mort's) insistence on the importance of developing theory first can be applied to the popular book *Getting to Yes* by Roger Fisher and William Ury. The book has its own brilliance and has reached a wide audience, but it does not propose its own theory. It does not acknowledge as a theoretical basis any of Mort's theories. Mort nevertheless affirms the usefulness of the book. "I think Roger Fisher is a very creative practitioner who has very good ideas and is able to formulate them in a way that is often very useful, and particularly understandable for people who are not in the field."

Carol Liebman a specialist in mediation and negotiation from Columbia Law School says that *Getting to Yes* was extraordinarily important, at least in the business world, because it was the first book on negotiation. "Even if it was over simple, it had a message that stuck, that resonated with huge numbers of people. It was quickly accessible, and it used to be all there was to teach from." Ivan Lansberg says that books such as *Getting to Yes* are popularizing Mort's work to the point that people are not aware of the connection from the powerful influence of Mort's basic ideas. Roger Fisher himself acknowledges the influence of Mort's ideas and research on his own work and that of others.

Dean Tjosvold: Business and Industry

One of David Johnson's students, Dean Tjosvold, took Mort's work and applied it to business and industry. David describes Dean as one of Mort's "grandchildren," of whom there are now many. Dean was there at the beginning of a lot of the work David did on controversy and they developed a version for decision-making in business and industry, a field he has extensively researched and written about.

Dean used Mort's theory of cooperation and competition to develop an understanding of interdependence within and between organizations. His work has helped to show how we can understand constructive controversy and, more recently, positive power. His research has also shown how the theory generalizes to China and Asia and how Chinese values affect cooperative and competitive dynamics.

He points out that the dynamics induced by cooperative goals and contributing to effective joint work has been characterized as constructive controversy, which occurs when persons discuss their opposing views about how a problem should be solved. Research indicates that it is through open-minded, controversial discussion that people combine and integrate their ideas to resolve issues and strengthen their relationships.[7] Through controversy, people develop and express their own perspectives on an issue. When confronted with another's opposing views, they feel uncertain about the most effective solution and search for additional information and a more adequate way of understanding the issue. Then they are prepared to integrate other ideas to create new, more elegant conceptualizations of the problem. This exploration of positions and the creation of new solutions during controversy results in high quality, high commitment decisions.

Constructive Controversy and Democracy

Thomas Jefferson believed that free and open discussion, not the social rank in which a person was born, should serve as the basis of influence within society. Based on the beliefs of Jefferson and his fellow revolutionaries, American democracy was founded on the premise that "truth" results from free and open-minded discussion in which opposing points of view are advocated and vigorously argued.[8]

David's eyes light up when he recalls that he and Dean wondered whether Mort would come if they invited him to a theory weekend. It took a couple of years for them to work up the nerve to ask Mort if he'd come to Minnesota for a weekend to meet with them to talk about theory. Mort said yes, and the Theory Institute was born. "This summer," says David, "we'll have either a third or fourth Theory Institute. The aim of the weekend is to take social interdependence theory and tear it to pieces and then try to reconceptualize it in a more insightful way. It's very difficult to tear Mort's work to pieces because it's so good, but it's good for us to try. I'm glad to hear he thinks well of our Theory Institute because it's such a privilege to be able to do this. It's the high point of my year. There's nothing like it."

Susan Opotow: Education

Susan Opotow is Associate Professor in the graduate program in conflict resolution at the University of Massachusetts. She is quite certain about the importance of Mort's influence in the social sciences. She says that Mort's work has "passed through the membrane and gone into other fields because it's so exportable. The ideas are so applicable. He was incredibly influential in social psychology and I think all social sciences. One of the faculty members, Roger Myers, said to me when I was Mort's student, 'Pound for pound, Mort's is probably one of the most prestigious faculty members here at Columbia and that takes into account the Nobel Laureate.' That's a pretty amazing statement because we're talking of Columbia, not of some small college."

Susan says, "Mort's very, very well-known as a psychologist. His work is well-known and his work has a kind of a pervasive quality to it. In conflict studies he is *the* most important theorist. I don't think there's another who is close to him."

The Orange Conflict

Mort uses Mary Parker Follett's famous example of two young people, a brother and sister, who have a conflict over an orange. Each wants the one orange that is available. But then one day when they talk about their interests and make it clear what they really want, it turns out that the girl wants the peel of the orange to make marmalade and boy wants the inside of the orange to eat. So once they understood their true interests, the conflict disappeared.[9]

Before she met Mort, Susan Opotow was a counsellor in a high school in New York City. She had come to the conclusion that she was seeing too many social problems and was not doing enough in the way of solutions. She felt she was at the output end of the problems but wanted to address problems closer to their source. So she decided she would go to graduate school and work in educational evaluation. She thought that if she could understand what makes education work it would be a lot more helpful than giving out psychological band-aids to students and just helping wherever she could. She considered the education evaluation program but chose social psychology instead and went to Teachers College to work with Mort. "I'd never heard of this field and I hadn't heard of Mort, but it was very clear when I came here that he was the person I wanted to work with."

"The richness of Mort's work is like a goldmine that has barely begun to be mined. There's just a little shaft where people have taken out some ideas, but if you leave aside a book like *The Resolution of Conflict*, which was published nearly thirty years ago, there are just thousands of ideas that are not even part of the field yet. It's such rich stuff! And yet there's a clarity to it too. For example, the theory of cooperation and competition had incredible clarity and in a way incredible simplicity, but there's a deceptive complexity too — like a good work of art which is completely accessible but there is also more there than meets the eye. And it's going to last the test of time," she says.

She was impressed by the breadth of his work. Mort seemed to be focusing on the really big issues when other people were concentrating on the smaller ones, and it struck her that the question she wanted to deal with was a very big one indeed. The other thing she found very attractive was that he had this extra-large group of students working with him.

"It was like an overlap of students who were actually before me — all this rich intellectual stuff coming and going. The vigor of the work going on created an atmosphere of real excitement. It just felt like the right place to be. This was in 1979, before the ICCCR had been established. By then Mort's research program was well under way and many of the students had already become important in the field in their own right."

Susan did a study with another professor first, on how people in organizations react to changes in the design of their space. She found it a wonderful project in many ways but it was seriously flawed in its design so she stopped working on it. She moved on to work with Mort and decided she was going to design better studies. So she did a study testing a theory of interdependence and psychological orientation, which involved the use of photography.

"The theory behind this was published in 1982[10] and describes all human relationships in terms of four dimensions: the cooperative/competitive, the equal/unequal, the socio-emotional versus task-oriented, and the formal/informal. It's both crystal clear and incredibly complex; the framework is really useful, and I loved it. What was so exciting was that I learned to take a theory and test it in ways that revealed some of the complexity. Sometimes experiments can be overly simple. I loved this one because I like things to be rich, really provocative. Mort was a pleasure to work with on that."

From there she did her dissertation, which was on moral exclusion. Mort had begun thinking about the importance of the *scope* of justice. "Between the interdependence paper and my dissertation there were three or four years of solid thinking, during which time my back broke when I was in a car accident and I had a baby and the whole time I took notes on what I was thinking. Part of the reason that I took so long to think about it was my ambition that my dissertation was to become my life's work, just as Mort's had been. I wanted it to really set a firm foundation I could build on. I wanted to make sure that the theory was sturdy and that it could be applied to a wide range of social situations."

"I designed some little studies, one of which was hysterical. I followed people walking their dogs around the neighborhood. I watched to see what they would do with the dog's dropping, whether they'd pick it up and throw it away or whether they'd leave it. We were at a time in New York where it had been the norm to leave dog poo on the streets, and while this was changing, removing it wasn't completely established as the correct thing to do. Once I saw what they did I would interview them."

"What I discovered was that people who respected the neighborhood scooped up the poo. Mort's response to this was 'Oh, you're interested in the scope of justice.' So that's what launched me on my dissertation. I started thinking about what it would mean to like your neighborhood or others and to behave in a morally responsible way towards that entity, whether it's a neighborhood, a person, a dog or anything. And that's what I spent the next couple of years doing, just thinking about it."

"I think my work actually expanded Mort's basic concepts and theories. At least from 1974, he talked about the scope of justice as something important. For instance, a Nazi can treat his family and neighbor with incredible courtesy but behave very differently to those outside — a bit like the stories of Nazi commandants going home to pet their horses after a day's work at the gas chambers. In different contexts there are different responses. It's provocative work. I'm fascinated that Mort has elaborated on it a lot since I did my work because I think that my work had already elaborated on it."

"I loved the fact that Mort was breathing life into a concept that needed life breathed into it. He is one of the few people who has never abandoned the concept. People have always looked at injustice, but mostly after the event, like after World War II or the My Lai massacre. Then they forget about it. It's dirty, it's distasteful; it's horrible research to do. And it's disheartening to some extent because it's so messy; it doesn't present a clean variable like visual perception. But I'm perfectly willing to muck around with a messy variable like morality."

"I could count the justice researchers I know are doing good work on one hand. It's always stayed as a very small subset within applied social psychology, which itself is a very small subset of psychology. So you end up with very few people doing it. And some of the people who have done good work on it have left the field. In contrast, areas like mediation and conflict resolution have gained a momentum that has carried them into many fields as a kind of seminally important notion."

Ellen Raider:
A Conflict Resolution Program for the Schools

For Ellen Raider, the appropriate application of Mort's work was in education. In the 1990s, in the context of a lot of violence in New York, she set up a program in conflict resolution.[11]

"A black man named Hawkins had just been killed. He was in a fight with some white kids and he ran out into traffic and was run over. There was a big to-do. At the time the Feds [Federal

Government] were giving a lot of money for safe streets and safe schools. I went to the Flom Foundation and asked them for money to bring teachers and administrators from different districts to the college for a semester of training."

The project followed the effects of training in cooperative learning and conflict in an alternative high school in New York City (described in Chapter 4). Ellen's successful work in this study led into a major project at the Board of Education. She received $300,000 to train two professionals in every high school in New York City. One became the mediation specialist and the other the negotiation specialist. She also institutionalized this program at the Board. Each of New York City's six districts appointed a conflict resolution coordinator and each of the schools received a 0.2 allocation, so 0.2 part of a person's job was allocated to these classes. She had 300 people and twelve cohorts and she hired ten people to run it. She became the outside training arm of the ICCCR, and Mort was there as her support.

After a while they had to ask themselves, were they really changing Teachers College and were they reaching the teacher educators? They raised funds and set up a special training for twenty-four faculty members at the College. They tried to get the College to seed this program in such areas as adult education, curriculum and teaching, social studies and English. The training was successful, but it became very clear that the most the faculty people could do was add 90 minutes to their curriculum. So they were really looking to Ellen and her colleagues to offer more for their students.

At around this time Mort and Ellen decided that they would like to start a graduate studies program in conflict resolution at Teachers College. After an unsuccessful attempt to have the program accepted by the Adult and Higher Education Department, it was successfully introduced as an area of specialization in the program of social and organizational psychology. Degree students in the program could take a master's degree in conflict resolution or a PhD degree with a specialization in conflict resolution. In addition, non-degree students could obtain a certificate of attendance after taking a sequence of six courses. The latter was an opportunity for people who already had degrees or did not want to take a degree, but wanted to attend courses on conflict resolution. Ellen taught the basic program in Negotiation and Mediation while Mort taught the theory course, which Peter Coleman took over later. Ellen also taught an advanced practicum course in conflict resolution, which she developed with Susan Coleman, and a train the trainer course.

When the basic practicum class started it comprised only sixteen people. It now has ten classes a semester and more than 200 people are going through the class every semester. There are ten or fifteen trainers who teach this course, and they say it is their "basic bread and butter."

Len Solomon: Social Justice

Len Solomon, Professor Emeritus of Psychology at Boston University, was Mort's research assistant at Stuart Cook's Research Center for Human Relations at NYU. He thinks Mort's genius lay in recognizing that irrational or self-defeating behavior in group members was a function not only of the cooperative/competitive/individualistic goal structure but also of the emotional relationships that grew out of that goal structure. These relationships could take on a life of their own. They could sometimes become dramatically malevolent or highly altruistic; the intense social emotions could easily result in either self-defeating or mutually self-defeating behavioral outcomes.

Len says it is the Prisoner's Dilemma game studies that show the need for social trust if both players are to maintain their rationality and maximize their potential gain. When suspicion arises between people, rational behavior becomes impossible, and a lot of other negative emotions such as retaliation or revenge appear. The laboratory experiment with the game provided a royal road to understanding how cooperation and rationality could deteriorate into the opposite.

It was a small step to transfer these ideas from the laboratory to the larger context of natural groups and group therapy. Mort's work could arm the group therapist with tools for understanding the way in which love or hate, altruism or competition could arise among members of a therapy group. His work also gives insights into the kinds of interventions a therapist can make in order to transform someone's defensiveness or distrust into openness and trust. He could see couples and family members struggling with mixed motives and conflicts of motives, much as in the game.

Len thinks it is not surprising that Mort is currently involved in social justice work, since that notion was implicit in the earlier studies of social trust. He was strongly influenced by Mort's ideas in this area. He embraced the work of Ivan Nagy, who had been working with theories that grafted onto psychoanalytic theory the importance of the concept of fairness in family relationships. Nagy focused on the ways in which forms of fairness and social equity governed a variety of family relationships, all of which the family therapist had to take into account. The therapist had to have a balanced commitment to all members of the family and not take sides. Len recognized the power of these ideas and the ways in which Nagy had come to them independently in the context of family dynamics. It was a good example, he says, of great minds working independently and moving in the same direction.

Michelle Fine: Victims of Injustice

Michelle Fine taught at the University of Pennsylvania for twelve years and is now at the Graduate Center of the City University of New York. She thinks of her work as both Lewinian and Deutschian. She sees it broadly as the social psychology of injustice, the conditions under which people blame victims or look at structures. This is what she has been doing in urban education, with school dropouts, teachers, and kids. Now she is working in a women's prison.[12]

"Mort and I have talked about what our theory of change is when we do this work on injustice. What's the theory of intervention, or where are the fractures and social arrangements where we could introduce a kind of counter-hegemonic analysis that might get us there? I feel that he has trained me well and I can figure out how to rate policy, how to rate community, how to rate scholarship, and what's hard these days. We're in a very conservative moment. The public purse has been shrunk and the public sector of schooling diminished and notions of equity trivialized. They're bringing in privatized prisons and the next thing we'll see is the rise of a discourse of disposability. That would be going back to Nazi Germany."

"I asked Mort what he thinks about his legacy and he started out with an apology and said, 'Well, I haven't been much of an activist.' But he has given us a language and a way of reaching the world. I have a sense that it's profound because with every conversation I'm in I'm there with Susan Opotow. It used to be Jeff Rubin, or somebody, because Mort has got a strong legacy of students who have carried this language. Susan and I have carried his legacy to schools, Jeff to bargaining and marriage, Janice Steil to marriages, and Barbara Bunker to a variety of applied settings."

"I just said to him, 'I don't know if you've ever met your intellectual grandchildren.' My students are profoundly affected by his work. They read him. We have a comprehensive exam where you have to take a classic article in social psychology and track its influence over time. The people from whom you can begin include Karl Marx, Kurt Lewin, Mort Deutsch, Fritz Heider, and Lev Vygotsky — there are a whole set of people — and then you track a key idea and track it to the citation index. Through this process students get to know his work."

Janice Steile: Family Relationships

Janice was a student who came to Mort at the time he was moving into the justice area, so her research addressed the psychology of injustice. It looked at the perception of the advantaged over the disadvantaged. A key question was what are the conditions under which the advantaged act on behalf of the disadvantaged? She now runs a clinical psychology program at the Gordon F. Derner Institute of Advanced Psychological Studies at Adelphi University. Her interests are in issues of power, in particular, family power, "his and her marriage."[13] She found that there was a relationship between psychological wellbeing and the amount of power people had in a relationship. Employed husbands had the most power and unemployed wives had the least, while employed wives were somewhere in the middle. She now concludes that equal relations are more beneficial. But why are equal relationships so difficult to achieve? And so her research continues. While her work has always been around equality, like Mort she sees the issue of equality in relationship to need.

Ivan Lansberg: Business

Ivan Lansberg says that the most interesting part about Mort's work is his capacity to synthesize ideas and then borrow, reshape and contribute his own original thinking to the ideas, without being limited by disciplines. He has the capacity to trust the integrity of an idea and to go from the idea to multiple arenas of influence in ways that other people might not even perceive.

Ivan has been interested in issues of economic development and some of his work has been with business and corporations. One of the first things that appealed to him about Mort was his capacity to bridge social psychology, with its focus on laboratory research, and the bigger issues. Mort was constantly going from the specific psychological and sociopsychological issues of particular problem and he was able to tie it in with larger world issues. Ivan's entry into the doctoral program coincided with a grant Mort had just received from the National Science Foundation to do work on the psychology of justice. This sparked a new phase of Mort's work on conflict where he homed in on the issue of justice. A lot of the most difficult conflicts hinged on issues of injustice and people's thoughts and feelings about it.

"In the philosophical tradition, a lot of the issues around justice are anchored on two definitions. The Greek definition is the equal treatment of your equals, which focuses on the sort of social comparison process among people who are alike, or feel themselves to be alike; the Roman definition focuses not so much on equality but on inequality, and says to give each person their due, the assumption being that not everybody is entitled to the same thing, and that the work of justice is actually about how you go about differentiating the merits of different people."

"What I tried to do in my dissertation was actually look at the psychological implications of both definitions and put them together. In any moment or situation or system, people have to be constantly monitoring their comparisons with others along two fronts. One front is 'who are my equals' and by virtue of defining who my equals are I expect to be treated like them, namely okay. So my sense of entitlement about what I deserve is anchored to a process of social comparison, where I map out the universe, in any given context, and say, okay, he is my equal, and therefore I take a look at what he's getting and then I say, well, at a minimum I'm entitled to that, and if I don't get that then an issue of justice arises for me."

"At the same time I'm also mapping by definition those who are not my equals, and then the question becomes 'How do I legitimize the distinction that happens between me and those below me, or between me and those above me? What are the criteria that are brought to bear for me to legitimize the distinction?' If I'm in a corporation among the middle executive, I'm in a little office with a crummy view and I have a little desk and all my little things, and then I look up to a CEO's office and I see that he's got a huge office, huge salary, huge bonus, a helicopter picks him up every day and all that."

"Why don't I feel a sense of resentment or that an injustice has been committed? The reason is because I buy into the criteria that I use to legitimize why he gets more than I do — he's been here longer, he's a superb performer, he's been given ten assignments and he's done an amazing job with all of them. You somehow rationalize whats he's entitled to versus what you are. And you see your underlings likewise. The point of the dissertation was to take a look at what conditions bring about that comparison. I was basically following Mort's lead here, trying to bring a big issue into a lab situation in a way that would inform the issue."

Ivan has also been interested in how family businesses work. He believes that at the core of family companies is the fundamental issue of how families collaborate. The family is at the heart of the enterprise, and that gives them a task that either adds meaning, depending on how they play their cards, or erodes their capacity to stay together as a family. So the notion of collaboration and creating conditions for collaboration is central to success in these businesses, and particularly in the case of continuing the business from one generation to the next. The other issues, to do with justice, are also central, because one of the most fundamental problems any family confronts is how to transfer the assets or wealth that one generation built to the next generation. The most fundamental distribution dilemma human beings face is how they are going to leave their children whatever they have built in their lifetime. And how do you discriminate or how do you make allowances for need if you have a son or daughter who is sick?

Along with some colleagues, Ivan has developed a model for thinking about family businesses that differentiate the ownership issues, the family issues, and the business issues. A lot of the work in making a family business function effectively revolves around building the capacity of people to understand that differentiation is structural, not personality-based, and once they do that, setting the processes in motion that would foster cooperative ways of resolving their inherent differences.

He sees Mort's thinking as very Marxist in fundamental ways: for instance, the notion of the structure of ownership, or the structure of relationships, the nature of the interdependence that gets set by the circumstances people are in, which determine the social processes that follow. In family enterprises, how the ownership of an enterprise is distributed has a profound impact on these social processes.

"What is interesting is that because ownership is such a sensitive and emotionally loaded issue, people typically don't look at it, so they are often spending a lot of time trying to negotiate the shadows of the ownership issues without addressing it in a more direct way. This comes back to issues of inheritance, to issues of justice within the family — the kinds of things you see, for instance, with women being given smaller portions or shares without votes, so they end up becoming disenfranchized members of the system, and that resentment gets played out in the subsequent social processes that are elicited by that original distribution."

Jeff Rubin: The International Arena

Jeffrey Rubin is one of Mort's graduates who had a great impact, during a relatively short career, on the field of international relations. He was a very productive, creative man who had a great capacity to get people together. By the time he died in a mountaineering accident in 1995, he had written a number of books jointly and edited a lot more; he organized many symposia and did much work in the international arena. He was executive director of the program on negotiation at Harvard that Roger Fisher started, and he was the founding editor of the *Negotiation Journal*.

Jeff enrolled in the doctoral program in social psychology at Teachers College in 1964 to study with Mort because of his interest in conflict. As an undergraduate at Antioch College, he had read some of Mort's writings on interpersonal bargaining and deterrence theory, and also his co-edited book, *Preventing World War III*. He was very interested in doing work on the social psychology of conflict, particularly international conflict.

Jeff's first paper as a doctoral student, for a theory seminar was a passionate critique of US policy in the Vietnam War. Mort told Jeff that his paper was unacceptable because it was not sufficiently analytical, nor did it have much psychological substance. Mort, in the Preface of a book honoring Jeff's work, has written about this and another aspect of Jeff's doctoral work:

> Jeff took my critique well and as not at all defensive and within a week he gave me a superb paper which was characterized by sharp, analytic thinking based upon social science theory and research; it was also written beautifully. This incident reflected a central feature of Jeff's character which contributed to his very productive career. His non-defensive reaction to constructive criticism and his readiness to grow intellectually in response to it.[14]

Jeff's interest in international affairs was clear very early on. His doctoral dissertation, "The Nature and Success of Influence Attempts in a Four-Person Mixed-Motive Bargaining Game," reflected another aspect of his personality which characterized his career: his intellectual ambition. His study was a very ambitious and complex experiment which was in part stimulated by the then-current Middle East crisis, in which the two superpowers, the United States and the USSR, were each supporters of a different weaker state in conflict with each other — Israel and Egypt respectively. His dissertation was on the idea of looking at a conflict that had four parties to it: two principal parties, as in the Middle East, with two superpowers, one on each side. He set that up in an experimental situation and looked at it. According to Mort, it was the first experimental bargaining study that involved four complexly interdependent parties. "It was one of the most intellectually ambitious dissertations that I have ever sponsored."[15]

Along with his many other interests in the study of conflict, Jeff's interest in international conflict and negotiation was actively pursued until his premature death. At the time of his death, he and I.W. Zartman, the distinguished scholar of international relations, had almost completed editing their important book *Power and Negotiation*, which has much wisdom to offer concerning the effects of power asymmetries in international and other arenas of negotiation. This is one of a number of books that he co-authored, co-edited, or edited which have relevance to international conflict. These books include *Conflict, Cooperation, and Justice* (1995); *Social Conflict: Escalation, Stalemate, and Settlement* (1994); *Culture and Negotiation* (1993); *Mediation in International Relations* (1992); *Leadership and Negotiation in the Middle East* (1988); and *Dynamics of Third Party Intervention: Kissinger on the Middle East* (1981). In addition, Jeff has published many articles relating to international conflict and negotiation.[16]

Jeff contributed to the development of the field of conflict resolution not only through his many publications but also as an educator, executive, organizer of conferences, founder and editor of an important journal, trainer, and consultant. He was a very energetic, multifaceted person who was able to fulfill many responsibilities simultaneously. He was Professor of Psychology and Professor of Diplomacy at the Fletcher School of Law and Diplomacy at Tufts University, Executive Director of the Program on Negotiation at the Harvard Law School, and in addition, the founding editor of the *Negotiation Journal*. He also served as President of the Society for the Psychological Study of Social Issues and the International Society of Political Psychology and was very active in the Processes of International Negotiation (PIN) project of the International Institute for Applied Systems Analysis, an Austrian-based organization of scholars from around the world. Jeff also served as a negotiation consultant and trainer at workshops for universities in the United States and abroad, to Fortune 500 companies, non-profit organizations, and the United Nations.

Mort, who was shocked and deeply saddened by Jeff's death, wrote in Kolb's book honoring Jeff:

> I am proud to have had Jeff as a student and I am indebted to him, as are other scholars throughout the world, for his invaluable contributions to the development of the field of conflict resolution. All of us will miss our warm personal contacts with him as well as the further important contributions he would have made were it not for his premature death.[17]

"The first book he did on social psychology, bargaining and negotiation," Mort recalls, "was a very important book that helped bring together all the work that had been done in this area. I can't say there was any specific theory underlying his work. I'm sure he was influenced by me and he certainly acknowledged that, but he was a guy who drew from a large range of experience and used it in a kind of creative way. He did a lot of consulting as well as writing."

Peter Coleman: International Relations

Peter Coleman is also becoming an influential contributor to work in international relations. He has written a number of important theoretical papers on intractable conflict[18], which provide a very useful conceptual framework for understanding and intervening in such conflicts. When Mort retired as Director of the ICCCR in 1998, Peter assumed this role. Since then, the ICCCR has continued to be active in training and consultation to the United Nations Secretariat. It has been offering collaborative negotiation, mediation, and crosscultural training and consultation to all levels of management and employees at the UN Headquarters and at all UN Field Duty Stations worldwide. In addition to this work at the UN, since Peter became Director, ICCCR has co-sponsored and co-taught a course with the UN Studies Program and the Conflict Resolution Program of the Columbia School of International and Public Affairs (SIPA) on "Preventative Diplomacy and Conflict Resolution: UN Cases" which includes as its students UN ambassadors and desk officers as well as Columbia graduate students.

Peter has also been active in a consortium of conflict resolution which holds regular meetings or seminars. It has had some leading figures from different disciplines. Its main purpose, he says, "is to bring together people from different disciplines within the university who are interested in the general area of conflict and negotiation and to see if some kind of joint programs of teaching and research and maybe service can be developed. It's often very difficult to get real integration across disciplines, but the university management thought that since there was this consortium already in existence which was meeting regularly and people were presenting and discussing things from different perspectives, it would be useful to try to give it more support to encourage its development."

As Peter tells the story, "about three years ago this Italian, Andrea Bartoli, showed up in our midst. He had the audacity to look around the university and say, 'you know, there are a lot of people who are really interested in this stuff [i.e., conflict resolution]. Why don't we talk to each other?' So we started informal meetings over breakfast and lunch where people would talk about their research and their interests. Everybody had something in common where usually they were scholars who were also interested in practice because of their applied arenas."

"We had an anthropologist at Barnard who studied mafia talk, we had a woman who was from Columbia, a Presbyterian who was a bioethicist who did grievances in bioethics, we had a social psychologist, we had international affairs people, political science people, attorneys interested in Alternative Dispute Resolution (ADR), people in the business school. It was an eclectic group. We came together formally for a while and talked and the list of participants grew and then at some point we put together a steering committee, which consisted of Carol Liebman, who's an attorney at the law school, Andrea and myself and another woman from the business school."

"We put together a proposal to put out a multidisciplinary conference and to get some part-time help. We went to the university for funding, but our proposal ran into some obstacles. In international affairs, conflict resolution is a new paradigm and there's the Institute of War and Peace at SIPA, which was founded by Eisenhower, and they're about the security paradigm. Many of the regular faculty at SIPA are affiliated with the Institute of War and Peace."

We had to put together a Faculty Advisory Board, which is chaired by the Dean at SIPA. She had a brilliant strategy: to put together a taskforce at SIPA, mostly of these folks, whose objective was to look at human rights, conflict resolution and security and see what they have in common and what the school should do in the future. It was really an educational intervention for them to learn about these things."

Mediation

According to Carol Liebman, a law professor and director of the mediation clinic and the negotiation workshop at Columbia Law School, Mort's work has had a major impact on mediation, but his influence is much broader than that. His work is read in many law school courses on alternative dispute resolution (ADR), mediation, and conflict resolution.

Although psychology's contribution to an understanding of mediation is rarely acknowledged by the legal profession, Carol Liebman acknowledges the work that has been done in psychology, and says it is basically Mort's work of which she is a "huge" fan.

Deutsch and Coleman's *Handbook of Conflict Resolution* (the *Handbook*) received an award from the Public Resources Center Institute for Dispute Resolution, a group of prestigious law firms and lawyers involved in negotiation and mediation, and the book has met with a great deal of interest from the legal profession. David Johnson says that he keeps hearing from some lawyers that it is a very useful book for them. They feel they need more understanding of the social-psychological process involved in helping people learn to resolve their conflicts in a cooperative way.

Carol had come across Mort's 1973 book *The Resolution of Conflict* and used it for four or five years. She felt it made so much of the theory accessible to people like her who are not experts. When she moved to Columbia she noticed on the dust jacket that its author was at Teachers College. She did something she had not done since she was a youngster. She picked up the phone and said. "I've just moved here. I love your work. Can I come and meet you?" She felt like a kid chasing a movie star. "He was so nice, so sweet, and I went over and had a wonderful conversation with him. It was just fabulous to find somebody who has been so influential, so smart, and yet such a nice person. And really you could see what a great teacher he was, and why everyone in the field who's doing really great work has been to his workshops at some point or another."

With Peter Coleman and Andrea Bartoli, Carol helped to start the University Conflict Resolution Network to bring together people from the university who were interested in conflict resolution. People present their works in progress and outside speakers are sometimes invited. Mort has been a part of it but in his usual modest way as just another contributor, not expecting it to revolve around him.

Carol was impressed when she found that the books that had been the most influential to Mort were those by Cohen, Nagel, Marx, and Freud. "He's just such a true intellectual," she says, "so broad in his tastes." She decided to make the *Handbook* better known. "What I wanted to do was celebrate the book and celebrate Mort." She invited 200 people from around the country to a dinner "because it was another way to say 'Hey, you guys ought to know about this book.' We had a discussion panel and a book launch and

Peter Coleman and Chris Honeyman talked very briefly about why the book was so important. Then we had a lawyer, a law professor, and a mediation center director respond by talking about a chapter that had been meaningful to them. And that was really quite rich and wonderful. There was this crazy mix of people, at different tables, and the conversation happened informally, without any attempt to steer it."

A Definition of Mediation

Mediation may be defined as a process in which disputants attempt to resolve their differences with the assistance of an acceptable third party. The mediator's objectives are typically to help the parties search for a mutually acceptable solution to their conflict and to counter tendencies toward competitive win-lose strategies and objectives ...

Although mediation is a pervasive and fundamental human activity — try to imagine family life devoid of parents interceding in their children's squabbles — in the last two decades formal mediation has begun to play a role at all levels of society and in virtually every significant area of social conflict. Some of the most prominent examples are divorce mediation, peer mediation in the schools, community mediation, mediation of public-resource disputes, judicial mediation, mediation of disputes within organizations, and increasing visibility for mediation in international conflicts between and within nations.[19]

Even better, Carol and Chris Honeyman — a mover in the field of mediation who focuses on bridging the gap between theory and practice — assembled a two-day meeting at the University of Massachusetts in Boston to work out how they would get their insights from the book into the hands of practitioners. The deal was that each person had to pick a chapter that they wanted to spend a day and a half working out how to teach. Almost 100 people came and included some of the top names in conflict resolution. David Johnson was in a group working on the chapter on social justice in conflict and he found it fascinating.

Mediation is about how a third party can help two parties who are having difficulty in establishing a cooperative problem-solving relationship. Mort says that mediation is not a new process. In the

Jewish tradition there are conciliation courts and in many societies there are mediators — the village elder, the rabbi, the priest, for example. There is a well-established folklore about mediation, and a lot of wisdom is to be found there. What people like Mort have done is make the ideas and the process more systematic than the folklore. "Formal mediation has been increasingly applied to an ever-widening array of disputes in such areas as divorcing, small-claims cases, neighborhood feuds, landlord–tenant relations, environmental and public-resource controversies, industrial disputes, school conflicts, and civil cases."[20]

When students are unable to negotiate a resolution to their conflict, they may request help from a mediator. A *mediator* is a neutral person who helps two or more people resolve their conflict, usually by negotiating an integrative agreement. In contrast, *arbitration* is the submission of a dispute to a disinterested third party (such as a teacher or principal) who makes a final and binding judgment as to how the conflict will be resolved. Mediation consists of four steps:

1. Ending hostilities: break up hostile encounters and cool off parties.

2. Ensuring disputants are committed to the mediation process: to ensure that disputants are committed to the mediation process and are ready to negotiate in good faith, the mediator introduces the process of mediation and sets the ground rules that (a) mediation is voluntary, (b) the mediator is neutral, (c) each person will have the chance to state his or her view of the conflict without interruption, and (d) each person agrees to solve the problem with no name calling or interrupting, being as honest as they can, abiding by any agreement made, and keeping anything said in mediation confidential.

3. Helping disputants successfully negotiate with each other: the disputants are carefully taken through the problem-solving negotiation steps.

4. Formalizing the agreement: the agreement is solidified into a contract.

The two mediation role plays below illustrate the kinds of situations that can arise in ordinary dealings between people that can be solved by mediation.

Examples of Disputes Requiring Mediation in a School Setting

Classroom Situation

Jason is a 12-year-old student who is not attending school regularly. The school has suggested to him and his parents that he attend another school which might be more to his liking. The suggested school is some 10 kilometres from his home and requires him to use several public transport routes by bus and train. Jason's parents are concerned that this would encourage and enable him to continue to play truant. They feel that the problem could be remedied at the current school if Jason were to become more engaged in his work and receive additional assistance with some of his educational difficulties. The school feels that they have tried several ways to interest him and assist him in his schoolwork but without success. The parents feel that the school is not doing enough. A school counsellor has been called in to mediate between the principal and Jason's parents.

Dispute Between Staff

Two teachers, Lauren Grant and Jim Kostas, are working at Carradine High School. Lauren teaches History and Jim teaches English. They are both enrolled in doctoral studies at different universities in their city. The school policy is to support staff in their pursuit of higher educational qualifications. Both are required to attend classes on Wednesday afternoons at their respective places of study but both have been scheduled to teach classes on Wednesday afternoons. They have consulted with the principal and he in turn has consulted with the senior staff member drawing up the year's timetable. A ready solution does not appear to be available for the current school year. Both classes have a large enrolment of students. Lauren and Jim feel that they cannot lose two semesters of their studies. A meeting has been called between Lauren and Jim and the timetabling senior member of staff. The principal has done a course in mediation and has accepted the role of mediator because he believes that he can conduct the meeting impartially.

The most obvious arena for mediation, however, is the law, that fundamentally adversarial, conflictual activity. Conflict has always produced the need for mediation in the form of legally binding arbitration. Mort got involved in mediation many years ago with Ken Kressel, another of his students. Ken had heard about Mort's research and he started to do some work with him. This became Ken's real interest, and he became a leading figure in developing mediation.

Teaching lawyers mediation is not always easy. The fact-finding and judging skills that lawyers need are very different from the kind of listening and facilitative skills that good mediators need, and judges really struggle when they take mediation courses.

Today, it is the courts that use mediation. Judges will send people off to mediation rather than have them continue in court. When people go into mediation they get a chance to tell their story — the facts as they see them — which is something they do not get to do in a courtroom. The client, therefore, tends to be pleased with mediation. Ken cites the high figure of seventy to ninety per cent of disputing parties being pleased with the process.[21]

He also says that roughly half of mediations result in a formal settlement, and though this figure is well below that achieved by lawyers who arrange settlements out of court, these successful mediations are often the intractable conflicts that lawyers have not been able to resolve. Compliance with a mediated agreement is also around eighty per cent, and there is evidence that "compared to adjudication mediation results in more compromise and more equal sharing of resources; produces settlements more quickly; and is less costly, both to the parties and the courts that provide the service."[22]

Examples of Legal Disputes Requiring Mediation

These three legal cases illustrate the kinds of legal situations where a mediator can resolve a problem without the parties going to court.

Family Court Dispute

Mary and John have recently separated. They have two children, Paul, 12 years, and Sharon, 10 years. Both children have been attending a private school until now.

There are disputes about who has the children and when and the maintenance contributions of each party. Mary is a nurse and works shift work, which involves her using the services of a child minding agency during her evening shifts. Close to the time of the separation, Paul moved to a state secondary school. He has had specific learning difficulties which were being addressed at his former school. Sharon has two more years to complete her junior school. She has difficulties making friends so a change of school is not advisable. Tom works in insurance and his work frequently takes him into the country. He finds it difficult to commit to regular days or weekends on which to have the children. His income is not totally predictable and he finds it difficult to continue a commitment to private school fees. Mary believes he is not living up to his responsibilities, and is becoming increasingly frustrated by his vagueness about his income and time commitments. At present, she cannot even organize her own work schedule to enable her to make arrangements for the children.

There is no possibility that the marriage will continue. The issues to be sorted out are ones concerning responsibilities to the children and settlement of property. They have been referred to mediation in the family court setting.

Business Dispute

Mr Saint contracted Dean Small, whom Mr Saint had been friends with since his school days. Following agreement about the design, materials, and so forth, a building contract was drawn up and signed by both parties. When the building was finished Mr and Mrs Saint found many things that were not completed to their satisfaction. Since Mrs Saint was expecting her third child and wanted to move in prior to the birth they asked for a legal document from Mr Small to say that the job was completed according to building regulations so that they could move in. Following the receipt of this document the list of complaints about the building grew. Dean had a number of other contracts which were now going over the agreed date and he would stand to lose money if he did not complete them. The Saints were not forthcoming with the balance of payment and Dean Small was getting further into debt, to the extent that the legal action which was looming over the dispute was debilitating. His lawyer advised mediation between him and the Saints.

Partnership Dispute

Jack Strong and his wife Jane are in partnership with Ted Lee. Jane Strong runs the catering firm for an agreed wage. The partners have had a gentleman's agreement to keep the business for four years and then to try and sell it if all parties were in agreement. The four years came and went and the business was thriving, so neither party wished to sell. But by the sixth year Jane Strong was weary of running the business and the trio agreed to put it on the market. They could not agree on a sale price. The potential buyers came and went. By the eighth year Jane Strong was desperate, Ted Lee was reluctant and posed all sorts of solutions for keeping the business while the market was down. Jack Strong was caught between the wishes of his wife and his agreement with his partner. A mediator with legal experience was suggested to the partners to resolve the dispute.

In the book Ken Kressel co-authored with Dean Pruitt, they bear witness to the success of mediation, which is found to be more robust than the legal system's traditional procedures. It seems, however, that in some circumstances mediation is unlikely to succeed: "Intensely conflicted disputes involving parties of widely disparate power, with low motivation to settle, fighting about matters of principle, suffering from discord or ambivalence within their own camps, and negotiating over scarce resources are likely to defeat even the most adroit mediators."[23]

Peter Coleman is aware that without a social justice perspective, mediation can be used to maintain the status quo and protect those in power. He sees a negative use of mediation to some degree in the law but especially in business. People can say, "I'm the leader of an organization and I want it to go wherever I want it to go, but I want to capitalize on the conflict inherent in the system so that people feel motivated and innovate and collaborate and go where I want them."

Mort says that his theory provides a framework for a mediator to use even in unpropitious circumstances. "The third party seeks to produce a cooperative problem-solving orientation to the conflict by creating the conditions which characterize an effective cooperative problem-solving process: these conditions are the typical effects of a successful cooperative process."[24]

The Skills of the Mediator

Mediators of all kinds need four kinds of skills: those related to establishing an effective working relationship with the conflicting parties; those related to establishing a cooperative problem-solving attitude among the parties toward their conflict; those involved in developing a creative group process and group decision-making; and considerable substantive knowledge about the issues in the conflict.

Kressel (2000) classifies mediator style into two main types: task-oriented and social-emotional. A subtype of the latter is transformational mediation, which aims at the personal transformation of the conflicting parties, whether or not they are able to reach a settlement. Its advocates believe that task-oriented mediation narrows "the parties' opportunity to become self-reflective and autonomous as well as aware of the other's separate reflective and distinctive reality." But Kressel says there is no evidence for preferring one style over another, and that the different styles suit different situations.[25]

The key word here, of course, is "cooperative. Everything hinges on individuals making the effort to cooperate, in spite of what they see as non-negotiable issues, such as their identity, security, and self-esteem. Mort lists four conditions that can help such people become aware that they could be better off if they recognize that the conflict is a joint problem that requires a joint effort:

1. Critical to this awareness is the recognition that you cannot impose a solution that may be acceptable or satisfactory to you upon the other. In other words, there is recognition that a satisfactory solution for you requires the other's agreement and this is

unlikely unless the other is also satisfied with the solution. Such recognition implies an awareness that a mutually acceptable agreement will require at least a minimal degree of cooperation.

2. To believe that the other is ready to engage in a joint problem-solving effort, you must believe that the other has also recognized that he or she cannot impose a solution — that is, the other has also recognized that a solution has to be mutually acceptable.

3. The conflicting parties must have some hope that a mutually acceptable agreement can be found. This hope may rest upon their own perception of the outlines of a possible fair settlement or it may be based on their confidence in the expertise of third parties, or even on a generalized optimism.

4. The conflicting parties must have confidence that if a mutually acceptable agreement is concluded, both will abide by it or that violations will be detected before the losses to the self and the gains to the other become intolerable. If the other is viewed as unstable, lacking self-control, or untrustworthy, it will be difficult to have confidence in the viability of an agreement unless one has confidence in third parties who are willing and able to guarantee the integrity of the agreement.[26]

In the case of a husband and wife that Mort dealt with in his clinical practice, non-negotiable conflict became negotiable when, with the help of the therapist, they were able to "listen and really understand each other's feelings *and the ways in which their respective life experiences had led them to the views they each held.* Understanding the other's position fully and the feeling and experiences which were behind them made them each feel less hurt and humiliated by the other's position and more ready to seek solutions that would accommodate the interests of both."[27]

Mort concludes from this case that "even though understanding and empathy do not imply agreement with the other's views, they indicate an openness and responsiveness which reduces hostility and defensiveness and which also allows the other to be more open and responsive."[28]

Intractable conflict occurs in what Mort calls a "malignant social process."

> Perfectly sane and intelligent people, once caught up in such a process, may engage in actions that would seem to them rational and necessary but would be identified by a detached observer as contributing to the perpetuation and intensification of a vicious cycle ... In such a social process both sides are right in believing the other is hostile, malevolent, and intent on harm ... Participants see no way of extricating themselves without becoming vulnerable to an unacceptable loss in a value central to their self-identities or self-esteems.[29]

In several presidential and other addresses through the 1960s, Mort's message was that to achieve an enduring, stable peace you have to work toward establishment of a cooperative relationship, whether this is in a marriage or in a relationship between nations. He tried to diagnose some of the characteristics of a malignant conflict that was entrapping individuals or groups or nations in a mutually destructive spiral.

Key elements that contribute to a malignant social process are as follows:

1. an anarchic social situation
2. a win-lose or competitive orientation
3. inner conflicts (within each of the parties) that express themselves through external conflict
4. cognitive rigidity
5. misjudgments and misperceptions
6. unwitting commitments
7. self-fulfilling prophecies
8. vicious escalating spirals
9. a gamesmanship orientation that turns the conflict away from issues of what in real life is being won or lost to an abstract conflict over images of power.

Mort has articulated basic principles for establishing cooperative relations after bitter conflict: mutual security, mutual respect, humanization of the other, fair rules for managing conflict, curbing the extremists on both sides, and gradual development of mutual trust and cooperation. More than ever now, we need these guidelines. We are surrounded by conflict. At the personal level relationships are breaking down faster than ever. Culture is pitted against culture, religion against religion. Industrial and organizational culture is steeped in conflict. And the nations that are not at war stand uneasily, wondering what is coming next.

Asked how theoretical insights on mediation could inform conflicts such as those between parents and children, Mort refers to an article he wrote for pediatricians.[30] First of all, he says, the parents themselves can learn to manage their conflicts better so that they really set a model of constructive conflict management that will be very important for their children. Then there are the conflicts between parents and children, then conflicts among siblings. Parents can help in these situations by constructive mediation and by helping children to learn how to manage conflicts, not only by example but also by direct tutelage — providing alternative behaviors that children may not have thought of as a way of dealing with the conflict.

For mediators to be effective, they need to understand the nature of conflict. David and Roger Johnson attribute to Mort "the most influential definition ... that a conflict occurs whenever incompatible activities occur."[31] As well as this, mediators know the importance of preventing a conflict from escalating to the point where negotiation is no longer possible. Mort has also been instrumental in developing understanding about the "negative spiral" of threats, counter-threats and self-fulfilling prophecies.[32]

Finally, Mort's research on justice emphasizes how vital the fair hearing given to parties in the mediation process is; it establishes the significance of mediation as a community service, because, in the absence of justice, frustration and anger thrive. The court system does not always allow parties to express their viewpoint as it may be considered inadmissible and parties mostly speak through their legal representatives.

Even with the excellent work that has been done, Mort thinks there is still not enough understanding of "how to mediate difficult conflicts in adverse circumstances or how to make the most effective match between mediator characteristics and the characteristics of the case to be mediated."[33]

Within an interpersonal, social emphasis, Morton Deutsch's work has been mainly very general and theoretical. He has mostly left the application of his theories to others, for he believes that a sound theoretical foundation is all-important for any specific work. His gift to psychology has been to formulate a body of theory on fundamental issues of human interaction — cooperation, competition, conflict, trust and distrust, and justice — that others can apply to specific situations, all with the aim of making the world a more livable place.

For one of the remarkable things about this man is that underneath the rigorous intellectual exterior there is a peaceful centeredness along with a passionate concern about the way the world is. He has had the self-discipline to use both these qualities in a systematic program of work, and his reward is not his name up in neon lights but the ongoing use of his theories in the cause of peace.

Chapter 6

Conflict Resolution in a Post-9/11 World

"I am not going to let these bastards destroy my world"

On the day the world changed, September 11, 2001, Morton Deutsch had an appointment to see a cardiologist whose office was directly across town from his apartment on West 86th Street. A new restaurant had opened between 85th and 86th Street on Madison Avenue and he had planned to have lunch there. In both directions, he saw, the buses were not running, the taxis were not allowed through the crossways, and a ghastly pall of smoke from the collapsed towers reared overhead. Walking through Central Park, his immediate response was, "I am not going to let these bastards destroy my world."

The day recaptured some of the sense of dread he had felt during his service in World War II. This was going to be a dangerous time. Emotionally, he had no personal doubt that he could cope with the danger, whatever it was, but he had a sour feeling that the world would change for the worse as a result of this calamity. Intellectually, his ideas were ones he wanted to share with his colleagues and he wrote a short piece that outlined, with characteristic clarity, evenhandedness and common sense, the way ahead (reproduced as Appendix A at the end of this book). It was circulated to colleagues in different universities and it received wide support.

Mort sees the world as going through a period of drastic change and crisis, but he thinks it will survive the crisis and a better world will emerge from it. It will be a more integrated world. There will be more participation in democratic processes in many areas where there are not democracies now, and the standard of living generally will rise. He thinks this is likely to happen over the next fifty years.

Asked how this optimism squares with the intractable nature of the world's conflicts, Mort invokes an historical perspective to examine the fundamentalisms that lie behind the 9/11 events and the ongoing hostility in the Middle East. He reminds us that fundamentalism is nothing new. Citing the example of the Spanish Inquisition (to which one could add examples from every civilization on earth) he says that we've had various groups at various times in history representing the narrow persecuting point of view with regard to difference, and that this has gradually been overcome in many areas. He thinks the dogmatic, extremist viewpoint of orthodoxy is a way of getting personal security in the face of very difficult times. Extremism can be overtaken by exposure to more open and more prosperous ways of living. If people's experience of life is a terrible one they are tempted to look to the afterlife for consolation or reward, so, like the Muslim suicide bombers, they have nothing to lose. But if their earthly life improves, they will be more oriented toward increasing their wellbeing and that of other people.

Of the seemingly impossible conflict between Israel and the Palestinian States, Mort says that the resolution of the conflict should be taken out of their hands. Their leaders are at a stalemate. They are not in a condition to resolve anything because their personal animosity is too bitter and too entrenched, and because the ongoing violence has generated enormous hostility in their followers. So at this point there's neither willingness on the part of the leaders nor political support from the population for a constructive agreement. Mort thinks, therefore, that the United States and Europe and moderate Arab countries probably have to unite to impose a solution that will be acceptable to the considerable majority on both sides, once they see it as a real solution to their conflict. The international community may have to be ready to intervene with military support to prevent violence while the agreement is made and until more positive attitudes develop.

Pressed on which of his empirical works might help US authorities to formulate useful strategies, Mort sidesteps and cites others with similar ideas, who work more directly in international conflict situations. He mentions Herbert Kelman, who has focused on the Palestinian–Israeli conflict. People in the conflict resolution community, he says, pretty much agree on what is required.

Mort considers his empirical works are secondary in the sense that they support the ideas. It is the ideas that give the lead. By implication, he is saying that his body of theory on cooperation and competition shows us the way. In a conflict, the most productive thing you can do is try to work together to reframe that conflict so that it's perceived as a mutual problem to be worked on in a cooperative way.

That cooperative, mutual orientation is the essence of Morton Deutsch's approach. From it flows the crucial ability to *reframe the conflict to take account of the other person's point of view*. Often people who are embedded in their own narcissism as a result of the conflict simply cannot do this, and they need a third party, the mediator, to help them develop that perspective.

Reframing an issue means you can at least understand that it's acceptable to be able to differ without violent consequences. Despite the differences, you can still cooperate on the main issues. Mort has seen this work with married couples and ethnic groups in conflict. He also knows people who have seen it work in international conflict.

For example, in the Balkans conflict of the early 1990s, one of the problems was that Milosovic and Trudjman had a narrow view of their own political interests, which they thought could be furthered by stirring up ethnic hatred. Milosovic is now before the international court being tried as a war criminal. Trudjman was reviled within his own community because of his leadership, which was oriented toward his own power rather than the good of the community.

What motivates such people is very important. Generally, it's crucial that people understand that power can be *for* others as well as *against* others, and that by being *for* the other you increase your power rather than diminish it. Unfortunately, much in our social and educational systems encourages the view that power is not something that is able to be shared. Power is something you use to coerce other people to do what you want them to do rather than the ability to influence and persuade people to do what you both want to accomplish.

Mort's work in conflict resolution therefore has the enormous task of counteracting the very way people are taught, in most cultures in the world, to think and act — out of fear, suspicion, distrust, defensiveness, hostility toward those outside the group — in other words, to tackle human nature in a way that neither religion nor democratic freedom has been able to do. Acting cooperatively takes immense courage and immense support from others.

In 2002, Mort continued to effect the cause of conflict resolution study and opinion worldwide from his cramped ICCR office overlooking West 120th Street at New York Teachers College. In that year he was put forward for yet another American Psychological Association Distinguished Scientific Award for the Application of Psychology, joined the list of the One Hundred Most Eminent Psychologists of the Twentieth Century and participated in a variety of conferences and think tanks about conflict around the country. In the summer, he travelled to Osnabruck in Germany at the invitation of Gunter Bierbrauer to teach in a program on Peace and Conflict Studies and, at the invitation of Kjell Tornblum of the University of Skövde, gave a plenary address at the annual meeting of the International Society of Justice Research in Skovde, Sweden.

His address in Sweden highlighted the continuing relevance of his work on conflict weaving the messages of key figures such as Martin Luther King and Nelson Mandala into a compelling tale of oppression as the root cause of the most serious conflicts of today. He discussed the nature of the psychodynamic relationship between the oppressor and the oppressed. How each participant has some of the latent qualities of the other; in controlling the oppressed, oppressors control themselves. And in being controlled, the oppressed also have their rage controlled. He highlighted the structural similarities between the sadomasochistic and the oppressor–oppressed relationships.

He talked of 'awakening the sense of injustice' to overcome oppression, and of the tactics needed. He identified five types of systematic injustice caused by oppression: distributive injustice, procedural injustice, retributive injustice, moral exclusion, and cultural imperialism. He spoke of oppressors who dominate by control, intimidation, indoctrination, and socialization and legitimize their actions by citing 'the law of nature,' 'the will of god' or 'survival of the fittest.'

Mort also discussed the psychodynamics of tactics to combat injustice. Persuasion can overcome oppression, through appeal to moral values (superego), self-interest (ego) and self-realization (id) — although when intense emotions such as rage or fear dominate, cooperative tactics are less effective. The power of the 'haves' depends largely on the control of 'tangibles such as instruments of force, an effective communication system, an effective transportation system and upon such intangibles as prestige and an aura of invincibility'. Low-power groups have difficulty interfering with the tangibles, but can still combat oppression by 'techniques of embarrassment and inventiveness', for example, picketing.

He concluded the address with the hope that:

> 'this framework can be usefully applied to understand and change oppressive relations between specific groups such as those between men and women, the economically privileged and the disadvantaged, managers and workers, parents and children, and between racial, religious, and ethnic groups.'

Others have also looked again at the legacy of Morton Deutsch's work in recent years. David and Roger Johnson (2002) drew a connection between their work and that of Morton Deutsch and other major figures in psychology. They identified the clear historical links between Kurt Koffka's contribution to Gestalt theory and Kurt Lewin's early theories of cooperation and competition and Mort's social interdependence theory of positive cooperation (interdependence) and negative cooperation (competition). In addition to his obvious contribution to international conflict and peace-building, the brothers pointed to Mort's legacy in the field of education: while cooperative learning was relatively unknown in the 1960s, in the new millennium it is used throughout the world, making it 'the most successful application of psychology to practice'. They also highlighted his influence in the fields of business, mediation, community development, and individual therapy.

In 2004 Mort continues his involvement with ICCR's Graduate Studies Program as well as his own work on the integration of theory and practice of conflict resolution; research projects about social systems locked in dominance and oppression; interviews with practitioners engaging hostile disputants in constructive conflict resolution; studies investigating factors associated with resistance and defensiveness; and conceptual models for addressing institutionalised oppression in schools and communities.

For Mort there are enough issues to warrant his continued writing and thinking about conflict and oppression. There is much unfinished business, and the aftermath of war in Iraq remains a great concern to him as to many others following in his footsteps.

There is no doubt that the life and legacy of Morton Deutsch will continue to influence theoreticians, practitioners and researchers for years to come.

Endnotes

Chapter One

1 p. 11, Deutsch (1999).

Chapter Two

1 Several of the quotations in this chapter are from Mort's autobiographical paper, "A personal perspective on the development of social psychology in the 20th century" (Deutsch, 1999).
2 Cohen & Nagel (1934).
3 p. 5, Deutsch (1999).
4 p. 6, Deutsch (1999).
5 p. 4, Deutsch (1999).
6 p. 7, Deutsch (1999).
7 pp. 7–8, Deutsch (1999).
8 pp. 9–10, Deutsch (1999).
9 p. 10, Deutsch (1999).
10 p. 187, Marrow (1969).
11 For more information about the Research Centre for Group Dynamics, the reader is referred to Marrow (1969). For an informed history of the development of sensitivity training see Kurt Bach's book on sensitivity training or Deutsch's autobiographical chapter (1999).
12 p. 13, (Deutsch 1999).
13 Deutsch (1948).
14 Deutsch (1999).
15 An issue of the *Journal of Social Issues* was devoted to the first NTL workshop.
16 p. 14, Deutsch (1999).
17 Based on pp. 14–15, Deutsch (1999).
18 p. 19, Deutsch (1999).
19 Deutsch (1999).
20 Deutsch (1949a); (1949b).
21 Campbell, D.T. (1979).

Chapter Three

1 Siegel & Fouraker (1960).

Chapter Four

1 For a fuller description of these ideas, with appropriate acknowledgement of the work of other scholars, I refer the reader to Mort's following publications: Deutsch (1949a), (1949b), (1949c), (1962), (1973), (1985), (1999); Opotow & Deutsch (1999); Deutsch & Coleman (2000).
2 Deutsch (1999).
3 Deutsch (2003).
4 Lewin's work was on intrapsychic conflict while Deutsch's was on interpersonal and intergroup conflicts. They are two quite different intellectual frameworks.
5 Deutsch (2003). An outline of Mort's ideas about cooperation and competition is included in this text.
6 Deutsch (1999).
7 Deutsch (2003).
8 pp. 22–23, Deutsch (2000).
9 See Johnson & Johnson (1989) for a comprehensive summary.
10 Opotow & Deutsch (1999)
11 Deutsch (2003).
12 Deutsch (2003).
13 Deutsch (2003).
14 Deutsch (2003).
15 pp. 25–26, Deutsch (2000).
16 p. 246, Opotow & Deutsch (1999).
17 Deutsch (2003). This list also appears, with an additional item on ethnocentrism ("understand and accept the reality of cultural difference") in Opotow & Deutsch (1999).
18 Opotow & Deutsch (1999).
19 Johnson, Johnson, & Holubec (1986). See also pp. 21–22, Opotow & Deutsch (1999).
20 pp. 21–22, Opotow & Deutsch (1999).
21 p. 209, Johnson & Johnson (2002).
22 Opotow & Deutsch (1999).
23 Opotow & Deutsch (1999).
24 Opotow (1991).
25 Bunker, Pearlson, & Schultz (1975); Judd, Smith, & Kidder (1991); Fine (1992).
26 Deutsch (2003)
27 Deutsch (1982).

Chapter 5

1 Deutsch (1999).
2 p. 40, Johnson & F.P Johnson (2000).
3 p. 42, Johnson & F.P Johnson (2000).
4 p. 42, Johnson & F.P Johnson (2000).
5 p. 417, Bunker & Rubin (1995).
6 Deutsch (1964).
7 Tjosvold (1985); (1998). See also Johnson, Johnson, & Tjosvold (2000).

8   p. 38, Johnson, Johnson & Tjosvold (2000).
9   Mary Parker Follett (1868–1933) was an early and original contributor to the science of administration and management whose work was neglected for some years. Her example of the orange dispute was made famous because it was used in *Getting to Yes*, which is where Mort first heard of both her and the story. See Follett (1940).
10 Deutsch (1982).
11 Raider (1995).
12 Fine (1992).
13 A term made famous by Jessie Bernard.
14 Kolb (1999).
15 pp. 9–10, Kolb (1999) — a preface written by Morton Deutsch.
16 See Kolb (1999), for a select bibliography.
17 p. 11, Kolb (1999) — a preface written by Morton Deutsch.
18 Coleman (1997); (2000).
19 p. 522, Kressel (1997).
20 Deutsch (2003).
21 p. 523, Kressel (2000).
22 p. 524, Kressel (2000).
23 p. 405, Kressel & Pruitt (1989).
24 Deutsch (2003).
25 Deutsch (2003).
26 Deutsch (2003).
27 (emphasis added) Deutsch (2003).
28 Deutsch (2003).
29 p. 263, Deutsch (1985).
30 Deutsch & Brickman (1994).
31 p. 379, Johnson & Johnson (2000).
32 pp. 61–62, Rubin, Pruitt, & Kim (1994).
33 Deutsch (2003).

References
and Bibliography
of Relevant Works

Bercovitz, J., & Rubin, J.Z. (Eds.). (1992). *Mediation in international relations: Multiple approaches to conflict management*. New York, NY: St Martin's Press.

Brown, J.F. (1936). *Psychology and the social order structure of Riemonmian Geometry*. New York: McGraw Hill.

Bunker, B.B., & Rubin, J.Z. (Eds.). (1995). *Conflict, cooperation, and justice: Essays inspired by the work of Morton Deutsch*. San Francisco: Jossey-Bass.

Bunker, B.B., Pearlson, H.B., & Schultz, J.W. (1975). *A student's guide to conducting social science research*. New York: Human Science Press.

Campbell, D.T. (1979). For vigorously teaching the unique norms of science: An advocacy based on a tribal model of scientific communities. *Communication and Cognition, 12*(3–4): 245–64.

Cohen, M.R., & Nagel, E. (1934). *An introduction to logic and scientific method*. New York: Harcourt.

Coleman, P.T. (1997). Redefining ripeness: A social psychological perspective. *Peace and Conflict: Journal of Peace Psychology, 3*, 81–103.

Coleman, P.T. (2000). Intractable conflict. In Deutsch, M., & Coleman, P.T. (Eds.), *The handbook of conflict resolution: Theory and practice* (pp. 428–450). San Francisco: Jossey-Bass.

Coleman, P, T., & Deutsch, M. (2000). Some guidelines for developing a creative approach to conflict. In M. Deutsch, & P.T Coleman (Eds.), *The handbook of conflict resolution: Theory and practice* (pp. 355–365). San Francisco, CA, US: Jossey-Bass/Pfeiffer.

Corti, W.R. (Ed.). (1977). *The Philosophy of George Herbert Mead*. Geneva: Winterthur.

Deutsch, M. (1949a). A theory of cooperation and competition. *Human Relations, 2*, 129–51.

Deutsch, M. (1949b). An experimental study of the effects of cooperation and competition upon group process. *Human Relations 2*, 199–231.

Deutsch, M. (1949c). The directions of behavior: A field theoretical approach to the understanding of inconsistencies. *Journal of Social Issues, 5*, 43–51.

Deutsch, M. (with C. Selltiz, M. Jahoda & S.W. Cook) (1959). *Research methods in social relations* (2nd ed.). New York: Holt & Dryden.

Deutsch, M. (1961). The interpretation of praise and criticism as a function of their social context. *Journal of Abnormal and Social Psychology, 62*, 391–400.

Deutsch, M. (1962). Psychological alternatives to war. *Journal of Social Issues, 18*, 97–119.

Deutsch, M. (1964). On producing change in an adversary. In R. Fisher (Ed.), *International conflict and the behavioral sciences* (pp. 145–60). New York: Basic Books.

Deutsch, M. (1965). A psychological approach to international conflict. In G. Sperazzo (Ed.), *Strategic interaction and conflict*. Washington, DC: Georgetown University Press.

Deutsch, M. (1966a). Comments on Kelley's comments. In K. Archibald (Ed.), *Psychology and international relations*. Berkeley: University of California Press.

Deutsch, M. (1966b). Communication, threat, and bargaining. in K. Archibald (Ed.), *Psychology and international relations*, Berkeley: University of California Press.

Deutsch, M. (1969a). Conflicts: Productive and destructive. *Journal of Social Issues, 25,* 7–41.

Deutsch, M. (1969b). Socially relevant science: Reflections on some studies of interpersonal conflict. *American Psychologist, 24,* 1076–92.

Deutsch, M. (1973). *The resolution of conflict: Constructive and destructive processes*. New Haven, CT: Yale University Press.

Deutsch, M. (1974). Awakening the sense of injustice. In M. Lerner & M. Ross (Eds), *The quest for justice* (pp. 19–42). Toronto: Holt, Rinehart & Winston.

Deutsch, M. (1979). Education and distributive justice: Some reflections on grading systems. *American Psychologist, 34,* 391–401.

Deutsch, M. (1982). Interdependence and psychological orientation. In V. Derlega & J.L. Grzelek (Eds.), *Cooperation and helping behaviour: Theories and research* (pp. 15–42). New York: Academic Press.

Deutsch, M. (1983). The prevention of World War III: A psychological perspective. *Political Psychology, 2,* 3–31.

Deutsch, M. (1985). *Distributive justice: A social psychological perspective*. New Haven, CT: Yale University Press.

Deutsch, M. (1992). Kurt Lewin: The tough minded and tender hearted scientist. *Journal of Social Issues, 48,* 31–43.

Deutsch, M. (1993). Conflict resolution and cooperative learning in an alternative high school. *Cooperative Learning 13,* 2–5.

Deutsch, M. (1995a). Commentary: The constructive management of conflict: Developing the knowledge and crafting the practice. In Bunker & Rubin (Eds.), *Conflict, cooperation, and justice*. San Francisco, CA: Jossey Bass.

Deutsch, M. (1995b). *A framework for thinking about research on conflict resolution*. Paper presented at the conference "Conflict resolution in the schools: Research agenda for the next decade," Teachers College, Columbia University, New York.

Deutsch, M. (1999). A personal perspective on the development of social psychology in the 20th century. In A. Rodrigues and R. Levine (Eds.), *Reflections on social psychology*. Boulder, CO: Westview Press.

Deutsch, M. (2000). Cooperation and competition. In Deutsch & Coleman (Eds.), *Handbook of conflict resolution* (pp. 21–40). San Francisco, CA: Jossey Bass.

Deutsch, M. (2002, June). *Oppression and conflict*. Plenary address given at the annual meeting of the International Society of Justice Research in Skovde, Sweden.

Deutsch, M. (2003). Cooperation and conflict. In M.A. West, D.J. Tjosvold, & K.G. Smith (Eds). *International handbook of orgnaizational teamwork and cooperative working.* NY, New York: Wiley.

Deutsch, M., & Brickman, E. (1994). Conflict resolution. *Pediatrics in Review, 15*(1), 16–22.

Deutsch, M., & Coleman, P.T. (Eds.). (2000). *The handbook of conflict resolution: Theory and Practice.* San Francisco, CA: Jossey-Bass.

Deutsch, M., & Coleman, P.T. (2000). A theory of cooperation and competition. *Human Relations, 2,* 129–51.

Deutsch, M., & Collins, M.E. (1951). *Interracial housing: A psychological evaluation of a social experiment.* Minneapolis: University of Minnesota Press.

Deutsch, M., & Gerard, H.B. (1955). A study of normative individual judgement. *Journal of Abnormal and Social Psychology, 51,* 629–636.

Deutsch, M., & Hornstein, H.A. (Eds.). (1975). *Applying social psychology: Implications for research, practice, and training.* Hillsdale, NJ: L. Erlbaum Associates.

Deutsch, M., & Krauss, R.M. (1965). *Theories in social psychology.* New York: Basic Books.

Deutsch, M., & Coleman, P.T. (Eds.). (2000). *The handbook of conflict resolution: Theory and practice.* San Francisco: Jossey-Bass.

Deutsch, M., & Hornstein, H. (Eds.). (1975). *Applying social psychology: Implications for research, practice and training.* Hillsdale, NJ: L. Erlbaum Associates.

Deutsch, M., Mitchell, V., Zhang, Q., Khattri, N., Tepavac, L., Weitzman, E.A. & Lynch, R. (1992). *The effects of training in cooperative learning and conflict resolution in an alternative high school.* New York: International Center for Cooperation and Conflict Resolution, Teachers College, Columbia University.

Deutsch, M., Pepitone, A., & Zander, A. (1948). Leadership in the small group. *Journal of Social Issues, 4*(2), 31–40.

Deutsch, M., Selltiz, C., Jahoda, M., & Cook S.W. (1951). *Research methods in social relations.* New York: Holt & Dryden.

Dewey, J. (1915). *The school and society* (2nd ed.). Chicago: University of Chicago Press.

Eron, L.D., Gentry, J.H., & Schlegal, P. (1995). *Reason to Hope: A Psychological Perspective on Violence and Youth.* Washington, DC: American Psychological Association.

Faure, G., & Rubin, J.Z. (Eds.), (1993). *Culture and negotiation.* Newbury Park, CA: Sage.

Fine, M. (1992). *Disruptive voices: The possibilities of feminist research.* Ann Arbor: University of Michigan Press.

Fisher, R., Ury, W., & Patton, B. (1991). *Getting to yes: Negotiating agreement without giving in* (2nd ed.). New York: Penguin.

Follett, M.P. (1940). Constructive conflict. In H.C. Metcalf & L. Urwick (Eds.), *Dynamic administration: The collected papers of Mary Parker Follett* (pp. 30–49). New York: Harper.

Freud, S. (1937). Analysis terminable and interminable. *International Journal of Psycho-Analysis, 18,* 373–405.

Frydenberg, E. (Ed.). (1999). *Learning to cope: Developing as a person in complex societies.* Oxford: Oxford University Press.

Haggbloom, S. J., Warnick, J. E., Jones, V. K., Yarbrough, G. L., Russell, T. M., Borecky, C. M., et al. (2002). *Review of General Psychology, 6*(2), 139–52.

Jahoda, M. (1949). Consistency and inconsistency in intergroup relations. *Journal of Social Issues, 5*(3), 4–11.

Johnson, D.W., & Johnson, R.T. (1989). *Cooperation and competition: Theory and research.* Edina, MN: Interaction Book.

Johnson, D.W., & Johnson, R.T. (1991). *Teaching students to be peacemakers.* Edina, MN: Interaction Book.

Johnson, D.W., & Johnson, F.P. (2000). *Joining together: Group theory and group skills* (7th ed.). Boston: Allyn & Bacon.

Johnson, D.W., & Johnson, R.T. (2000). Paper presented at the 2002 Social Interdependence Theory Conference, Silver Wind Farm, Minnesota, July 12–14.

Johnson, D.W., & Johnson, R.T. (2002). Coping with adversity: The three C's. In Frydenberg (Ed.) *Beyond Coping: Meeting goals, visions, and challenges.* Oxford: Oxford University Press.

Johnson, D.W., Johnson, R.T., & Holubec, E.J. (1986). *Circles of learning: Cooperation in the classroom* (rev. ed.). Edina, MN: Interaction Book Co.

Johnson, D.W., Johnson, R.T. & Tjosvold, D. (2000). Constructive controversy: The Value of Intellectual Opposition. In Deutsch & Coleman (Eds.), *Handbook of conflict resolution: Theory and practice* (pp. 65–85). San Francisco: Jossey Bass.

Judd, C.M. (1978). Cognitive effects of attitude conflict resolution. *Journal of Conflict Resolution, 22*, 483–498.

Judd, C.M., Smith, E.R. & Kidder, L.H. (1991). *Research methods in social relations.* Fort Worth: Holt, Rinehart & Winston.

Kolb, D.M. (Ed.). (1999). *Negotiation eclectics: Essays in memory of Jeffery Z. Rubin.* Cambridge, MA: PON Books (Program on Negotiation at Harvard Law School).

Koffka, K. (1935). *Principles of Gestalt Psychology.* Oxford, England: Harcourt, Brace.

Kressel, K. (1987). Clinical implications of existing research on divorce mediation. *American Journal of Family Therapy, 15*(1), 69–74.

Kressel, K. (1997). Practice-relevant research in mediation: toward a reflective research paradigm. *Negotiation Journal, 13*(2), 43–160.

Kressel, K. (2000). Mediation. In Deutsch & Coleman (Eds.), *Handbook of conflict resolution: Theory and practice* (pp. 522–46). San Francisco: Jossey Bass.

Kressel, K., & Pruitt, D. (1989). *Mediation Research* San Francisco: Jossey-Bass.

Lewicki, R.J., (1988). *Experiences in management and organizational behavior.* New York: Wiley.

Lewicki, R.J., Saunders, D.M., & Minton, J.W. (2001). *Essentials of negotiation.* Boston: Irwin/McGraw-Hill.

Lewin, K. (1935). A dynamic theory of personality. New York, NY: McGraw-Hill.

Lewin, K. (1936). *Principles of topological psychology,* New York, NY:McGraw-Hill.

Marrow, A.J. 1969. *The practical theorist: The life and work of Kurt Lewin.* New York: Basic Books.

Mead, G.H. (1934) *Mind, self and society : From the standpoint of a social behaviorist.* Oxford, England: Uni.Chicago Press.

Miller, D.L. (1980). *George Herbert Mead: Self, language, and the world.* Chicago: University of Chicago.

Opotow, S. (1991). Adolescent peer conflicts. *Education and Urban Society, 23*(4), 416–441.

Opotow, S., & Deutsch, M. (1999). Learning to cope with conflict and violence: How schools can help youth. In E. Frydenberg (Ed.), *Learning to cope: Developing as a person in complex societies* (pp. 198–224). Oxford: Oxford University Press.

Pfeutze, P.E. (1954) *The social self.* New York: Bookman Associates. (Reprinted with revisions as Self, Society, Existence: Human Nature and Dialogue in the *Thought of George Herbert Mead and Martin Buber* (1961). New York: Harper Torchbooks).

Pruitt, D., & Rubin, J.Z. (1986). *Social conflict.* New York: Random House.

Raider, E. (1995). Conflict resolution training in schools: Translating theory into applied skills. In B.B. Bunker & J.Z. Rubin (Eds.), *Conflict, cooperation, and justice: Essays Inspired by the Work of Morton Deutsch* (pp. 93–121). San Francisco: Jossey-Bass.

Rubin, J.Z. (Ed.). (1981). *Dynamics of third party intervention: Kissinger on the Middle East.* New York: Praeger .

Rubin, J.Z., & Faure, G.O. (Eds.). (1993). *Culture and negotiation.* New York: Sage.

Rubin, J.Z., & Kellerman, B. (Eds.). (1988). *Leadership and negotiation in the Middle East.* New York: Praeger.

Rubin, J.Z., & Zartmann, I.W. (Eds.). (2000). *Power and negotiation.* University of Michigan Press.

Rubin, J.Z., Pruitt, D.G. & Kim, S.H. (1994). *Social conflict: Escalation, Stalemate, and settlement* (2nd ed.). New York: McGraw-Hill.

Schachtel, E.G. (2001). *Metamorphosis: On the conflict of human development and the psychology of creativity.* Hillsdale, NJ, US: Analytic Press, Inc.

Siegel, S., & Fouraker, L.E. (1960). *Bargaining and group decision making: Experiments in bilateral monopoly.* New York: McGraw-Hill.

Tjosvold, D. (1985). Implications of controversy research for management. *Journal of Management, 11*, 21–37.

Tjosvold, D. (1998). Cooperative and Competitive goal approach to conflict: Accomplishments and challenges. *Applied Psychology: An International Review, 47,* 285–342.

Von Neumann, H., & Morgenstern, O. (1944). *The theory of games and economic behavior.* New York: Wiley.

Wenck, W.A. (1981). The effect of distributive systems on psychological orientation and task performance. *Dissertation Abstracts International, 42,* 2608–9.

Wright, Q., Evans, W.M., & Deutsch, M. (1962). *Preventing World War III: Some Proposals.* Oxford, England: Simon and Schuster.

Appendix A

—

Letter to colleagues from Morton Deutsch post-9/11.

September 20, 2001

Dear Colleagues,

We are all horrified and shocked by the horrendous events which have occurred recently in which thousands of innocent victims were killed by well organized terrorists actions directed against people and buildings in New York City, Pennsylvania, and Washington, D.C.

From various news reports and statements by US government officials, it seems that our government believes that:

1. The terrorist actions were planned, organized, and carried out by the bin Laden group

2. The Taliban government in Afghanistan has provided harbor for the bin Laden group

3. Elements within the government of Iraq, and possible others, have provided support of various kinds for the bin Laden group

The US government, with the support and possibly cooperation of other nations, is preparing a series of responses directed at the bin Laden group, the Taliban government, the Iraqi government, and to the general problem of terrorism. Among the likely responses is a strong military action by the US and its allies.

What can those of us who have been working for a just, peaceful, humane and sustainable world do in the light of the above? I suggest that we should be sending the following message to our political leaders: to the President and members of his Cabinet, to members of Congress, and to other people who influence policy:

1. It is important to encourage thoughtful, deliberate policy-making which has a long-term perspective and which fully takes into account the possible long-term consequences of one's action. *There should be every effort to resist premature judgements and actions. Time must be taken for careful policy-making.* Hot-tempered actions, based upon a primitive impulse for revenge, are likely to be ineffective, costly, unduly dangerous to ourselves and to many innocent people, and to produce long-term consequences which promote rather than eliminate terrorism.

I suggest that the best long-term *strategy* will involve:

(a) Differentiating Islam and the terrorist groups so that the terrorist groups are perceived to be anti-Islam rather than acting as agents of Islam. This will involve very strong opposition to anti-Muslim actions in the US and elsewhere. It will also require getting the active support of Muslim religious authorities in denouncing terrorism and terrorist groups. We do not want our actions against terrorist groups to provoke a war with Islam (this is exactly what the terrorists want). We want to cooperate with Islam in de-legitimizing violence against civilians whatever their religious background. We should encourage leading Islamic religious figures to broadcast statements that people who engage in terrorism are not acceptable in the Islamic community, will not be allowed to enter paradise in the after-life, and will be condemned for eternity.

(b) Addressing the causes which engender hatred and terrorism toward the United States. The causes are discussed below under point 3. Although it would be a mistake to feel that the actions and policies of the United States in any way justify the terrorist actions, it is well to examine in what ways we can prevent or reduce the animus against the United States.

2. We can support diplomatic, political, economic, and limited military actions to bring to justice those who planned, organized, or provided support to the terrorist actions. The implementation should be so focused and

limited that it results in no or minimal harm to the population of the countries attacked. Through disproportionate and cruel actions we do not want to create a backlash which will only create more terrorists and a continuous cycle of destruction.

3. *We must begin to think seriously about the causes of terrorism and address its causes* rather than believe that violence against terrorism will eliminate it. Long-term effective action to eliminate terrorism and other forms of violence will mainly involve positive action to eliminate its causes. Its causes are manifold: psychological, economic, political, religious, educational, and the easy availability of highly destructive weapons. Each of these causes are addressed briefly:

(a) *Psychological:* It is important to understand the underlying motivations and cognitive perspectives of both the leaders and also the followers of organized terrorist groups. At a deep level, it has been well stated that "violence is the expression of impotence grown unbearable." At a more direct level, the leaders of terrorist groups such as those connected with the drug traffic are mainly seeking to protect and promote their illegal business. In contrast, the leaders of such groups as bin Laden's are seeking to promote a political-religious ideology under conditions in which they feel impotent to achieve their objectives through peaceful means. Osama bin Laden apparently seeks to destroy the modern, secular, democratic, dominating, globalizing capitalism as symbolized by the United States and return to a more medieval, pre-capitalistic theocratic world (such as found in the Taliban-controlled Afghanistan). The leaders of terrorist groups are often well educated, from backgrounds of upper-middle or higher social-economic backgrounds, but often of marginal, disrespected ethnic, nationalist, or religious groups within their society. They often harbor deep resentment against the leaders of their own society and those who are allied with them.

The active followers of the terrorist leaders are often alienated, educated people from petit bourgeois families who are seeking a power and prestige-enhancing self-identity as well as the emotional and economic support of being a member of a close-knit group. The political-religious ideology of their leaders provides them with an acceptable moral justification for their violent behavior.

(b) *Economic:* During the past decade, the United States has gone through a period of considerable economic prosperity but many people throughout the world, as well as in the US, have not shared in this prosperity and a considerable number have seen their economic situation worsen. Some believe that those who have prospered have done so because they have exploited those nations and people who have not. There is considerable envy and resentment toward the US as a result. To overcome these feelings, as well as for other good reasons, it is important for the US to take an active, leading, and visible role in improving the economic well being of those nations and people who are suffering economic difficulties.

(c) *Shortsighted policy-making:* In the past, we were so anti-Communist that we supported any group (including bin Laden's and the Taliban) that fought against the Soviets whether or not, they shared any of our other values. Our bombing of Sudan was seen to be an unjustified terrorist attack against a Muslim state which, in turn, justifies an attack against us. Apparently, our limited foresight can produce policies which are destructive to our own interests.

(d) *Political:* Political violence, to paraphrase, grows out of unbearable political impotence. In other words, political violence is less apt to be stimulated in a democracy where one has the freedom to express one's political views and to openly try to persuade others to elect to political power and leadership those who represent your views and interests than in the dictatorial nations of the Middle East. Dictators are, often, able to prevent internal violence by severe, repressive controls and by deflecting the pent-up rage on to other targets. The United States, partly because of its support of Israel as well as its leading role in the modern globalizing world, has become a handy target for this displaced rage. It is evident that the US has much to gain by supporting the development of democratic institutions and leadership to replace the backward autocratic governments in this region.

(e) *Religious:* The central tenets of all the major religions — Christian, Muslim, Hindu, Buddhist and Jewish — respect the sanctity of human life. They all oppose violence against innocent human beings. However, there are deviant radical "fundamentalist" groups in some of the religions who distort the basic teachings of their religion to condone and, even, encourage politically inspired violence against innocent victims. Although this has been particularly true, recently, in the Middle East, where deviant "fundamentalists" have legitimized and even glorified people who have engaged in terrorist violence, it has also occurred in the United States, Israel, Ireland and other countries. The United States should encourage the religious leaders of all religions to take very active leadership in de-legitimizing violence against innocent victims.

(f) *Educational:* Education in many parts of the world, as well as in the United States, does not provide students with the knowledge, attitudes, and skills to become active participants in — and advocates of — a peaceful world. Too often, it is narrowly ethnocentric, glorifies violence by one's own group and dehumanizes members of outgroups. It predisposes students to use zero-sum power strategies and tactics in conflict with outgroups, rather than cooperative, problem-solving methods. Clearly, if we are to have a world free of terrorism, much effort will have to be directed at educating our students to have the knowledge, attitudes, and skills for constructive conflict resolution.

(g) *Availability of Weapons:* The US government's pursuit of an anti-missile defense program is likely to lead to a

> unilateral ending of an important arms control treaty and hamper the development of international agreements to limit and control the production and widespread availability of weapons of mass destruction. Our emphasis should be on developing effective international control of such weapons rather than on taking actions to militarize space unilaterally.

To sum up, we are in a win-lose conflict with terrorism; we must not allow it to escalate to a conflict with Islam or Muslims. We must also prevent it from battering our democratic freedoms as we take steps to decrease our vulnerability to terrorism and to de-legitimize as well as undermine terrorist groups. And, of course, we must continue our active efforts to create a world that is characterized by a cooperative peace, social justice, and a sustainable environment.

Respectfully Yours,

Morton Deutsch
E. L. Thorndike Professor Emeritus of Psychology
and Education, and Director Emeritus, International
Center for Cooperation & Conflict Resolution (ICCCR),
Teachers College, Columbia University

P.S. Please feel free to circulate this message.

Appendix B

Vita — Morton Deutsch

Born February 4, 1920

Higher Education

B.S. City College of New York. 1939
M A.. University of Pennsylvania. 1940;
Ph.D , Massachusetts Institute of Technology. 1948;
Certificate in Psychoanalysis. Postgraduate Center for
Mental Health' 1958.

Professional Positions

Assistant Professor. New York University. 1948–1952; Associate
Professor, New York University, 1952–1956; Member of Technical Staff
(in charge of Interpersonal Process), Bell Telephone Laboratories,
1955–1963; Adjunct Professor, N.Y.U., 1961–1963; Staff, Postgraduate
Center for Psychotherapy, 1954–63; Professor, Teachers College,
Columbia University. 1963–present; Edward Lee Thorndike Professor
of Psychology and Education, Teachers College, Columbia University,
1981–present; Director, International Center for Cooperation and
Conflict Resolution, 1986–1998; Professor Emeritus, 1990–present.

Professional Memberships

Fellow, American Psychological Association; Fellow, American
Association for the Advancement of Science; New York State
Psychological Association; Society for the Psychological Study of
Social Issues; International Society of Political Psychology; Society of
Experimental Psychology; European Association of Experimental
Social Psychology; International Association of Conflict Management

Areas of Specialization

Conflict resolution, distributive justice, social perception, intergroup relations, developmental social psychology, small group processes, social psychology of mental health.

Offices and Awards

President, Society for the Psychological Study of Social Issues (1961–61); President, Division of Personality and Social Psychology of the American Psychological Association (1964–65); President, New York State Psychological Association (1965–66); President, Eastern Psychological Association (1968–69); President, International Society of Political Psychology (1981–82); first President. Division of Peace Psychology. American Psychological Association (1990–91); consulting editorships: Journal of Experimental Social Psychology, Journal of Applied Social Psychology, Journal of Conflict Resolution, Journal of Personality and Social Psychology, Contemporary Psychology, Contemporary Psychoanalysis, Journal of Applied Behavioral Science. Journal of Peace Research, International Journal of Conflict Management, Peace and Conflict; Journal of Peace Psychology; the social psychological prize of the American Association for the Advancement of Science, 1961; the Samuel Flowerman Memorial Award of the New York Society for Clinical Psychologists. 1963; the Hovland Memorial Award Lectures, Yale University, 1967; the Kurt Lewin Memorial Award Address at the American Psychological Association Annual Meeting. 1968; Research Scientist Fellowship, National Institute of Mental Health, 1970–71; the Gordon Allport Prize, 1973; Visiting Scholar, Russell Sage Foundation, 1976–77; the Kurt Lewin Award of the New York State Psychological Association, 1980; the Cattell Fund Sabbatical Fellowship, 1983–4; the Nevit Sanford Award of the International Society of Political Psychology, 1984; the Distinguished Scientist Award of the Society of Experimental Social Psychology, 1985; the Distinguished Scientific Contribution Award of the American Psychological Association, 1987; elected a William James Fellow of the American Psychological Society. 1988; Honorary Doctorate of Humane Letters by the City University of New York, 1989; the Helsenki Medal for Distinguished Contributions to Psychology by the

University of Helsenki, 1990; the Teachers College Medal for Distinguished Contributions to Education, 1992; Life-time Achievement Award, International Association of Conflict Management, 1993; Distinguished Visiting Fellowship, La Trobe University, 1993; Division of Cooperative Learning of the American Education Research Association, 1993; International Association of Conflict Management, 1993; Society for the Psychological Study of Social Issues, 1995; Society for the study of Peace, Conflict, and Violence, 1995; Levinson Award of the Division of Consulting Psychology of the American Psychological Association, 1998; the Book Award (for *the Handbook of Conflict Resolution: Theory and Practice*), The CPR Institute for Dispute Resolution, 2000; Annual Awards named the Morton Deutsch Award: The Society for the Study of Peace, Conflict, and Violence Award for distinguished work in the field of Conflict Resolution, 2003– ; The International Society for Justice Award for distinguished work in the field of social justice, 2004– ; Teachers College, Columbia University Award for a distinguished graduate student paper related to social justice, 2005– ; Teachers College, Columbia University Award for distinguished scholarly/activist contributions to social justice.

Publications

Books

Deutsch, M. (1951). The effect of public policy in housing projects upon interracial attitudes. *Readings in Social Psychology.* New York: Henry Holt.

Deutsch, M. (1964). Some psychological aspects of social interactions. In *Scientific psychology*, New York, NY: Basic Books.

Deutsch, M. (1973). *The resolution of conflict: Constructive and destructive processes.* New Haven: Yale University Press.

Deutsch, M. (1985). *Distributive justice: A social psychological perspective.* New Haven: Yale University Press.

Deutsch, M., & Brewster Smith. (1984). *Preventing Armageddon: A Social Issue Release.* Washington, DC: American Psychological Association.

Deutsch, M. & Coleman, P.T. (Eds.) (2000) *The handbook of conflict resolution: Theory and practice.* San Francisco, CA; Jossey-Bass.

Deutsch, M., & Collins, M. E. (1951). *Interracial housing: A psychological evaluation of a social experiment.* Minneapolis: University of Minnesota Press.

Deutsch, M., & Hornstein, H. (Eds.). (1975). *Applying social psychology: Implications for research, practice and training.* Hillsdale, NJ: L. Erlbaum Associates.

Deutsch, M., & Krauss, R., M. (1965). *Theories in social psychology*. New York: Basic Books.

Deutsch, M., Selltiz, C., Jahoda, M., & Cook S.W. (1951). *Research methods in social relations*. New York: Holt & Dryden.

Deutsch, M., Wright, Q., & Evan, W. M. (Eds.). (1962). *Preventing World War III: Some proposals*. New York: Simon & Schuster.

Journal Articles and Chapters in Books

Coleman, P. T., & Deutsch, M. (1995). The mediation of interethnic conflict in schools. In W. D. Hawley, & A. W. Jackson, (Eds), *Toward a common destiny: Improving race and ethnic relations in America* (pp. 371–396). San Francisco, CA, US: Jossey-Bass.

Coleman, P. T., & Deutsch, M. (2000). Some guidelines for developing a creative approach to conflict. In M. Deutsch & P. T. Coleman (Eds.), *The Handbook of Conflict Resolution* (pp. 355–366). CA: Jossey-Bass.

Coleman, P., & Deutsch, M. (2001). Introducing cooperation and conflict resolution into schools: A systems approach. In D. J. Christie, & R. V. Wagner, (Eds), (2001). *Peace, conflict, and violence: Peace psychology for the 21st century* (pp. 223–239). Upper Saddle River, NJ, US: Prentice Hall.

Deutsch, M. (1949). A theory of cooperation and completion. *Human Relations, 2*, 129–151.

Deutsch, M. (1949). An experimental study of effects of cooperation and competition upon group processes. *Human Relations, 2*, 199–231.

Deutsch, M. (1949). The directions of behavior: A field theoretical approach to the understanding of inconsistencies. *Journal of Social Issues, 5*, 43–51.

Deutsch, M. (1951). Task structure and group process. *American Psychologist*.

Deutsch, M. (1951). Social relations in the classroom and grading procedures. *Journal of Educational Research, 45*, 145–152.

Deutsch, M. (1953). Problems and progress of research in housing in its bearing upon race relations. *Inventory of Research in Racial and Cultural Relations, 5* (2–3), 65–95.

Deutsch, M. (1954). Field theory and projective techniques. *Journal of Projective Techniques, 18*, 427–434.

Deutsch, M. (1954). Field theory in social psychology. In L. Gardner (Ed.). Handbook of social psychology (pp. 181–222). Oxford, England: Addison-Wesley Publishing Co.

Deutsch, M. (1955). Conditions affecting cooperation. *ONR Research Reviews*. Washington, DC: Office of Naval research, Department of Navy.

Deutsch, M. (1958). Trust and suspicion. *Journal of Conflict Resolution, 2*, 265–279.

Deutsch, M. (1959). Some factors affecting membership motivation and achievement motivation in a group. *Human Relations, 12*, 81–95.

Deutsch, M. (1960). Trust, trustworthiness and the F. Scale. *Journal of Abnormal and Social Psychology, 61*, 138–140.

Deutsch, M. (1960). The effect of motivational orientation upon trust and suspicion. *Human Relations, 13*, 123–139.

Deutsch, M. (1960). The pathetic fallacy: An observer error in social perception. *Journal of Personality, 28*, 317–332.

Deutsch, M. (1961). The face of bargaining. *Operations Research, 9*, 886–897.

Deutsch, M. (1961). Some considerations relevant to national policy. *Journal of Social Issues, 17,* 57–68.

Deutsch, M. (1961). The interpretation of praise and criticism as a function of their social context. *Journal of Abnormal and Social Psychology, 62,* 391–400.

Deutsch, M. (1962). Dissonance or defensiveness? *Journal of Personality, 30,* 16–28.

Deutsch, M. (1962). A psychological basis for peace. In M. Deutsch, Q. Wright & W. M. Evan (Eds.), *Preventing World War III: Some proposals.* New York: Simon & Schuster.

Deutsch, M. (1962). Psychological alternatives to war. *Journal of Social Issues, 18,* 97–119.

Deutsch, M. (1962). Cooperation and trust: Some theoretical notes. In M. R. Jones (Ed). *Nebraska Symposium on Motivation,* (pp. 275–320). Oxford, England: University of Nebraska Press.

Deutsch, M. (1964). Humans in the Skinner box. *Sociological Inquiry.*

Deutsch, M. (1964). On producing change in an adversary. In R. Fisher (Ed.), *International conflict and the behavioral sciences* (pp. 145–160). New York: Basic Books.

Deutsch, M. (1965). A psychological approach to international conflict, in G. Sperazzo (Ed.), *Strategic interaction and conflict.* Washington, DC: Georgetown University Press.

Deutsch, M. (1968). Group behavior. *International Encyclopedia of the Social Science, 5,* (pp. 406–416). Oxford, England: Macmillan.

Deutsch, M. (1968). Field theory. *International Encyclopedia of the Social Science, 6,* (pp. 265–276). Oxford, England: Macmillan.

Deutsch, M. (1969). Conflicts: Productive and destructive. *Journal of Social Issues, 25,* 7–41.

Deutsch, M. (1969). Socially relevant science: Reflections on some studies of interpersonal conflict. *American Psychologist, 24,* 1076–1092.

Deutsch, M. (1971). Toward an understanding of conflict. *International Journal of Group Tensions, 1,* 42–54.

Deutsch, M. (1971). Conflict and its resolution. In C. Smith (Ed.), *Conflict resolution* (pp. 36–58). Notre Dame: Notre Dame University Press.

Deutsch, M. (1974). Awakening the sense of injustice. In M. Lerner & M. Ross (Eds.), *The Quest for Justice* (pp. 19–42). Holt of Canada.

Deutsch, M. (1974). The social-psychological study of conflict: Rejoinder to a critique. *European Journal of Social Psychology, 4,* 441–456.

Deutsch, M. (1975). Equity, equality, and need: What determines which value will be used as the basis for distributive justice? *Journal Social Issues, 31,* 137–150.

Deutsch, M. (1976). On theorizing in social psychology. *Personality & Social Psychology Bulletin, 2,* 134–141.

Deutsch, M. (1976). On cursing the darkness versus lighting a candle. In *Social Psychology in Transition.* New York, NY: Plenum.

Deutsch, M. (1977). Recurrent themes in the study of social conflict, *Journal of Social Issues, 33,* 222–225.

Deutsch, M. (1978). The social psychology of justice. In Proceedings of the *International Symposium on Social Psychology, 23*–46. Kyoto, Japan: The Japanese Group Dynamics Association.

Deutsch, M. (1979). Justice in "The Crunch" *Alternatives.*

Deutsch, M. (1979). Education and distributive justice: Some reflections on grading systems. *American Psychologist, 4,* 391–401.

Deutsch, M. (1979). A critical review of "equity theory": An alternative perspective on the social psychology of justice, *International Journal of Group Tensions, 9,* 20–49.

Deutsch, M. (1979). Some comments on the current status of American social psychology. *Japanese Journal of Experimental and Social Psychology, 18,* 167–171.

Deutsch, M. (1980). Socially relevant research: Comments on "Applied" versus "Basic" research. In R. F. Kidd & M. J. Saks (Eds.), *Advances in applied social psychology* (pp. 97–112). Hillsdale, NJ: Erlbaum Associates.

Deutsch, M. (1980). Fifty years of conflict. In L. Festinger (Ed.), *Retrospections on social psychology* (pp. 46–77). New York: Oxford University Press.

Deutsch, M. (1981). Justice in "The Crunch". In M. J. Lerner & S. Lerner (Eds.), *The justice motive in social behaviour* (pp. 343–357). New York: Plenum Publishing.

Deutsch, M. (1982). Interdependence and psychological orientation. In V. Derlega & J. L. Grzelek (Eds.), *Cooperation and helping behavior: Theories and research* (pp. 15–42). New York: Academic Press.

Deutsch, M. (1983). Conflict resolution: Strategies of inducing cooperation. In H. H. Blumberg, A. P. Hare, V. Kent. & M. Davies (Eds.), *Small groups and social interaction*. John Wiley & Sons.

Deutsch, M. (1983). Conflict resolution: Theory and practice. *Political Psychology, 4,* 431–453.

Deutsch, M. (1983). Preventing World War III: A psychological perspective. *Political Psychology, 2,* 3–31.

Deutsch, M. (1983). Current perspectives on justice. *European Journal of Social Psychology, 13,* 305–319.

Deutsch, M. (1983). What is political psychology? *International Social Science Journal,* 222–236.

Deutsch, M. (1986). Cooperation, conflict, and justice. In H. W. Bierhof, R. L. Cohen & J. Greenberg (Eds.), *Justice in social relations,* (pp. 3–18). New York: Plenum.

Deutsch, M. (1986). "Folie a deux": A psychological perspective on Soviet-American relations. In M. P. Karns (Ed.), *Persistent patterns and emergent structures in a waning century,* (pp. 185–196). New York: Praeger.

Deutsch, M. (1986). The malignant (spiral) process of hostile interaction. In R.White (Ed.), *Psychology and the prevention of nuclear war,* (pp. 131–154). New York: New York University Press.

Deutsch, M (1986). Strategies of inducing cooperation. In R. White (Ed.), *Psychology and the prevention of nuclear war,* (pp. 162–170). New York: New York University Press.

Deutsch, M. (1987). Experimental studies of the effects of different systems of distributive justice. In J. Master & W. Smith (Eds.), *Social comparison, social justice, and relative deprivation,* (pp. 151–164). Hillsdale, NJ: Erlbaum.

Deutsch, M. (1987). A theoretical perspective on conflict and conflict resolution. In D. J. Sandole & I. Sandole-Staroste (Eds.), *Conflict management and problem-solving,* (pp. 38–49). London: Pintner.

Deutsch, M. (1987). Going beyond "Beyond Deterrence." *Journal of Social Issues, 43,* 149–153.

Deutsch, M. (1988). On negotiating the non-negotiable. In B. Kellerman & J. Rubin (Eds.), *Leadership and negotiation in the Middle East*, (pp. 248–263). New York: Praeger.

Deutsch, M. (1989). Equality and economic efficiency: Is there a trade-off? In N. Eisenberg, J. Reykowski, & E. Staub (Eds.), *Social and moral values*, (pp. 139–154). Hillsdale, NJ: Erlbaum.

Deutsch, M. (1990). Forms of social organization: Psychological consequences. In H. Himmelweit & G. Gaskell (Eds.), *Societal psychology*, (pp. 57–176). London: Sage Publications.

Deutsch, M. (1990). Enthusiasm for the work. In S. Wheelan, E. Pepitone & V. Abt (Eds.), *Advances in field theory*, (pp. 23–26). London: Sage Publications.

Deutsch, M. (1990). Psychological roots of moral exclusion. *Journal of Social Issues, 46*(1), 21–25.

Deutsch, M. (1990). Cooperation, conflict, and justice. In S. Wheelan, E. Pepitone, & V. Abt (Eds.), *Advances in field theory*, (pp. 149–164). London: Sage Publications.

Deutsch, M. (1990). A framework for teaching conflict resolution in the schools. In B. Sheppard, M. Bazerman, & R. Lewicki (Eds.), *Negotiation in Organizations* (pp. 189–203), Connecticut: JAI Press, Inc.

Deutsch, M. (1990). Subjective features of conflict resolution: Psychological, social, and cultural influences. In R. Vayryen (Ed.) *New directions in conflict theory: Conflict resolution and conflict transformation*, (pp. 26–56). London: Sage Publications.

Deutsch, M. (1991). Egalitarianism in the laboratory and in the workplace. In R. Vermunt & H. Steensma (Eds.), *Social Justice in Human Relations* (pp. 195–210). New York: Plenum Press.

Deutsch, M. (1992). Educating beyond hate. In A. Bjerstedt (Ed.), *Peace, environment and education, 2*, 3–19.

Deutsch, M. (1992). *The effects of training in cooperative learning and conflict resolution in an alternative high school.* New York: International Center for Cooperation and Conflict Resolution, Teachers College, Columbia University.

Deutsch, M. (1992). Kurt Lewin: The tough-minded and tender-hearted scientist. *Journal of Social Issues, 48,* 31–43.

Deutsch, M. (1993). Educating for a peaceful world, *American Psychologist, 48,* 510–517.

Deutsch, M. (1993). The effects of training in cooperative learning and conflict resolution in an alternative high school. *Cooperative Learning, 13,* 2–5.

Deutsch, M. (1994). Constructive conflict resolution: Theory, research, and practice. *Journal of Social Issues, 50,* 13–32.

Deutsch, M. (1994). Constructive conflict resolution for the world today. *International Journal of Conflict Management,* 5, 111–129.

Deutsch, M. (1994). William James: The First Peace Psychologist. *Peace and Conflict: Journal of Peace Psychology, 1,* 17–26.

Deutsch, M. (1999). A personal perspective on the development of social psychology in the 20th century. In A. Rodrigues and R. Levine (Eds.) *Reflections on social psychology.* Westview Press.

Deutsch, M. (1999). Hope with optimism: A commentary on Brewster Smith's article. *Peace and Conflict: Journal of Peace Psychology, 5,* 17–22.

Deutsch, M. (1999). *Psychological aspects of ethno-political conflict.* Address given at the university of Massachusetts, Boston

Deutsch, M. (2000). Commentary on "Civil political discourse in a democracy". *Peace and Conflict: Journal of Peace Psychology*, 6(4), 319–323.

Deutsch, M. (2000). Introduction. In M. Deutsch & P. T. Coleman (Eds.) (pp. 1–19), *The Handbook of Conflict Resolution*. CA: Jossey-Bass.

Deutsch, M. (2000). Cooperation and Competition. In M. Deutsch & P. T. Coleman (Eds.), *The Handbook of Conflict Resolution* (pp. 21–40). CA: Jossey-Bass.

Deutsch, M. (2000). Justice and Conflict. In M. Deutsch & P. T. Coleman (Eds.), *The Handbook of Conflict Resolution* (pp. 41–64). CA: Jossey-Bass.

Deutsch, M. (2000). A framework for thinking about research on conflict resolution training. In M. Deutsch & P. T. Coleman (Eds.), *The Handbook of Conflict Resolution* (pp. 571–590). CA: Jossey-Bass.

Deutsch, M. (2003). Content, yes! And theory, yes! *Journal of Dispute Resolution*, 367–375.

Deutsch, M. (2001). Cooperation and conflict resolution: Implications for consulting psychology. *Consulting Psychology Journal: Practice & Research*, 32(2), 76–81.

Deutsch, M. (2002). Social psychology's contributions to the study of conflict resolution. *Negotiation Journal*, 19(4), 307–320.

Deutsch, M. (2003). Cooperation and conflict: A personal perspective on the history of the social psychological study of conflict resolution. In D.J. Tjosvold, M.A. West, & K.G. Smith (Eds.), *International Handbook of Organizational Teamwork and Cooperative Working*, 9–43. Chichester, England: Wiley and Sons.

Deutsch, M., Canavan, D., & Rubin, J. (1971). The effects of size of conflict and sex of experimenter upon interpersonal bargaining. *Journal of Experimental Social Psychology*, 7, 258–267.

Deutsch, M., Chein, I., Hyman, H., & Jahoda, M. (Eds.). (1949). Consistency and inconsistency in intergroup relations. *Journal of Social Issues*, 5, 4–11.

Deutsch, M., & Collins, M. E., (1950). Interracial housing. III. Influence of integrated, segregated occupancy on racial attitudes measured. *Journal of Housing*, 7, 127–129.

Deutsch, M., & Coleman, P. (in preparation). *The Theory and Practice of Conflict Resolution*.

Deutsch, M. & Coleman, P. (1998). The mediation of inter-ethnic conflict in schools. Reprinted in Weiner (Ed.) *The Handbook of Interethnic Coexistence* . New York: Continuum.

Deutsch, M., & Coleman, P. (2000). Cooperation, conflict resolution and school violence: A systems approach. Brief developed for the *Choices in Preventing Youth Violence* initiative. Institute for Urban and Minority Education, Teachers College, Columbia University.

Deutsch, M., & Gerard, H. B. (1955). A study of normative and informational social influences upon individual judgment. *Journal of Abnormal & Social Psychology, 51,* 629–636.

Deutsch, M., & Hornstein H., (1970). The social psychology of education. In J. Davitz & S. Bell (Eds.), *Psychology of the educational process*. New York: McGraw-Hill.

Deutsch, M., Hulett, J. E. Jr., & Stagner, Ross (Eds). (1952). Social environment and attitudinal change: a study of the effects of different types of interracial housing. *Problems in social psychology: an interdisciplinary inquiry.* Oxford, England: University of Illinois.

Deutsch, M., & Kinnvall, C. (2002). What is political psychology? In Kristen Renwick Monroe (Ed.), Political psychology (pp. 15–42). Mahwah, NJ, US: Lawrence Erlbaum

Deutsch. M., & Kotik, P. (1978). Altruism and bargaining. In H. Sauermann (Ed.), *Bargaining behavior* (pp. 1–21). Tubingen: Mohr.

Deutsch, M., & Krauss, R. M. (1960). The effect of threat upon interpersonal bargaining. *Journal of Abnormal and Social Psychology, 61,* 181–189.

Deutsch, M. & Krauss, R. M. (1962). Studies of interpersonal bargaining. *Journal of Conflict Resolution,* 6, 52–76.

Deutsch, M. & Krauss, R. M. (1966). Communication in interpersonal bargaining. *Journal of Personality and Social Psychology, 4,* 572–577.

Deutsch, M., & Lewicki , R. (1970). "Locking-in" effects during a game of chicken. *Journal of Conflict Resolution, 14,* 367–378.

Deutsch, M., Pepitone, A., & Zander, A. (1948). Leadership in the small group. *Journal of Social Issues,* 2, 31–41.

Deutsch, M., & Schichman, S. (1986). Conflict: A social psychological perspective. In M.G. Hermann (Ed.), *Political psychology* (pp. 219–250). San Francisco: Jossey-Bass.

Deutsch, M., & Brickman, E. (1994). Conflict resolution. *Pediatrics in Review, 1*L, 16–22.

Deutsch, M., & Solomon, L. (1959). Reactions to evaluation by others as influenced by self-evaluations. *Sociometry, 22,* 93–112.

Deutsch, M., Tuchman, B., Kressel, K., Watson, C., Weinglass, J., & Jaffe, N. (1977). Mediated negotiations in divorce and labor disputes. *Conciliation Courts Review, 15,* 9–12.

Deutsch, M., Wish, M., & Biener, L. (1972). Differences in perceived similarity of nations. In R. N. Shepard, A. K. Romney, & S. B. Nerlove (Eds.) *Multidimensional scaling: Theory and applications in the behavioral sciences: I. Theory.* Oxford, England: Seminar Press.

Garner, K., & Deutsch, M. (1974). Cooperative behavior in dyads: Effects of dissimilar goal orientations and differing expectations about the partner. *Journal of Conflict Resolution, 18,* 634–645.

Gumpert, P., Deutsch, M., & Epstein, Y. (1969). Effect of incentive magnitude on cooperation in the Prisoner's Dilemma game. *Journal of Personality & Social Psychology, 11,* 66–69.

Heilman, M. E., Slochower, J., & Deutsch, M. (1976). The effects of victimization on reactions to other victims. *Journal of Applied Social Psychology, 6,* 193–205.

Hornstein, H. A., Deutsch, M. (1967). Tendencies to compete and to attack as a function of inspection, incentive and available alternatives. *Journal of Personality & Social Psychology, 5*(3), 311–318.

Janis, I. L., Deutsch, M., Krauss, R. M., Goktepe, J. R., & Schneier, C. E. (1991). Group behavior . In W. A. Lesko (Ed.). *Readings in social psychology: General, classic, and contemporary selections* (pp. 317–341). Needham Heights, MA, US: Allyn & Bacon.

Kelley, H. H., Deutsch, M., Lanzetta, J. T., Nuttin, J. M. Jr., Shure G. H., Faucheux, C., Moscovici, S., & Rabbie, J. (1970). A comparative experimental study of negotiation behavior. *Journal of Personality and Social Psychology, 16,* 411–438.

Kressel, K., & Deutsch, M. (1977). Divorce therapy: An in-depth survey of therapists' views. *Family Process, 16,* 413–443.

Kressel, K., Lopez-Morillas, M., Weinglass, J., & Deutsch, M. (1978). Professional intervention in divorce: A summary of the views of lawyers, psychotherapists, and clergy. *Journal of Divorce, 2,* 119–155.

Lichtenberg, P., & Deutsch, M. (1955). A descriptive review of research on the staff process of decision-making. *USAF Personnel & Training Research Center Research Bulletin. No. AFPTRC-TR-54-129.*

Muney, B. F., & Deutsch, M. (1968). The effects of role-reversal during the discussion of opposing viewpoints. *Journal of Conflict Resolution, 12,* 345–356.

Opotow, S. &, Deutsch, M. (1999). Learning to cope with conflict and violence: How schools can help youth. In E. Frydenberg, (Ed). *Learning to cope: Developing as a person in complex societies* (pp. 198–224). London, Oxford University Press.

Proshansky, H. M., Deutsch, C., Deutsch, Martin; Deutsch, Morton. (1973). Behavior and heredity: Statement by the Society for The Psychological Study of Social Issues, *American Psychologist, 28,* 620–621.

Sandy, S. V., Boardman, S., & Deutsch, M. (2000). Personality and Conflict. In M. Deutsch & P. T. Coleman (Eds.), *The Handbook of Conflict Resolution* (pp. 289–315). CA: Jossey-Bass.

Steil, J., Tuchman, B., & Deutsch, M. (1978). An exploratory study of the meanings of injustice and frustration. *Personality & Social Psychology Bulletin, 4,* 393–398.

Weinglass, J., Kressel, K., Deutsch, M. (1978). The role of the clergy in divorce: An exploratory survey. *Journal of Divorce, 2,* 57–82.

Wish, M., Deutsch, M., & Biener, L. (1970). Differences in conceptual structures of nations: An exploratory study. *Journal of Personality and Social Psychology, 16,* 361–373.

Wish, M., Deutsch, M., & Kaplan, S. J. (1976). Perceived dimensions of interpersonal relations. *Journal of Personality & Social Psychology, 33,* 409–420.

Appendix C

Students Whose Doctoral Dissertations Were Conducted with Morton Deutsch as Principal Advisor

Name	Date Degree Awarded
New York University	
Harold Proshansky	1952
Seymour Levy	1953
Joseph B. Margolin	1954
Harold Yuker	1954
Leonard Solomon	1957
James L. Loomis	1957
Robert M. Krauss	1964
Teachers College, Columbia University	
Harvey A. Hornstein	1964
David W. Johnson	1966
Stephen Thayer	1966
Bert Brown	1967
Peter Gumpert	1967
Abaineh Workie	1967
Yakov M. Epstein	1968
Miriam G. Keiffer	1968
Roy J. Lewicki	1968
Jeffrey Z. Rubin	1968
Donnah Canavan	1969
Barbara B. Bunker	1970
Mary Chase	1971
Ella Lasky	1971
Lois Biener	1972
Madeleine E. Heilman	1972
Lida Orzeck	1973
Kenneth Kressel	1973
Lorenz J. Finison	1973
Rebecca C. Curtis	1973
Antonietta Graciano	1974
Barbara J. Stembridge	1974
Charles M. Judd Jr.	1975

Teachers College, Columbia University (continued)

Sharon P. Kaplan	1975
Joyce Slochhower	1976
Nancy L. Hedlund	1977
Janice Steil	1979
Michelle Fine	1980
Sherry Deren	1980
William A. Wenck, Jr.	1981
Cilio R. Ziviani	1981
Dolores Mei	1981
Shula Shichman	1982
Bruce Tuckman	1982
Ivan Lansberg	1983
Louis Medvene	1983
Janet Weinglass	1983
Susan Boardman	1984
Ellen Cooper	1984
Nefertari Crummey	1984
Sandra Horowitz	1984
Lorinda Arella	1985
Eric Marcus	1985
Rachel Solomon-Ravich	1985
Susan Opotow	1986
Rony I. Rinat	1987
Marilyn Seiler	1987
Cathie M. Currie	1989
Jorge da Silva Ribeiro	1990
Nisha Advani	1991
Curtis Dolezal	1991
Adrienne Asch	1992
Lela Tepavac	1992
Quanwu Zhang	1992
Martha Gephart	1993
Judith K. Herschlag	1993
Nidhi Khattri	1993
Eben Weitzman	1993
Peter Coleman	1998
John Barkat	2000
Ying Ying Joanne Lim	2003